ISBN 978-0-282-20340-5
PIBN 10314193

1 MONTH OF
FREE
READING

at
www.ForgottenBooks.com

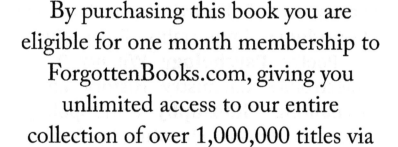

By purchasing this book you are
eligible for one month membership to
ForgottenBooks.com, giving you
unlimited access to our entire
collection of over 1,000,000 titles via
our web site and mobile apps.

To claim your free month visit:

www.forgottenbooks.com/free314193

The Book

of the

Settlement of Iceland.

TRANSLATED FROM THE ORIGINAL ICELANDIC OF

ARI THE LEARNED,

BY

REV. T. ELLWOOD, M.A.

RECTOR OF TORVER,

Author of " Lakeland and Iceland."

KENDAL:

T. WILSON, PRINTER AND PUBLISHER, 28, HIGHGATE.

—

1898.

To EIRÍKR MAGNÚSSON, Esq., M.A.

To you, to whom I owe much of what I know in Icelandic, with its exhaustless stores of literature and legend, I respectfully inscribe this translation as a slight acknowledgment of the kindness with which you have aided me by your suggestions and counsel in the study and annotation of the work.

T. ELLWOOD.

PREFACE.

IT is about eleven years since I first began the translation of the Book of the Settlement of Iceland. The remarkable resemblance of its Place-Names and language generally to the Place Names and Dialect of my native county, Cumberland, as also of Westmorland and North Lancashire, having been that which set me going, and which through so many years has kept me to the work.

I did it first of all in single isolated chapters, singling out the chapters from any portion of the original work as they might seem to have an especial bearing on the local Place Names or dialect with which I was engaged.

I then wrote these out again as a whole. This translation of it as a whole was first completed in the spring of 1895. The work of writing it out occupied me almost incessantly during the winter and spring of that year.

Since then the translation has been copied and corrected, most of it twice over. The original Icelandic copy first used was one from the edition of Copenhagen, 1843. For a considerable portion of the work I used an edition taken from the Mela Bók and bearing that date of 1770 or thereabouts.*

The Table of Contents, the Notes in a great measure, and the list of Place Names with references, are my own work. This I say not as claiming credit, but as acknowledging responsibility.

E. Magnússon, Esq., M.A., a distinguished Icelander, whose works in his own department of literature are too well and widely known to need comment from me, has throughout assisted me with his kind counsel and advice; to him, therefore, I have inscribed the translation. The character of this

---

* The great discrepancy in places between the two editions used will account for some differences between those in the Register at the end and the names, &c., in the body of the work.

immortal

immortal work of Ari may be well summed up in the words
of this gentleman when he says :—" It is a classic of all
classics in the mediæval literature of the whole Germanic
world," and the present is an attempt to render, however
imperfectly, that work from Icelandic, a language spoken by
only about 60,000 or 70,000 people, all told, into English,
spoken as it is by a kindred people, a race numbering over
one hundred millions, whose maritime enterprize * followed
by settlement and colonization derived apparently from the
Norsemen, have given them the dominion of a great part of
the earth.

The Settlement of Iceland is contemporary, and in a great
measure identical with that national migration which resulted
in the Norse Settlement of the north-western portion of Great
Britain. The glimpses of Early British Church History †
that run through the following pages, show that Iceland
derived its first knowledge of Christianity from British
settlers, that when the Norsemen first left Norway they were
heathen, but that their sojourn in the Hebrides or the north-
west of our island, generally had the effect of converting
them to the Christian faith.

This work in the original is unique as a record, for no
other country in the world has such an account of its Earliest
History, and no other country in the world affords such an
unimpeachable testimony to the truth of its Earliest History
by having preserved its original language, place names, men's
names, and traditions, essentially unaltered and unimpaired.

T.E.

---

* The author of the Book of the Settlement contrasts early Norse discovery
with more recent discovery, when he says of Floki using the ravens to guide
him : "Floki had consecrated the ravens to this service in Norway that they
might lead him in his discoveries, as navigators in the north had not, at that
time, any knowledge of the compass (leiðarstein) to guide them. See note in
the original Icelandic edition, Copenhagen, 1843, I, 2, page 30.

† For notices of Early Church History see Prologue and I, 9, 12, 15; II, 15,
16, 17, 18, 19 and Notes; III, 12; V, 15.

TABLE OF CONTENTS.

PROLOGUE.

Pages.

Iceland before the Settlement. Testimony of Bede. Anchorites from Britain.   1-2

FIRST PART.

CHAPTER I.—*Settlement. Contemporary Sovereigns. Position of Iceland, and discovery by Naddod and Gardar*   -   -   -   -   -   -   2-4

CHAPTER II.—*Discovery of Iceland by Floki. Name of " Iceland " first given*   -   -   -   -   4-5

CHAPTER III.—*Discovery of Iceland by Bjornolf*   -   5-6

CHAPTER IV.—*Ingolf and Leif gather a band and set out from Norway for Iceland*   -   -   -   -   6-7

CHAPTER V.—*Leif's expedition to Ireland*   -   7

CHAPTER VI.—*Ingolf sets out to settle in Iceland, A.D. 874*   -   -   -   -   -   -   8-9

CHAPTER VII.—*Ingolf takes vengeance on the murderers of Leif*   -   -   -   -   -   -   9-10

CHAPTER VIII.—*Settlement at Reykjavik*   -   10

CHAPTER IX.—*Thing first set up. Thorkell Moon, Speaker-at-law. Christianity introduced A.D. 1000*   10-11

CHAPTER X.—*Tale of Bjorn Buna*   -   -   11-12

Pages.

CHAPTER XI.—*Harald Fairhair subdues the Hebrides* - 12-13

CHAPTER XII.—*Orlyg from the Hebrides lands at Patrick's-firth, and after settles near Kjalarness* - - 13-14

CHAPTER XIII.—*Svartkel, a settler from Caithness in Scotland* - - - - - - 14-15

CHAPTER XIV.—*Settlement at Hvamm* - 15-16

CHAPTER XV.—*Early Christian Settlers* - - 16-17

CHAPTER XVI.—*Asolf's miraculous power of drawing fish. His final settlement at Holm* - - 17

CHAPTER XVII.—*Bekan and other early Settlers* - 18-19

CHAPTER XVIII.—*Kveldulf's last voyage. His last words and death. The chest containing his dead body cast overboard. His companions find it cast ashore* - 19-21

CHAPTER XIX.—*Borg the home of Kveldulf's descendants* 21-22

CHAPTER XX.—*Other Settlements round Borgarfirth. Slaughter of Torfi* - - - - 23-24

CHAPTER XXI.—*Raud settles Rodgill. Grim settles Grimsgill. Koll settles Koll's-stream (læk). Ulf settles between White-river and South glacier* - 24-26

Note on the Godi and the institution of the Althing, A.D. 930 - - - - - - 26-27

SECOND PART.

The Settlement in the Quarter of the Western Firths.

CHAPTER I.—*Kalman from the Hebrides and his Settlements* - - - - - 27-29

CHAPTER II.—*Settlements by the Kjarr-river and Hvit (White) river. The ancestors of those who fought in the Battle upon the Heath. Snorri of Melar* - 29-31

Pages.

CHAPTER III.—*Settlements of Arnborg, Thorbjorn, Geirmund, Orn, Rauda Bjorn, Karl, and the freedmen of Skallagrim* - - - - - 31-32

CHAPTER IV.—*Settlement of Bersi godless and the freedmen of Grim* - - - - - 32-35

CHAPTER V.—*Grim draws up a mereman (marmennil) while fishing, which he compels to foretell place of settlement. First appearance of Volcano Eldborg to Thorir, his son, in old age* - - - 35-37

Note on Eldborg and Raudamel - - - - 37-38

CHAPTER VI.—*Settlements by Straumfjord-river. The Holmgang. Ancestors of the Sturlungs of Hvamm. Hospitality of Thora. Story of the interment of Asmund* - - - - - - 38-40

CHAPTER VII.—*Deadly conflict between the party of Laugarbrekka-Einar and the party of Lon-Einar about alleged witchcraft. Einar's grave mound* - 40-42

CHAPTER VIII.—*Settlements of the descendants of Grimkell. Thorarin Korni, the hamramr mjök, i.e., the great wizard who could change his shape* - - 42-43

CHAPTER IX.—*Gerveld accused of witchcraft. Her trial by Duradóm is broken up by a free fight. Settlement of Herjolf. Slays a wood-bear* - - - 43-46

CHAPTER X.—*Settlements upon the lava plains. Appearances of a mysterious horse* - - - - 46-47

CHAPTER XI.—*Descendants of Ketil Flatnose. Dispute with Harald Fairhair. Hrolf the Ganger* - - 47-48

CHAPTER XII.—*Settlement of Thorolf Mostbeard, A.D. 884. His high seat posts come to land in Broadfirth. He finds them at Temple-stead on Holy-fell. Temple set up there and District Assembly. Fight and consequent feud between the men of Thorsness and the followers of Kiallak the Old, A.D. 932 to 934* - 48-51

Pages.

Note upon the High Seat Pillar, öndvegis sula - - 51-52

The Holy Hill or Helga Fell on Snœfellness; the earthly Paradise of Thorolf and his descendants who settled around Broadfirth (Breiðafjörð.) - . - 52-54

Note on Thorolf's Temple at Temple-stead - 54-55

Note on the Stone of Thor, Blot-steinn or Stone of Sacrifice - - - - - - 55-56

CHAPTER XIII.—*Settlement of Geirrod and Ulfar. Hospitality of Geirrid his sister. Duel at the Holmgang between Thorolf and Ulfar. Death of Ulfar. Settlements in the Eyri. Origin of the community whose history is related in the Eyrbyggja Saga* - 56-58

CHAPTER XIV.—*Discovery (A.D. 982) and Settlement (A.D. 986) of Greenland by Eirek the Red* - 58-62

CHAPTER XV.—*Olave the White, King of Dublin, marries Aud, daughter of Ketil Flatnose. Thorstein their son and Sigurd conquer more than half of Scotland. Thorstein falls in battle* - - - 62-63

CHAPTER XVI.—*Queen Aud settles all the Dale-lands, A.D. 892* - - - . - - 63-65

CHAPTER XVII.—*Queen Aud gives lands for settlement to her shipmates and freedmen* - - - 65-67

CHAPTER XVIII.—*Other settlements made by Queen Aud's followers* - - - - - 67-69

CHAPTER XIX.—*Death of Queen Aud. Her Arval Feast and Burial within the Sea Shore* - - - 69-70

Note on the Arval Feast of Queen Aud - - 70-71

Note on the voyages and settlements of Queen Aud - 71-73

Pages.

Settlement of Kjallak. His blood-feud. Births of Hamund and Geirmund, sons of King Hjor. Bragi's prophecy concerning them. Battle in Hafursfirth, A.D. 885. Settlement of Geirmund in Broadfirth - - 73-77

CHAPTER XX.—Settlements, wealth, and retainers of Geirmund "Hellskin" - - - - 77-78

CHAPTER XXI.—Settlements of Steinolf, Slettu-Bjorn, Olaf Belg, and Gisl Skeid-neb - - - 79-80

CHAPTER XXII.—Settlements of Thorarin Crook, Ketil Broad-sole, and Ulf the Squinter. Ari is drifted over the ocean to Whitemen's land or Ireland the Great, conjectured to be South America - - 80 82

CHAPTER XXIII.—Hallstein settles Codfirth; makes High-seat posts from drift-wood. Thorbjorn "Loki" settles Deepfirth to Steamfirth. Ketil "Gufa" comes from Viking raids in Ireland and settles Gufuscales and Gufuness. Flight and feuds of his thralls. "Burning in" by thralls at Lambistead. The "burning in" is avenged - - - - 82-85

CHAPTER XXV.—Koll, Knjuk, Geirstein, Geirleif, and sundry other settlers - - - - 85-87

CHAPTER XXVI.—Settlements of Armod, Thorolf Sparrow, Ketil Broadsole, and Orn. An Redfell harries Ireland in a Viking-raid to the west, afterwards settles in Iceland with his relations - - 87-89

CHAPTER XXVII.—Eirek settles Ditch Dale. Vestein and Dyra settle Dyrafirth. Thord, son of Harald Fairhair and his connections - - - 89-91

CHAPTER XXVIII.—Settlements of Ingiald and Ljot the Sage. Gest foretells the death of Ljot. The sons of Grim "Kogr" fulfil the prophecy - - - 91-93

Pages.

CHAPTER XXIX.—*Settlements of Onund, Hallward Soughing, Thurid Soundfiller, Helgi son of Hrolf, Eyvind Knee, Vebjorn, Gunnstein, and Haldor* - 94-96

CHAPTER XXX.—*Settlements of Snæbjorn, brother of Helgi the Lean. Terrible blood feud between Snæbjorn and Hallbjorn, on account of the murder of Hallgerd, Hallbjorn's wife* - - - - - 96-99

CHAPTER XXXI.—*Settlements of Olaf " Jafnakollr,' Orlyg, son of Bodvar, and Eirek Snare. The landtakes of Geirmund in their order* - - - 100-101

CHAPTER XXXII.—*Settlements of Onund Treefoot, Bjorn Steingrim, Koll, Thorbjorn " Bitra," Balki, and Aindis* - - - - - - 101-103

CHAPTER XXXIII.—*Hromund the Halt and his sons Thorbjorn, Thorleif, and Hestein settle at Fairbrink. They summon Helgi and his clan of Viking Eastmen for horse stealing. Hromund and his sons are made wardens of the district. A poem relating the terrible and fatal conflict between Hromund and the Eastern Vikings; their final discomfiture and flight; names of chief settlers in Westfirth. Census* - - 103-109

Note to Chapter XXXIII. - - 113

THIRD PART.

The Settlement in the Northern Quarter.

CHAPTER I.—*Eysteinn " Meinfret" settles the Dales. Thorodd settles Ramsfirth and dwells at Thoroddstead. Fur Bjorn settles Midfirth. Midfirth Skeggi, his son, and his exploits. Harald Ring settles Waterness. Audun Skokil, grandson of Ragnar Lodbrog, settles at Auduustead. His connexions and their Settlements.* 110-113

Pages.

CHAPTER II.—*Ingimund the Old from Norway. Pre-diction of the witch wife concerning his Talisman. Its singular story. He settles Vatnsdale and resides at Hof* - - - - - 113-116

CHAPTER III.—*Ingimund finds three white bears at Hunavatn. Sends them to King Hrrald in Norway. Finds one hundred swine in Swinedale* - - 116-117

CHAPTER IV.—*Hrolleif the Great and Ljot his mother settle in Hrolleifsdale. Settlement results in a series of deadly family feuds* - ' - - - 117-123

CHAPTER V.—*Eyvindr settles Svindale. Ævarr comes to Blanda-river-mouth. Settles Langdale all across the Hause and shares his lands with his ship's crew. Vefreyd settles Moberg. Gaut settles Gaut's-dale aud Hauk settles near Hauk's pits. Holti at Holtisland. Fostolf and Thorstolf settle Engihlid in Langdale. Fatal feud between them and Ulfhedin* - - 123-126

CHAPTER VI.—*Eilif Eagle settles land from Manis-Hummock to Gunnguskeid-river and Lax-river-dale. Sæmund from the Hebrides brings his ship to the mouth of Gaunga-skards-river. Settles land from Sæmunds-slope to Vatn-skard. Skefil contemporary with Sæmund settles land beyond the Sand-river. Settlements of his descendants. Ulfljot settles Lang-holt. Alfgeir settles Algeirs fields up to Machfells-river. Settlement by Hrosskel in Svart-river-dale* - 126-129

CHAPTER VII.—*Eirek, a Norwegian, settles Goddale down to North-river. Contends with Vekell the Shapechanger* - - - - - 129-131

CHAPTER VIII.—*Eirek and Onund the Wise contend for land east of Mark Gill. Taking possession of the land by the fire arrow. Thorbrand's hospitality. Horse racing and fighting* - - - - 131-133

Pages.

CHAPTER IX.—*The Royal connexions of Gorm in Sweden and Russia. His settlements in Iceland. Ondott's settlements* - - - - - 134

CHAPTER X.—*Remarkable Arvals. A Drapa. Verses on the appearance of the sons of Hjalti at Thorskafjard Thing. The discovery of Vinland the Good, i.e. America. Thord and his nineteen children* - - 135-137

CHAPTER XI.—*Fridleif the Swede, Floki, and other settlers. Bard from the Hebrides, and Bruni the White settle Narrowdales. Rotation in the ownership of land* - ' - - - - 137-143

CHAPTER XII.—*Bjorn exiled from a burning in, in Sweden. Goes to Ireland in Vestrviking. Eyvind his son settles in Ireland. Helgi the Lean, son of Eyvind, brought up in the Hebrides. His adventures and final settlement in Iceland* - - - 140-143

CHAPTER XIII.—*Settlement of Thorstein Svarfad. Origin of the Saga of the men of Svarfaus-dale. Hamund Hellskin shares his lands with Orn* - 143-144

CHAPTER XIV.—*Settlement of Thord the Tearer and his relations in Horg-river-dale. Verses on the conflict between Steinraud and Blacksmith and Geirhild the witch-wife. Settlement of Audolf and Eyvind in Horg-rivers-dale* - - - - - 144-146

CHAPTER XV.—*Quick voyage of Thrand Much-sailing from the Orkneys. Grim slays Ondott. Grim burned in his house by the sons of Ondott. Terrible conflict resulting therefrom.* - - - - 146-148

CHAPTER XVI.—*Settlement of Hamund "hellskin," Audun, Thorgeir, sons-in-law, and Ingiald, son of Helgi the Lean* - - - - - 149-151

CHAPTER XVII.—*Gaut clears his forecastle of Vikings by a blow of his tiller, hence called "Tiller-Gaut." Verses on his settlement. Thorir worships the grove. Verses in welcome of Hallstein* - - - 151-153

Pages.

CHAPTER XVIII.—*Settlements of Bard of the Peak. Settlements of Kamp-Grim from the Orkneys and his descendants. Settlements of Heidan and Hoskuld, sons of the Giant* - - - - - 154-156

CHAPTER XIX.—*Settlements of Vestman, Ulf, Eyvind, Grenjad. Shipwreck and settlement of Bodolf. Foretelling the weather by means of ship's beaks. Grettis verses concerning Thorir* - - - 156-158

CHAPTER XX.—*Mani from Halogaland settles between Fljots and Raudaskridu (Red Screes). Einar, Vestman, and Vemund from the Orkneys consecrate to themselves by place-names, Axfirth, Eagle's hummock, and Cross-ridge. Ketil Thistle settles Thistle-firth* - 159-162

FOURTH PART.

The Settlement in the Quarter of the Eastern Firths.

CHAPTER I.—*Gunnolfsvik and Gunnolfsfell settled by Gunnolf Kroppa and others. Eyvind the Weaponed gives the name to Weaponfirth—Vapnafjord* - - 162-165

CHAPTER II.—*Weaponfirth settled by Thorstein Turf, Lyting, and Thorfid. Hakon settles Jokulsdale west of Jokul's-river. Tongue lands between Lagarfljots and Jokul's-river settled by Thord and his descendants. Arneid finds buried treasure* - - - 165-167

CHAPTER III.—*Porridge-Atli settles eastern shore of Lagarfljot to Gils-river (Gilsá). Thorgeir and others settle there. Hrafnkel's dream. Settles Hrafnkelsdal* 167-169

CHAPTER IV.—*Uni (son of Gardar first discoverer) and his companions slain by Leidolf in a deadly feud. Drawing and carving by Tjorvi. His satirical verses result in the death of Hroar and his sister's sons. Vertrlidi settles Borgfirth (Borgarfjord)* - - 169-171

                                                     Pages.

CHAPTER V.—*Lodmund the Old and Bjolf come from
    Norway to Iceland. Lodmund guided by his High
    Seat Pillars settles between Hegoat-river and Jokul's-
    river on Solheima-sand ; names his dwelling Solheim
    =Sunholme. Lomund and Thrasi agree that Jokul's-
    river shall divide the East and South Quarters* - 171-173

CHAPTER VI.—*Bjolf settles Seydisfjord. Egil the Red
    settles Northfirth (Nordfjord). Freystein the Fair
    settles Sandvik and Cavefirth (Hellisfjord). Thorir
    the High settles Krossavik (Crosswick), Reydarfjord
    (Troutfirth). Vemund settles Faskrudsfjord. Thor-
    hadd the Old settles Stodvarfjord* -   :   - 173-174

CHAPTER VII.—*Hjalti settles Broaddale. Herjolf settles
    Hvalness Screes. Thjodrek settles Berufjord and
    Bulandness. The ring in each Chief Temple. Form
    of the oath upon the ring* -   -   -   - 174-177

CHAPTER VIII.—*Thorstein Leg goes from the Hebrides
    to Iceland ; settles all lands from north of the Horn
    to Jokul's-river ; returns to the Hebrides. Rögnvald
    Earl of Mæri and his three sons, of whom Hrollaug
    is sent to Iceland and Einar volunteers for the
    Orkneys* -   -   -   -   -   - 177-179

CHAPTER IX.—*Voyage and settlement of Hrollaug ;
    keeps up allegiance with Harald Fairhair ; accepts
    from him sword, alehorn, and gold ring. Settlement
    of Hrollaug's sons* -   -   -   -   - 179-180

CHAPTER X.—*Ketil, Audun the Red, and Thorstein the
    Squinter buy land of Hrollaug. Vors-Ulf settles
    Papyli and Breidabolstead. Thord· Evilmind wrecks
    his ship upon Broadriversand. Settles between Jokul's-
    river and Folds-river. Sons of Asbjorn settle round
    Ingolf's-stead. Peak-bird settles Fljotsherfi and the
    Peaks* -   -   -   -   -   - 180-182

Pages.

CHAPTER XI.—*Eyvind Carp settles near Alhmens'-Fleet. Ketil the Foolish from the Hebrides settles between Geirland's-river and Firth-river; lives at Kirkby, former abode of the Papar. Vilbald from Ireland comes ashore at Kudafljot's-mouth and dwell at Buland* - · - - - - 182-184

CHAPTER XII.—*Hrafn Haven-key foretells a volcanic eruption. Death song of Vermund the Blacksmith. Mould-Gnup the Blacksmith, his brother, settles Kudafleet and Swan's-haunts. Bjorn, his son, dreams of the rock-dweller; his great prosperity resulting therefrom* - - - - - - 185-187

CHAPTER XIII.—*Eystein wrecks his vessel and settles Fairdale. Olver, son of Eystein, settles land east of Grim's-river. Sigmund Kleykir settles land from Grim's-river to Carlines-river. Names of most distinguished settlers in Eastfirth's Quarter* - - 187-189

FIFTH PART.

The Settlement in the Southern Firths.

CHAPTER I.—*Thrasi settles between Kadaklof-river and Jokul's-river. Hrafn the Foolish settles between Kaldaklof-river and Lambfell-river* - - 189-190

CHAPTER II.—*Asgeir "Kneif" settles land between Lambfell-river and Seljaland-river. Thorgeir settles land between Lambfell-river and Ira-river. Asgerd upon the murder of Ofeig, her husband, by Harald Fairhair, sets out for Iceland with her children; settles between Seljaland-mull and Markfleet. Ancestors of Burnt Nial* - · · · · 190-192

Pages.

CHAPTER III.—*Ketil Salmon avenges the murder of Thorolf by burning in their house Harek and Hrærek, two of Thorolf's deadliest enemies; afterwards goes to Iceland and settles land betweeu Rang-river and Hroarsbrook. His son, Sighvat the Red, settles above the Dealing or 'dividing' river. Three cornered plot of land hallowed by fire and set apart for a Temple* - 192-194

CHAPTER IV.—*Baug settles Fleet-Lithe. Fatal fight at Sandholar-ferry between the followers of Sigmund and followers of Stein the Snell. Sons of Stein outlawed from Lithe. Many and fatal blood suits result therefrom between Stein, Onund, and their families* - 195-197

CHAPTER V.—*Remarkable combat of Dufthak and Storolf in Oldugrof. Orm the Enthralled first to settle Westman-isles. Eilif from Sogn settles land up to Troutwater and Viking-brook. Bjorn from Sogn lives at Svinhagi and settles land along Rang-river. Kol, son of Oitar Ball, settles land east of Troutwater and Stot-brook with Troll-wood. Fatal fight of Egil, his son, with Gunnar; other fatal fights with Gunnar. Hrolf Redbeard settles land of Holm between Fish-river and Rang-river; resides at Force (the Falls); he worships the Force; his remarkable power of distinguishing his sheep; foretells his own death and destruction of his flocks* - - - - - 198-200

CHAPTER VI.—*Harald Fairhair causes Asgrim to be killed by Thororm. Thorstein Asgrim's son burns Thororm in, and then with Thorgeir, his brother, sails for Iceland. By advice of Flosi he settles the Rang-river plains above Viking-brook. Buried treasure at Tent-stead* - - - - - - 201-202

CHAPTER VII.—*Flosi goes from Norway to Iceland on account of manslaughter of King Harald's bailiffs. His settlements by the Rang-river. Ketil the Onehanded, Ketil Char, Orm the Wealthy, and other settlers by the Rang-river* - - - - 202-204

Pages.

CHAPTER VIII.—*Settlements of Rathorm and Jolgeir from the west, and Askel Knokan, Thorkel Furcoat, Lopt the son of Orm, Thorvid the son of Ulfar, and Thorarin, son of Thorkel* - - - - 204-205

CHAPTER IX.—*Ancestry of Harald Fairhair. Hastein driven by him from Sogn, betakes himself to Iceland; throws his Seat Stocks overboard for an omen; they come ashore at Stockkseyri; settles between Rothay (Red-river) and Olvis-river up to Full-brook. Settlements of Hallstein, Thorir, son of hersir Asi, Hrodgeir the Sage, and Onund Bil* - - - 206-208

CHAPTER X.—*Settlements of Ozur the White and his freedman Bodvar. Bodvar summoned for sheeplifting. After his death his house at Willowwood becomes the source of a fatal feud to rival claimants. Thord slays Rafn from an ambush* - - - 208-211

CHAPTER XI.—*Settlements of Thrand Much-sailing, Olvir Bairncarle, Thorbjorn Laxcarle, Thorbrand, and others who came out late in the Landnamtide* - 212-214

CHAPTER XII.—*Ketilbjorn from Naumdale in Norway with a ship (the Ellidi) gives that name to the Ellidi's-river. His settlements at Grimness, Laugardale, Bishop's-tongue, and Mossfell. Settlement of Asgeir at Lithe, Eilif at Head. Grim, son of Vethorm, settles Bowerfell. Hallkel fights with and slays Grim for his land upon Hallkel's-hillocks* - 215-217

CHAPTER XIII.—*Thorgrim Bill settles Bills-fell, and Steinraud, his freedman, gets the Waterlands. Hrolleif settles lands on the western side of the Axe-river, which flows across the Thingwall. Orm settles land east of the Warm-river (Hita). Alf of Agdir, from Norway, brings his ship into Alf's-os Inlet. Settles lands to west of Warm-river; resides at Gnupar* - 217-218

Note to Chapter XIII. The Plain of Thing Vellir. The Axe-river (Oxara) and the Althing - - 218-220

Pages.

CHAPTER XIV.—*Thorir Harvestmirk settles Sealcreek (Selvag) and Creasywick. Steinun the Old buys from Ingolf, her kinsman, Walrusness for a spotted cloak; gives land to her kinsman Eyvind. Herjolf, mentioned before, gets land from Ingolf between Reekness and Veg. Herjolf, his grandson, fares to Greenland and is drawn into the ocean-whirl. In his ship a man from the Hebrides writes the Poem of "The Ocean Whirl"* - - - - - 220-222

CHAPTER XV.—*Names of the noblest landtakemen. The land completely settled in sixty years. Names of the greatest Chieftains in the four Quarters at the end of 120 years. Most settlers from the west (British Islands) were baptised Christians. Relapse of their descendants into heathenism for about 120 years* - 222-223

Place Names, being the Register of all the Place Names, Farm Names, and Tribe Names contained in the Book of the Settlement - - - - - 224-243

INTRODUCTION.

ICELAND. ITS PHYSICAL FEATURES.

Iceland is an island in the north Atlantic Ocean, the northernmost point of it just touches the Polar circle. It lies between 63° 23' and 66° 22' north latitude and between 13° 22' and 24° 15' west longitude.

The distance from Iceland to Greenland * is about 250 miles, to Norway 600 miles, to the Faroe Islands 250 miles, and to Scotland 500 miles. Its superficial area is 40,300 square miles, more than one-third larger than Scotland, length from east to west 300 miles, breadth from north to south 200 miles. As will be seen upon the map, the north, west, and east coasts are very much indented by bays and firths, which are wanting on the south coast. Its circumference from point to point would be about 900 miles, but following in the indentations of the coast line, it is about 2,000 miles.

One of the most striking views to voyagers approaching Iceland from the west is the wide and magnificent coast line presented by Faxe Fiord or Faxis Inlet, which takes its name, as we are told by Ari, from Faxi, an early discoverer, who exclaimed when he first scanned it † " This must be a great land which we have discovered, for here are mighty rivers." Within this firth now stands Reykjavik ‡ with its 4000 inhabitants, and upon another branch of the same bay is Borg, § the settlement and home of that renowned family of Kveldulf, whose story is so pathetically related in the Egil's Saga. One of the latest writers upon Iceland, Lord

---

* For old Norse computation of those distances to Greenland, Norway and Ireland as estimated in days' sailing see pages 2 and 3.
† Page 4.
‡ Reykjavik, i, 8, page 10.
§ Borg, see i, 19; also Borg and Borgfjordr on Map.

Dufferin

Dufferin, approaching it from the western coast, thus describes that fiord to which Faxi had given the name over a thousand years before—" The panorama of the bay of Faxi Fiord is magnificent, with a breadth of 50 miles from Horn to Horn, the one running down into a rocky ridge, the other towering to a height of 5000 feet in a pyramid of eternal snow, while round the intervening semi-circle crowd the peaks of a hundred noble mountains. As you approach the shore you are very much reminded of the west coast of Scotland, except that everything is more *intense*, the atmosphere clearer, the light more vivid, the air more bracing, the hills steeper, loftier, and more tormented, as the French say, and more gaunt, while between their base and the sea stretches a greenish slope patched with houses, which themselves, both roof and walls, are of a mouldy green as if they had been fished out of the bottom of the sea."

The promontory of Snæfellness is the Horn which Lord Dufferin here describes as crowned with mountains towering to a height of 5000 feet in a pyramid of eternal snow. This mountain Snæfell (Snowfell), mentioned at I, 1, page 2, gives its name to the promontory Snæfellness. Physically or historically this is the most remarkable promontory in the whole island. Near its extremity is Arnar Stapi (now Stappen) or the Steeple Rock of the Eagles. Here too is Helga Fell,* in heathen days the most sacred spot in Iceland, while north of this promontory is Breidfjord, or Broadfirth, whose discovery by Thorolf is described at Part II, 12, page 48. Broadfirth abounds in islands. Round the head of one of its bays, Queen Aud from the British Islands, settled the dale lands and took up her permanent abode at Hvamm.

This was about the year 892.

Iceland generally consists of a table-land about 2000 feet in height. It slopes in some instances evenly down to the coast, especially on the south coast between Eyjafajallokul and Reykjanes. The lowland here is about 1400 square miles.

---

* For Arnar Stapi and Helga Fell see map.

Borgarfirth

Borgarfirth is the next largest lowland comprising about 400 square miles. *

As indicated by the numerous Place Names compounded with Hraun, the island is throughout volcanic. The whole of the interior is occupied by barren sands, lava tracts, and icefields. The largest of these tracts is Odathahraun, about 1200 square miles. The largest icefield † is that of Vatna-jökull, about 3000 square miles, all the icefields together cover 5360 square miles. The Ornæfa Jökull is the highest mountain in Iceland having a height of 6426 feet above the level of the sea. The snow line is between 3000 feet and 4000 feet above the sea level. There are twenty volcanoes in Iceland which have been in eruption at one time or other since the island was inhabited. The eruptions of Hecla have been most frequent. In 1783 Skapta threw out a lava stream 45 miles long and about 15 miles broad. As a result of such volcanic agency about 2400 miles of Iceland was covered with lava. The Book of the Settlement indicates the commencement of some of the outbreaks, more particularly that of Raudamel.

The Place Names are amongst the best records of the physical formation of Iceland, and a glance at the map upon its south-western extremity gives evidence that the volcanic agency has not been confined to the island itself. Three names of islands occurring together are Reyknes, Eldey, and Eldey-jardrangr—these are literally Reckness or promontory, Fire Island and Fire Island Rocks and indicate what their geological formation also abundantly proves, that those islands have risen from the sea by volcanic eruption. The word Reykr or Reykjar which occurs so often upon the map of Iceland has a striking significance. It is the English word Reek or smoke, and occurs in Reykja-á, Reykja-dalr, Reykja-holt, Reykja-vellir, Reykja-fjordr (twice in western Iceland) Reykjr-strand, and Reykja-vik, and indicates the numerous hot springs scattered all over the island connected with these

* See Borgarfjördar on Map and in Place Names.
† The various icefields will be found on map under Icelandic equivalent "jökull."

volcanic

volcanic fires. The singular Reykjar being used when there is only one spring, and the plural Reykja when there are more than one. The most famous of them are the Geysirs; they differ much in temperature, some being just warm enough for bathing, others convert their water into steam at a degree far above boiling point. A recent traveller thus vividly describes the largest : " The subterranean thunders commenced—a violent agitation disturbed the centre of the pool—suddenly a dome of water lifted itself up to the height of 8 or 10 feet, then burst and fell, immediately afterwards a shining liquid column, or rather a sheaf of columns, wreathed in robes of vapour, sprung into the air, and in a succession of jerking leaps, each higher than the last, flung their silver crests against the sky. The spectacle was certainly magnificent, but no description can give any idea of its more striking features. The enormous wealth of water—its vitality—its hidden power—the illimitable breadth of sunlit vapour, rolling out in exhaustless profusion, all combined to make one feel the stupendous energy of nature's slightest movements. The first burst upward till the time when the last jet retreated into the pipe occupied the space of seven or eight minutes. At no time did the crown of the column reach higher than 60 or 70 feet. Early travellers talk of 300 feet, more trustworthy persons have stated the eruption at 200 feet, while well authenticated accounts, when the elevation of the jet has been actually measured, makes it to have attained a height of upwards of 100 feet."

In the Book of the Settlement, rivers form perhaps the most important natural features, as affording inlets to the early settlers on the otherwise harbourless coasts, and as giving a line of demarcation to the landtakes, which, as will be seen, are almost invariably referred to the rivers or to the water shed of the country—Steer's river (Thjórsá) in the south and Glacier-river (Jokulsá) and Trembling-water (Skjalfandafljot) in the north are the largest rivers, each being over 100 miles long. Hot-river (Hvitá) and Cold-river (Kaldá) which bound opposite quarters of the same landtake as place-names need no comment. White-river (Hvita) implies the colouration of the water by a glacial

moraine

moraine while Gorge-river (Glufrá) is a sufficient evidence to the character of the bed within which it flows.

The most considerable lakes are Thingvalla Lake, of which a description is given in Part v, 13, and Midgewater or Myvatn in the north. This is often referred to in the Book of the Settlement.

The following sketch of Iceland has been written expressly for this work by Dr. Jón Stefánsson,* PhD. of the University of Copenhagen, a native Icelander, who spent a great portion of the summer of last year (1897) in re-visiting and exploring the island.

The western part of Iceland is the classic saga ground which specially centres round Broadfirth. With its innumerable islands and the wicks and voes, bays and fjords which cut into its coasts, it bears more similarity to Greece than any other part of Iceland. It varies much. Snæfell's-ness, with its mountain range that ends in the imposing dome of the glacier, at the extreme end of the peninsula, the dales, so like the glens in the Scottish and English borderland, the deep and narrow north-west fjords, Patrick's fjord with its steep and precipitous sides, where the rock ledges rise one above the other in parallel streaks. They throw the firth into shadow but give shelter from the winds. Bluff headlands rising behind each other on the horizon.

A great many of the islands in Broadfirth are inhabited, the best known of these is Flatey, on which one of the earliest monasteries in Iceland was built. Between some of the islands are rapid currents or swirls, which are dangerous to fishermen. Some of the islands are covered with luxuriant grass in summer, others are well-known as breeding places for seals or eiderducks.

Besides these islands, the Westman Islands south of Iceland, Grimsey north of it, and a few islands in the eastern and north-western fjords are inhabited. Grimsey is cut in two by the Polar Circle. It forms one parish and the church lies just in the line of the Arctic Circle. The Islanders seldom come the long way to the mainland.

---

* Dr. Stefánsson also kindly looked over and corrected for this work proofs of a portion of Part III, and Parts IV and V.

The

The capital of Iceland, Reykjavik, numbers 4000 inhabitants, and is the seat of all the highest officials in the island. Parliament is held there every other year, and it has a lively trade with the British Isles, Norway and Denmark. One of the islands (Videy) that form the harbour is inhabited and boasted of a famous cloister in the Middle Ages.

The next town in size in Iceland is Akureyri, on the Eyjafjord, with about 1000 inhabitants. It is pleasantly situated on the hillside overlooking the fjord and the scenery of Viga Glúm's Saga.

The third town in Iceland in size is Isafjord, in the north-west, with about 600 inhabitants. The harbour is shut in completely and land-locked.

The fourth town is Seydisfjord on the east coast, a little smaller than Isafjord, but being the nearest to Europe, it has more communication with it all the year round than any other port.

There are two made roads in Iceland, the one from Reykjavik to Thingvellir, 35 miles; the other from Reykjavik to Thjórsá or Steer's-river. This last road runs partly through the district devastated by the earthquakes in 1896; such earthquakes had not occurred in Iceland for a century, or since the great eruption of 1783-1784. New geysers opened and long cracks were to be seen in the ground. Several hundred farmhouses tumbled down but the loss of life was small.

The whole of Iceland is believed to have risen out of the sea by gradual volcanic eruptions. The basaltic formation of the east and the north-west seems, however, to date from an earlier geological period. Dr. Thorvaldar Throddsen has been engaged during the last sixteen years in exploring the country, and the new geological map of it which he is about to issue, will supersede Björn Gunnlaugsson's excellent map which is now half a century old.

Travelling in Iceland, away from the trading towns, is still very primitive. On pony back you scamper over the tracks made by horses hoofs, and put up at one of the farmhouses on your way, where the warmth of the welcome and the hospitality makes up for the scantness of the fare. The

Celtic

Celtic strain imparted to the settlers in Iceland by inter-marriage with Celts in Scotland, Ireland, and the Hebrides, is still noticeable in Iceland. They also brought a great number of Celtic slaves* with them to Iceland, and the result is seen in the number of dark-haired people in the island. The names of men and places have varied little from the time of Settlement until now. Iceland in this respect as in others is one of the most conservative countries in the world.

It has been noticed that Iceland is heart shaped, the point turning south, and so is its largest glacier, the Vatnajökull.

———

ARI THE LEARNED, Author of the Book of the Settlement.

Forefathers of Ari the Learned as given in the Book of the Settlement.

OLAF the white, marries Aud.
|
THORSTEIN the Red.
|
OLAF FEILAN.
|
THORD YELLIR marries ALFDIS OF BARA
|
EYOLF the Gray.
|
THORKEL.
|
GELLIR.
|
THORGILS.
|
ARI the Learned.

Ari the Learned was born in 1067, of a noble family sprung from Queen Aud and King Olaf the White, from whom he was eighth in descent. Of his lineal ancestors five were born in Iceland, two in the heathen days, three in the christian times, but only one died a heathen. His sixth lineal ancestor, the settler Olaf Feilan, was born in the western islands, probably in Dublin, but died in Iceland. On his father's side

---

* See Part I, 5, 6.

Ari

Ari was the great-grandson of Gudrun the heroine of the
Laxdala Saga, on the mother's side he was sprung from
Hall-o-side, up to whom it is remarkable that the three
great Icelandic historians trace their descent on the mother's
side, Thorey, Sæmund's mother being Hall's granddaughter,
and Joreid, Aris' mother, his great granddaughter, Gudrig,
Snorri's mother standing to him both in the sixth or seventh
degrees of descent.   It was from the Reyknessings that the
historian got his name of Ari=*the eagle.*   His father Thorgils
was drowned in his infancy, hence he was brought up at
Helgafell (Holy fell) the house of his grandfather.   He was
a godi and is once, in 1118, recorded among the chiefs of
Iceland who were in Holy Orders.   He was married and had
a son and a daughter.   He died in 1148, on Nov. 9th, aged 81.
   " Ari the Learned," says Snorri in his preface to the
Heimskringla, " was the first man of this land who wrote
down lore both old and new in the speech of the north.   He
came when seven winters old to Hawkdale,* to Hall the son
of Thorarin and abode there fourteen winters.   Hall was an
exceeding wise man of keen memory.   Teit the son of Bishop
Isleif also taught Ari much.   He was fostered at Hall's in
Hawkdale, and taught Ari the priest manifold lore, which
Ari wrote down afterwards.   Ari got manifold knowledge
from Thurid daughter of Snorri the priest, a woman wise of
wit.   She remembered Snorri her father who was near
thirty-five when Christ's faith came to Iceland, therefore
nothing wonderful it is that Ari knew many ancient tales
both of our lands and the outlands, inasmuch as he had
learned them from old men and wise, and was himself a man
of eager wit and fruitful memory."
   Ari was the true father of Icelandic letters, as well as the
first prose writer and first historian in the Icelandic language.
It would hardly be an exaggeration to say that whatever we
know for certain of the life, religion, and constitution of the
old days of the Scandinavian States is in one way or other
due to Ari.   And it is well for us that he lived when he did,

---

* See Haukadale on the map, remarkable as being but half-a-mile from the
famous Geysirs.

like

like Herodotus, just in time to gather up and garner for us traditions that were dying out or been driven out of men's minds by new interests and new ideas, and not in vain does Snorri perhaps half regretfully, notice his *age* and the opportunities it gave him, advantages which he himself was denied.

Ari's works : Three works of his are distinctly mentioned.

1. The Konung-Bók, or Book of Kings (Heimskringla).
2. The Landnama, or Book of the Settlement.
3. The Islendinga-Bók, or Book of the Icelanders.

The very use of the work " bók " is distinctive of Ari, for when he wrote, all preceeding histories were Sagas in the true sense of the word, that is, they were *vivâ voce* traditions which had never been written down, and it would seem he thus distinguishes his own *written* work, to distinguish it from what is recited orally, the Saga or what is recited or said.

THE LATER EDITORS OF THE BOOK OF THE SETTLEMENT.

The story of the discovery of Iceland and the Settlements of the west, north, and south quarters, Parts II, III, and V, were written by Ari.

Kolskegg Asbiornson, his contemporary, described the East Quarter as is said, Part IV, 4 : " Now has Kolskegg dictated the story henceforth as to the Settlements." This takes in the remaining portion of Book IV.

(*a*) The joint work of these two was again edited by Styrmir the Learned, son of Kari, who died (1245).

(*b*) This edition was again gone over and revised by the distinguished historian, Sturla Thordson* (1214-1284). The recensions (*a* and *b*) of Styrmir and Thordson were re-edited by Hauk Erlendson, his edition the " Hauks-bók," forming

---

* Thordson was cousin of Snorri Sturlason and the author of the largest and most important of all the Sagas, ''The Sturlunga Saga,'' describing the terrible struggle which terminated in the fall and extinction of the Icelandic republic in 1261. He himself was nearly related to the leaders, and took a most important share in the struggle.

one of the principal texts of the Landnama Bok. There is a special recension based on (*a* and *b*) the so-called Mela-bók, frequently referred to in the following translation. The author of this edition is not known. Brand Haldorson is mentioned as the author of the genealogies of the men of Broadfirth.

What these later editors did was to add to the Book of the Settlement its geneaological lore and bring down the lines to their more immediate predecessors.

HARALD FAIRHAIR.

The sixty years that mark the period of the Settlement of Iceland are in a great measure contemporaneous with the reign of Harald Fairhair. That reign which marks in its record the commencement of authentic history in Norway, seems throughout to have been employed to crush and subdue the Norwegian chieftains, over whom Harald held the nominal rule, and it was because they would not be crushed and because they would not be subdued that so many of them, as related in the following pages, set out with their families and all their belongings for Iceland, to seek that position of self rule and freedom which was so sternly denied them at home.

Carlyle in his early Kings of Norway, gives a forcible sketch of this state of things. "Till about the year of grace 860," he says, "there were no kings in Norway, nothing but numerous jarls, essentially kinglets, each presiding over a kind of republic or parliamentary little territory, fylke things or folk things, little parish parliaments reproduced by them in the quarter things, founded by those chieftains when they migrated to Iceland and forming when united, that assembly, which as a whole, makes up the Althing or representative and legislative assembly of the whole land."

Harald Fairhair was the first to put an end to this state of things, by reducing it under one head and making a kingdom of it, which it has continued to be ever since. His
father,

father, Halfdan the Black, had already commenced this process, hard fighting followed by wise guidance of the conquered, but it was Harald Fairhair, his son, who carried it out and completed it. Harald's birth year, death year, and chronology in general are known only by inference, but by the latest reckoning his birth is put down at 850, he began, under tutelage doubtless, his reign in 860, and died about the year 933 of our era, a man of 83.

The business of conquest lasted Harald about 12 years in which he subdued also the Vikings of the out-islands, Orkneys, Shetlands, Hebrides, and Man. His reign is counted altogether to have been over 70 years. These were the times of Norse colonisation, proud Norsemen flying into other lands, to freer scenes, to Iceland, more especially to the Faroe Islands, to the Orkney and the Shetland Islands, the Hebrides, and other countries where Norse squatters and Norse settlers already were.

Settlement of Iceland, settlement of the Faroe Islands, and settlement of Normandy by Rolf the Ganger,* according to the Saxon Chronicle 876. Anent this season of subduing and driving out the recalcitrant Norwegian jarls to Iceland and elsewhere by Harald, the following relation is made in the Heimskringla or History of the Kings of Norway, concerning his ten or twelve years of conquest and the epithet by which he was afterwards known. King Harald sent his messengers to a certain maiden called Gyda, the daughter of King Eric of Hordaland, to ask her in marriage. She replied to his messengers as follows : " Give this my word to King Harald, that only so will I engage to being his sole and lawful wife if he will first do so much for my sake, as to lay under him all Norway, and rule that realm as freely as King Eric rules the Swede realm, or King Gorm, Denmark, for only such an one may be called aright a King of the People." Harald replied as follows : " This oath I make, first and swear before the God who made me and rules over all things, that never more will I cut my hair or comb it, till I have gotten to me all

---

* See page 178 for Rolf the Ganger.

Norway and the tithe thereof, and dues, and will rule there-over or else I will die rather." Then follows the fierce fighting, crushing, and expatriation of the Norwegian chieftains for 10 or 12 years, at the end of which time we are told King Harald had got to him all the land. So King Harald had his hair combed and Earl Rognvald sheared it—for hitherto it had been uncombed and unshorn for ten winters. Aforetime he had been called Shockhead, but now Earl Rognvald gave him a by-name, and called him Harald Fair-hair, a name which he has ever since received.

THINGS, THE QUARTER THINGS, AND THE ALTHING.

In Icelandic the term Thing has a twofold meaning.

1st. *An assembly or meeting;* a general term for any public meeting, especially for the purpose of legislation, also the place where such assembly was held.

2nd. *A district; county; shire;* a thing community; a political division of a county.

A careful comparison of the notices upon the subject in the Book of the Settlement will give the best idea of what is meant by the Icelandic Thing, Part II, 12, page 48, will show how Thorolf, a distinguished chieftain from Norway, formed the first Icelandic Quarter or District Thing.

It was the legislative district assembly; the doom or law court and the temple parish; the godi or chieftain himself being the priest. An account of the godi will be found I, 20, page 26. It was formed apparently upon the methods of the Folk Things or parish Parliaments they had had in Norway. A reference to the map will show that they were thirteen such Quarter Things or spring Thing in the whole island, each having three godi or temple priests. The other twelve Quarter Things or spring Things were formed doubt-less by the chieftains as they landed and by omen, fire or battle, took possession of their respective districts, and they were doubtless upon very much the same lines as

Thorolf

Thorolf is recorded to have formed Thorsness Thing. An account of the division of the land into quarters and also the form of oath taken at the Thing will be found at IV, 7, page 177. In the year 930 Ulfljot united all those district Things and formed of them the Althing bringing a code of laws for their government from Norway. The Althing seems to have held the same relationship to the whole island that the districts Things had to their respective quarters, and it was the Parliament or general assembly of the Icelandic Commonwealth, invested with supreme legislative and judicial power. The President is called logmaðr or lögsögu-maðr, law Speaker, or Speaker-at-Law, and his office was to preside at the assembly, and as in heathen times the law was not written he had to say from memory on the Lögberg, or law hill, before the assembled people what was the law of the land.

The Logretta or law-righter was the legislative body of the Althing, and on the Lögretta depended the duty of making laws for the whole land, framing new laws, and deciding what should be the law when a point was doubtful though not connected with any actual suit.

Before 930, the general assembly met at Kjalarness, see I, 9, page 10, whence it was removed, in 930, under the name of Althing, to Oxara or the Axe river, see Alþing and þingvöllr upon the map. For a description of the place see Part V, 13, note. The Parliament at first met on the Thursday commencing which fell between the 11th and 17th of June, but by a law of the year 999 its opening was deferred until the next following Thursday between 18th and 24th of June, old style. It continued for two weeks.

The Quarter Things with the Quarters in which they are included.

The Quarter of the Western Firths, part II.
           Thverar-thing
           Thorsness-thing
           Thorskafjardar-thing
The Northern Quarter, Part III.
           Hunavatns-thing
           Hegraness-thing
           Vaðla-thing
           Thingeyjar-thing   The

The Quarter of the Eastern Firths, Part IV.
 Sunnudal-thing
 Kidjafells-things
 Skaptafells-thing
The Quarter of the Southern Firths, Part V.
 Rangar-thing
 Arness-thing
 Kjalarness-thing

CHRONOLOGY OF THE BOOK OF THE SETTLEMNET AND OF THE SPEAKERS-AT-LAW TO THE FALL OF THE ICELANDIC REPUBLIC.*

A.D.

852—The Norse Sea King, Olave the White, landed at Dublin and founded a Norse Principality.

860—Harald Fairhair becomes King of Norway.

871—Accession of Alfred the Great.

875—Ingolf first settled Iceland.

878—Alfred's Treaty with the Danes.

884—Thorolf Mostbeard took land at Thorsness.

886—Biorn the Eastman, and Hallstein, son of Thorolf, settle Broadfirth.

892 (about) Queen Aud came to Iceland and settled all the Dale lands.

901—Death of Alfred the Great.

901—Accession of Edward, son of Alfred.

913—Thorstein Codbiter born.

918—Death of Thorolf Mostbeard.

927—Ulfljotr brought a system of law from Norway to Iceland. He first promulged a system of law in Iceland and by his advice the Althing was established.

930—The Althing is inaugurated; Rafn, son of Ketil the Salmon, first had the office of Speaker-at-Law and said law for 20 years.

---

* For the History of the fall of the Icelandic Republic, see Islendinga Saga (A.D. 1196-1262) by Sturla Thordarson,

950—

950—Thorarin Ragabrodir, son of Olaf, was Speaker-at-Law for 20 years.

970—Thorkel Mani, son of Thorstein, was Speaker-at-Law for about 15 years.

985—Thorgeir, son of Thorkel, was Speaker-at-Law for 17 years.

1000—Christianity introduced into Iceland. Discovery of Vineland or America by the Norsemen, described in Saga of Eirek the Red.

1002—Grim, son of Sversting from Mossfell, was Speaker-at-Law for about 2 years.

1004—Skapti, son of Thorodd the Priest, was Speaker-at-Law for about 26 years.

1031—Stein, son of Thorgest, was Speaker-at-Law for 3 years.

1034—Thorkel was Speaker-at-Law (the second time) for 19 years.

1054—Gellir, son of Bolverk, was Speaker-at-Law for 9 years.

1056—Isleif was consecrated first Bishop of Iceland at Skalholt.

1063—Gunnar, son of Thorgrim the Seer, was Speaker-at-Law for 3 years.

1066—Kolbein, son of Flosi, was Speaker-at-Law for 6 years. That summer King Harald, son of Sigurd, fell in England.

1071—Gellir was Speaker-at-Law the second time for 3 years.

1075—Gunnar Speaker-at-Law the second time for 1 year.

1076—Sighvat Speaker-at-Law for 8 years.

1080—Gellir Speaker-at-Law the third time.

1084—Markus, son of Skegg, Speaker-at-Law that summer and died 1093.

1093—Bergthor, son of Hrafn, Speaker-at-Law.

1097—Tuindargjald took law to Iceland.

1106—Bergthor Speaker-at-Law the second time. About this time the Christian Scriptures were brought to Iceland.

1107—Ulfedin took law to Iceland.

1122—Gudmund, son of Thorgeir, was Speaker-at-Law for 17 years.

1139—Hrafn Ulfhedin's son Speaker-at-Law for 4 years.

1143—Finn, son of Hall, Speaker-at-Law for 6 years.

1149—Hrafn Ulfhedin's son Speaker-at-Law for 10 years.

1159—Snorri Speaker-at-Law for 15 years.

1174—Styrkar, son of Odd, Speaker-at-Law for 10 years.

1184—Gizur, son of Hall, Speaker-at-Law for 22 years.

1206—Hall, son of Gizur, Speaker-at-Law for 8 years.

1214—Styrmir, son of Kara, Speaker-at-Law for 5 years. Styrmir was one of the later editors of Book of Settlement.

1219—Snorri Sturluson, the Historian, Speaker-at-Law for 4 years.

1223—Teitr, son of Thorvald, Speaker-at-Law for 3 years.

1226—Snorri Sturluson second time Speaker-at-Law for 10 years.

1236—Styrmir second time Speaker-at-Law for 4 years.

1240—Teitar, son of Thorvald, second time Speaker-at-Law for 12 years.

1252—Olafr, son of Thord, Speaker-at-Law for 3 years.

1256—Olafr, son of Thord, second time Speaker-at-Law for 1 year.

1257—Teitr, son of Einar, Speaker-at-Law for 6 years.

1262—Final submission of Iceland to Norway.

———

SAGAS.

As most of the Icelandic Sagas* had their first origin in the historical events related by Ari in the Book of the Settlement or from persons mentioned there, some of the chief of those Sagas with their district and probable period are noted on next page.

---

* For an excellent translation of the chief and most interesting of the Sagas, including the Heimskringla or History of the Early Kings of Norway, the reader is referred to the series contained in the Saga Library, commencing its issue in 1891, the volumes of which are still coming out at intervals. For a Picture Book to illustrate the Sagas of Iceland and to supply the background of scenery which the ancient dramatic style of the Sagas takes for granted, the Translator of the Book of the Settlement would refer to " A Pilgrimage to the Sagasteads of Iceland," by W. G. Collingwood, M.A., and Dr. Jón Stefánsson, which is expected to appear about Christmas in the present year, and which will contain 13 coloured plates and 138 engravings from water colour drawings by W. G. Collingwood. The places are such as have all been named and particularized in this Book of Settlement. The illustrations were completed by Mr. Collingwood on the spot in a pilgrimage which took him and Dr. Stefánsson, his companion, in the summer of 1897, over a rough and roadless country in a journey of over a thousand miles.

Nials

Nials Saga—The Saga of Law—Terminates with the Battle
of Clontarf 1014—South, V, 2.

Erbyggja Saga—Treats chiefly on Politics—Commences with
settlement of Thorolf Mostbeard, 884—extends over a
. period of 140 years—West, II, 12. The Saga of the
Battle upon the Heath, 1021, referred to at II, 2, page
29, is contained in this Saga.

Laxdala Saga—The most romantic of the Sagas—West. Of
uncertain date—chief character and leading events
sketched at II, 17.

Egil's Saga—A family feud between Kveldulf and Harald
Fairhair carried on for three generations—Ninth and
tenth centuries—Norway, England, and Iceland, I,
18 and 19.

Grettis Saga—Seems formed from hints found in Book of
Settlement, 1010 to 1013. North of Iceland and Norway, III, 19, and note.

The Saga of Howard the Halt is founded upon the tragic
event related at II, 18, page 92.

Other Sagas are noted under the chapters with which they
they are connected.

THE BOOK
OF THE SETTLEMENT OF ICELAND.

PROLOGUE.

Iceland before the Settlement—Testimony of Bede—Anchorites from Britain.

THIS is the Prologue to this Book. In that Book *
on the reckoning of time, which the Venerable Bede †
drew up, there is mention made of the Island called Tili,
which in books is said to be six days' sailing north from
Britain. There he said day came not in winter, nor
night in summer, when day is at its longest. By wise
men the reason why Iceland is called Tili is held to be
this, that, wide about the land the sun shines all night
when the day is at its longest, and that wide about it the
sun is not seen in the day time when night is at its
longest.

But Bede, the Priest, died 735 years after the
Incarnation of our Lord, according to what is written,
and more than one hundred years before Iceland
was peopled by the Northmen. But before Iceland was
peopled from Norway there were in it the men whom the
Northmen call Papar; they were Christian men, and it is
held that they must have come over sea from the west,
for there were found left by them Irish books, ‡ bells, and

---

* Aldarfarsbók = De Ratione Temporum, a work by Bede.
† Venerable Bede, born about 673 A.D., died 26th May, 735 A.D. " He was,"
says Green, " first among English scholars, first among English theologians,
first among English historians, it is in the Monk of Jarrow that English literature strikes its roots."
‡ Bækr irskar bjöllur ok baglar.

croziers,

[PART I, CHAPTER I.]
croziers, and more things besides, from which it could be understood that they were Westmen * (Irishmen); these things were found east in Pap-isle † and Papyle, and it is stated in English books that in those times voyages were made between these countries.

PART FIRST.

CHAPTER I. Here beginneth the " Landnamabok " (or Book of Settlement), and in the first chapter is stated whither is the shortest way from Iceland. When Iceland was discovered and peopled from Norway, Adrian was Pope of Rome, and after him John, he who was eighth of that name in the Apostolic seat, Louis, son of Louis, was Kaisar north of the Alps, and Leo and his son Alexander over Constantinople. Then was Harold Fairhair King over Norway and Eric the son of Eymund in Sweden, and his son Biorn; and Gorm the Ancient in Denmark, and Alfred the Great in England, and afterwards Edward his son, and Kiarval in Dublin, and Earl Sigurd the Mighty in Orkney.

So wise men say, that from Norway, out of Stad, there are seven half-days' sailing to Horn, in eastern Iceland, and from Snowfells Ness, where the cut is shortest, there is four days' main west to Greenland. But it is said, that if one sail from Bergen straight west to Warf, in Greenland, then one must keep about 12 miles (sea miles) south of Iceland, but from Reekness, in southern Iceland, there is five days' main to Jolduhlaup, in Ireland, going south; but from Longness, in northern Iceland, there is four days'

---

* Westmen were those who came from the British Islands as distinguished from austmenn (eastmen) those who came from Norway and the Scandinavian continent.

† The Norse Name for these Anchorite Fathers is Papar. Three islets among the Hebrides, two in the Orkneys, two in the Shetlands, and others among the Faroes, bear the names of Pabba or Papa=Father's Isle. In the mainland of Orkney, and again in South Ronaldshay, we find places called Paplay=The Hermit's abode, and at Enhallow and at one of the Papas in the Orkneys the ancient Cell still remains.

main

[PART I, CHAPTER I.]

main north to Svalbard, in Hafsbotn, but one day's sail there is to the Wastes of Greenland from Kolbein's Isle in the north.

Discovery of Iceland by Naddod the Viking.

So it has been said that once men set out from Norway bound for the Faroe Islands; and some say that it was Naddod the Viking ; but they drifted west into the main and found there a great land. They went up aland, in the East Firths, to the top of a high mountain, and looked round about, far and wide, to see if they could observe smokes, or any inkling of the land being settled, but they could not oberve anything of the kind. They went afterwards, about autumn, to the Faroe Islands, and as they sailed from the land, much snow fell upon the mountains, and therefore they called the land Snaeland=Snowland. They praised the land much. The place where they arrived at is now called Reydar Fell, in the East Firths. So said Sæmund,* deep in lore, the Priest.

Discovery of Iceland by Gardar.

There was a man named Gardarr, the son of Svavar, a Swede by kin, he went to seek Iceland under the direction of his mother, who was a seer. He came to land east of the Eastern Horn ; there was a haven then. Gardar sailed round the land and so came to know that it was an island.

He was through the winter in the north in Husavik † in

---

* Sæmund Sigfusson of Oddi (b. 1056 d. 1133) an elder contemporary of Ari. In the Sagas he appears as the greatest churchman of his day, as an historia and as the founder ot a great fam.ly, the Oddverjar.

† Husavik lies at the termination of an inlet on the east side of Skialfandafiord. Consists of several houses, and several cottages. Lies at the height of more than 100 feet above the level of the sea on the brow of perpendicular precipices. The harbour is reckoned one of the most dangerous in Iceland, on account of rocks at the entrance and exposure to north and north-west winds, by which enormous masses of Greenland Ice are driven into it.—Henderson's Iceland.

bondswoman,

[PART I, CHAPTER II.]
Skjalfand and there he built a house. In the spring, when
he was ready for sailing, a man named Nattfari was drifted
from him in a boat, in which also was a thrall and a
bondswoman. He settled in the place which has since
been called Nattfara-vik. Gardar went from thence to
Norway, and he praised the land much. He was the
father of Uni, the father of Hroar, the godi of Tunga.
After that the land was called Gardar's Holme, and was
covered with wood between fell and foreshore.

Discovery of Iceland by Floki. Name of "Iceland" first given.

CHAPTER II. Floki, the son of Vilgerd, was the name
of a man, a great viking. He went to search for Gardar's
Holme, and put to sea where it is now called ' Flóka-Varði,'
=Flokis beacon. There Hordaland and Rogaland meet.
He went first to the to the Shetlands and lay there in
Flokis Bight ; there Geirhild, his daughter, perished in
Geirhild's Water- With Floki were in the ship a good-
man named Thoralf, and another called Herjolf. There
was also a man named Faxi, from Sodor,* who was in the
ship.

Floki took three ravens † with him to sea. When he
set free the first, it flew aft over the stem ; the second flew
up into the air and back to the ship again ; but the third
flew forth straightway over the stem, in the direction in
which they found the land. They hove in from the east
at the Horn, and then they coasted the land by the south.
But as they sailed west round Reykjanes, and the firth
opened out to them, so that they saw Snæfellness, Faxi
observed " This must be a great land which we have dis-

---

* The word in the Icelandic is ' Suðreyskr '=a man from Suðr-eyjar or the
Southern Islands=Sodor, i.e the Hebrides.
† In another copy of the Landnama it is stated that Floki had consecrated these
ravens to this service before he set out from Norway.

covered

[PART I, CHAPTER III.]

covered, and here are mighty rivers." Thence they called
that river's mouth 'Faxaóss'=Faxemouth. Floki and
his men sailed west over Broadfirth, and there he made
land where now is the bay called 'Vatns fjörðr'=Water
Firth, against Barda-Strand. The bay so abounded in fish,
that by reason of the catch thereof they gave no heed
to the gathering in of hay, so that all the live-stock
perished in the winter. The following spring was rather
cold; then Floki went up to the top of a high mountain
and discovered north, beyond the mountain, a firth full of
drift ice; therefore they called the land 'Iceland,' and
so it has been called since then. Floki and his men were
minded to go away in summer, but they were ready only a
short time before the beginning of winter. The remains of
their scale-toft are yet to be seen east of Branslæk, and the
shed that covered their ship, and the firestead. They could
not beat round Reykjanes, and the boat broke away from
them with Herjolf upon it. He came in at the place
which is now called Herjolf's Haven. Floki was, during
the winter, in Borg-Firth, and they found Herjolf again.
They sailed to Norway the summer after, and when men
enquired of them about the land, Floki spoke ill of it, but
Herjolf told both the good and the bad of the land, and
Thorolf said that butter dropped from every blade of grass
in the land which they had discovered, therefore he was
called Thorolf 'Smjör'*=Thorolf butter.

Discovery of Iceland by Bjornolf.

CHAPTER III.   There was a man named Bjornolf, and
another named Hroald, they were the sons of Hromund,
the son of Grip. They went from Thelmark on account

---

* Smjör or butter is elsewhere in Landnama applied as place names as Smjör-
hòlar in the west of Iceland, meaning 'Butter-hillocks.' Compare Lake and
Butterhilket. Smjör-hòlar so called is the place where the lady Ölöf stored her
butter. Also in Landnama are Smjor Sand and Smjor vatn.

[PART I, CHAPTER IV.]

of manslaughters, and they took up their abode at Dale's Firth, in Fjalir. The son of Bjornolf was Orn, the father of Ingolf and Helga, and the son of Hroald was Hrodmar, the father of Leif. The foster-brothers, Ingolf and Leif, went a-warring with the sons of Earl Atli the slim, of Gaular, these to wit, Hastein, Herstein, and Holmstein. Between them all dealings went well, and when they came home they bespoke an expedition in common the next summer, and in the winter the foster-brothers made an entertainment for the sons of the Earl, at which feast Holmstein vowed a vow that he would marry Helga, the daughter of Orn, or no other. To this vow little heed was given, but Leif reddened up at it, and little enough Leif and Holmstein would have to do with one another as they parted there at the feast.

CHAPTER IV. In the spring the foster-brothers prepared to go out warring, and went to meet the sons of Earl Atli, whom they met at Hisargafl, when Holmstein and his brothers immediately attacked Leif and Ingolf in battle. When they had fought for a while there came upon them Olmod the Old, son of Horda-Kari, a kinsman of Leif, and brought aid to Ingolf and Leif. In that battle Holmstein fell, but Herstein fled. Thereupon Leif and Ingolf set out on warfare. In the winter following, Herstein went against Leif and Ingolf, and was minded to slay them, but, being warned of his proposed attack upon them, they met him in battle, and there befell a great fight in which Herstein was slain. After that there drifted to the foster-brothers a great number of their friends and acquaintances from the Firth-folk; then men were sent to Earl Atli and Hastein, that they might make a reconciliation between them, which was settled on those conditions, that the foster-brothers should hand over to them all their estates. After that the foster-brothers fitted out a great vessel which they possessed, that they might go and seek

that

[PART I, CHAPTER V.]
that land which ' Hrafnafloki '=(Floki of the ravens) had
discovered, which was then called Iceland. They found
the land, and made a stay in the east country in the
southernmost Alptafirth (or Swans' Firth the southernmost). The land seemed to them to be better southward
than northward. They spent one winter in the land and
then they returned to Norway.

Leif's Expedition to Ireland.

CHAPTER V. After that Ingolf spent their money on
an expedition to Iceland, but Leif set out upon a viking
expedition to the west (Vestrviking). He harried Ireland
and found there a large underground house or cavern, he
went into it and within it was very dark until he advanced
till where he saw a light gleaming from a sword which a
man held in his hand. Leif slew the man and took the
sword and much treasure from him, and thereafter he was
called Hjorleif=Leif of the sword. Hjorleif harried
Ireland wide about, and took from thence much treasure;
he also took ten thralls who are thus named: Dufthak
and Geirrod, Skjaldbjorn, Halldor, and Drafdrit, more
are not named.

After that Hjorleif went to Norway and found there
Ingolf his foster-brother. He had before this married
Helga, the daughter af Orn, Ingolf's sister. That winter
Ingolf made a great sacrifice and consulted the oracles
concerning his destiny=(forlog or what is "laid" up)
but Hjorleif always contemned sacrifices. The oracle *
marked an abode for Ingolf in Iceland. After that each
of those kinsmen-in-law prepared his ship for the Icelandic
expedition, Hjorleif taking on board his ship his war-
booty; but Ingolf, on his, the wealth they owned in
fellowship; and when all their equipments were ready,
they set out to sea.

---

* Frétt=an inquiry of the gods or men about the future.

Ingolf

Ingolf sets out to settle in Iceland, A.D. 874.

CHAPTER. VI.   That summer when Ingolf set out with his companions to settle Iceland, Harald Fairhair had had been for twelve years King over Norway.   There had elapsed from the creation of the world six thousand and seventy three winters, and from the Incarnation of our Lord eight hundred and seventy four years.   They held together until they sighted Iceland, then they seperated.   When Ingolf sighted Iceland he cast overboard his high seat pillars for an omen, and he made the vow that he would settle there wherever his high seat pillar came ashore.

Ingolf landed at the place which is now called Ingolf's Head, and Hjorleif was driven to the west, along the land, when a great want of water overtook him.   Then the Irish slaves formed the plan of mixing meal and butter together, and they called that unthirsty fare (ùþorslàtt =not thirst awaking) ; they named it also minnthak* but when this had been fully prepared there came a great rain and they collected the rain-water in their awnings, and when the ninnthak began to mould, they threw it overboard, and it came to land in the place which is now called Minnthakseyr.†

Hjorleif let make there two Scales ‡ and the one toft § was 18 fathoms long, and the other 19 fathoms.   Hjorleif resided there during the winter; and in the following spring he determined to make a seed time or sowing.

He had one ox, but he made his slaves draw the plough. When Hjorleif was employed about the Scale, Dufthak gave this advice to the others, that they should kill the ox, and say a wood-bear had slain it, and that, when Hjorleif

---

* From a Gaelic word min=flour.
† Minnthak's Beach.
‡ Icelandic " Skàli "=Cumberland Scale, as Peat Scale.   Also in Place Names as Scales; Seascale; Scale Hill ; Sand Scale ; Nether Scales.
§ Toft=Cumberland Toft.

and

[PART I, CHAPTER VI.]

and his companions should seek for the bear, they should set upon them. Afterwards they told this story to Hjorleif, and then they went to seek the bear, and when they were dispersed in the woods, the slaves set upon them separately and murdered them all, as many as they were themselves. Then they ran away with their women, and the chattels, and the boat. The slaves went to those islands which they saw out at sea, towards the south-west, and took up their abode there for awhile. Vifill and Karli were the names of two slaves of Ingolf whom he sent westward along the sea coast, to try and find his High Seat posts, and when they came to Hjorleif'shof, they found Hjorleif dead and went back and told Ingolf the tidings ; he took the fate of Hjorleif much to heart.

CHAPTER VII. After that Ingolf went west to Hjorleif-shof, and, when he saw Hjorleif dead, he exclaimed "little indeed went here to the undoing of a brave man and true, that slaves should have put him to death, and thus I see it goes with every one who will do no sacrifice." Ingolf let array the burial of Hjorleif and his companions, and took charge of their ship and chattels. He then ascended the headland and observed some islands which lay out at sea, towards the south-west, and the thought came into his mind that they might have escaped thither, inasmuch as the boat had vanished. So they went to seek for the slaves, whom they found in the Islands, at a place which is now called Eid.* They were at meat when Ingolf came upon them. They fled, terror struck, each his own way. Ingolf slew them all. The place where Dufthak was killed is now called Dufthak's-scor or scar. The greater part of them threw themselves from the rocks which have taken their names from them. And these islands † where the slaves were slain have since been called

---

* Eid means Isthmus.
† See Westmannaeyjar in the Map.

islands

the Westmens' Islands,* because those who were slain
there were Westmen. Ingolf and his men took with them
the widows of the men who had been murdered, and
returned to Hjorleif'shof. Ingolf was there another
winter, and in the following summer he went west, along
the sea coast. He passed the third winter under Ingolf's
fell, to the west of Olfu's river (and some say that he was
interred there.)† In those seasons Vifill and Karli found
his High Seat Pillars in Orn's-Knoll, beneath the Heath.

Settlement at Reykjavik.

CHAPTER VIII. Ingolf went, in the following spring,
down over the Heath. He took up his abode where the
High Seat Pillar had come to land. He dwelt at Reykjavik. There are now his High Seat Pillars there in the
Eldhouse=Fire House. Then Ingolf took for himself
land between Olfu's‡ river and Hvalfjardar, or Whale
Firth, west of Brinjadal's river, and all between that and
the Axe-river and all the nesses to the south-ward. Then
said Karli, "To an evil end did we pass through goodly
country-sides that we should take up abode on this outlying
ness." He ran away and a bondswoman with him. Ingolf
gave to Vifil his freedom, and he settled at Vifil's Tofts;
and from him is named the mountain called ' Vifil's Fell.'
There he abode for a long time and was an upright man.
Ingolf let rear a Scale upon Scale-Fell—thence he saw
Reek=smoke or vapour, against Olfus water, and found
Karli there.

Thing first set up. Thorkell Moon Lawspeaker.
Christianity introduced A.D. 1000.

CHAPTER IX. Ingolf was the most renowned of all

---

* Westmenn or those who came from the Western, or British Islands, as dis-
tinguished from the Eastmenn, or Norwegians.
† This passage not found in some early copies of Landnama.
‡ See Olvus vatn on the Map.

the

[PART I, CHAPTER IX.]

the settlers of Iceland; for he came here to an un-inhabited land, and was the first to set up an abode upon it, and the others who settled there afterwards did so induced by his example. Ingolf married Hallveig, the daughter of Frodi, the sister of Lopt the aged. Their son was Thorstein, who set up the Thing at Kjalarness, before the Althing was established.

The son of Thorstein was Thorkell Moon, the Law-speaker, who, according to the general opinion of the men of that time, was the best amongst heathen men. In his last illness he caused himself to be borne out to where the rays of the sun would fall upon him, and committed himself into the hands of that God who had shaped the sun. His life was so pure that it was comparable with the lives of the best of the Christians.

His son was Thormod, who held the supreme priest-hood when Christianity was was first brought to the Island.

His son was Hamal, the father of Mar and Thormod and Torfi. Sigurd was the son of Mar, the father of Hamal, the father of Gudmund, the father of Thormod, the godi of Skeid.

CHAPTER X. Here the tale is of Bjorn Buna. There was a man, Bjorn Buna, a renowned 'hersir,' in Norway, the son of Verdrar-Grim, a 'hersir' of Sogni. The mother of Grim was Hervör, the daughter of Thorgerd, the daughter of Eylaug, a 'hersir'* from Sogn. From Bjorn are descended almost all the renowned men in Iceland. He was married to Velaug, the sister of Vermund the old; they had three sons, one was Ketil flatnose; another was Hrapp; the third Helgi. They were famous men, and of their decendants many things are told in this book.

Of Thord Skeggi, the son of Hrapp. There was a man

---

* Hersir, a chief or lord, was the name of the Norse chiefs of the earliest age; especially before the time of Harald Fairhair and the settlement.

named

[PART I, CHAPTER X.]

named Thord Skeggi; he was the son of Hrapp, the son of Bjorn Cuna. Thord married Vilborg, the daughter of Osvald. Their daughter was named Helga, whom Ketilbjorn the Old, married. Thord went to Iceland, and with the advice of Ingolf, took land in his landtake between Ulfar's river and Leiruvag. He dwelt at Skeggistead. From Thord are descended many distinguished men in Iceland.

CHAPTER XI. There was a man named Hall the godless. He was the son of Helgi the godless, neither father nor son would sacrifice but they trusted in their own might. Hall went to Iceland and took land with the advice of Ingolf from Leiruvag to Mogil's river. The son of Hall was Helgi, who married Thurid, the daughter of Ketilbjorn. Their son was Thord, in Alfsnes, who married Gudny, the daughter of Hrafnkel. Hall resided in Muli.

Harald the Fairhaired harried west over sea as is related in his Saga. He subdued to his power all Sodor,*=The Hebrides, so far west that no king of Norway has conquered further since his time. But when he returned from the west, Vikings threw themselves into those Islands as well as Scotchmen and Irishmen, and harried and plundered wide about. When Harald heard this, he sent to the west Ketil Flatnose, son of Bjorn Cuna, to recover those Islands. Ketil married Yngvild, daughter of Ketil Wether, a lord from Hringariki. Their sons were these: Bjorn the Easterner and Helgi Bjola; Aud the deep-minded, and Thorun the horned were their daughters. Ketil went west, and left behind Bjorn, his son. He subdued the whole of Sodor=The Hebrides, and made himself lord thereover, but paid no tribute for them as had been agreed upon, to Harald the King; then the King confiscated his possessions, which were in Norway, and expelled Bjorn his son.

[PART I, CHAPTER XI.]

Of Helgi Bjola. Helgi Bjola, the son of Ketil Flatnose, went to Iceland from Sodor=The Hebrides. He was with Ingolf the first winter, and settled under his advice the whole of Kjalarness, between Mogil's river and Mydal's river. He dwelt at Hof. His sons were Slaughter Hrapp, and Kollsvein, father of Thorgerd, the mother of Thord, the mother of Ogmund, the father of Bishop John, the Holy.

CHAPTER XII. Orlyg was the name of a man who was the son of Hrapp, the son of Bjorn Cuna; he was brought up by the Holy Patrick, Bishop of Sodor. He conceived the desire to go to Iceland, and asked the Bishop St. Patrick who had brought him up that he would make provision for his setting out. The Bishop provided him with wood, suitable for building a church and a plenarium and an iron bell, a golden penny and consecrated earth, to be put under the corner pillars. Afterwards the Bishop told him that he should take land where he should see two mountains rising out of the sea, and rear his dwelling under the southernmost mountain; in either mountain there should be a valley, and there he should take up his abode, and let build there a church and should consecrate it to the Saint Columba.* With Orlyg there was in the ship a man named Koll, his foster-brother, and another named Thorbjorn sparrow; a third named Thorbjorn talkni, and his brother Thorbjorn Skuma, they were the sons of Bodvar bladder pate.

These went to sea along with Orlyg, and they had a hard and difficult voyage and knew not whither they were going. Then Orlyg besought St. Patrick that he might have a landing, and vowed that he would assign his name as the place name to whatever land he might take. They were thenceforth but a little while upon the ocean until

---

* St. Columba, Apostle to the Hebrides and West of Scotland, born 521 A.D., died at Iona, 597, A.D.

they

[PART I, CHAPTER XII.]

they sighted land, and discovered that they had come west around the country. They brought their ship to port at Orlygshaven, and the bay which stretches inward from thence they called Patricksfirth. They were there for one winter, and in spring Orlyg fitted up his ship, and, taking all his possessions with him, sailed round Bard by the west, but when he had passed Faxemoth to the south, he saw there two mountains and a dale in each, and he recognised the mountains which had been before designated to him. He held there towards the southern mountain, which was Kjalarness, which Helgi his cousin had settled already.

Orlyg was with Helgi the first winter, and in spring he settled land by the advice of Helgi, between Mogil's river and Osvif's Brook. and dwelt at Esjuborg. He built a church there as he had vowed. Orlyg had many children. His son was Valthjof, father of Valbrand, the father of Torfi; another was Geirmund, the father of Halldora, the mother of Thorleif, from whom and his kinsmen the Esjubergings are descended. Orlyg and his kinsman believed in Columba. The daughter of Orlyg the Old was Velaug, whom Gunnlaug Ormstunga the son of Hromund in Thverarhlid * had for his wife. Their daughter was Thurid dylla, mother of Illug the black, at Gilsbank.

Svartkel, a settler from Caithness in Scotland.

CHAPTER XIII. There was a man named Svartkel, from Caithness: he settled land inward from Mydal's river, between that and Elifsdale-river, and dwelt first at Kidfell and afterwards at Eyri. His son was Thorkell, father of Glum, who thus prayed before the cross: "Ever good to old men; ever good to young men!" He was

---

* Thverarhlid is literally "cross river"; thver being applied to a tributary or cross river, as distinguished from the main river into which it flows as an effluent.

the

[PART I, CHAPTER XIII.]

the father of Thorarin, the father of Glum at ‘Vatn-lausa’=waterless. The sister of Svartkel was named Arnleif, the wedded wife of Thorolf viligisl, the father of Kleppjarn the Old from Flokadale, their daughter was named Hallgerd, who was the wife of Bergthorr, the son of Koll.

Valthjof, son of Orlyg the Old from Esjauberg, settled all Kjos and dwelt at Medalfell; from him are the Valthjoflings descended. His daughter was Signy, the mother of Gnup, the father of Birning, the father of Gnup, the father of Eirik, the Bishop of the Greenlanders.

Settlement at Hvamm.

CHAPTER XIV. Hvamm Thorir settled land between Lax river and Foss river, and dwelt in Hvamm.

He had a contention with Ref the Old concerning a cow which was called Brynja, and from her the Dale has its name, as she grazed out with 40 cattle (nauta=Scottish nwote) which were all bred from her. Ref and Thorir fought in Thorisholar, there Thorir fell and eight of his men.

Thorstein, the son of Solmund, the son of Thorolf butter, settled land between Botn’s river and Foss river, the whole of Brynjudale. He married Thorbjorg Katla, the daughter of Helgi Skarf, the son of Geirleif, who settled Barda-strand. Their son was Ref the Old, from whom the Bryndalers are descended. Now have been told those men who settled the landtake of Ingolf westward from him.

There was a man named Avang, an Irishman by race, he first settled in ‘Botn’=Bottom. The wood was at that time so abundant there that he built from it a seagoing ship, and put in her cargo at the place which is now called Hladhamar.* His son was Thorleif, the father of

---

* Cargo Crag.

Thurid

[PART I, CHAPTER XIV.]
Thurid, the wedded wife of Thormod, who was the son of
Thjoster at Alftanes, and of his wife Idunn, the daughter
of Molda-Gnup.

The son of Thormod was Bork, the father of Thord,
the father of Audun, in Brautarholt. Kolgrim the old,
son of Hrolf hersir * settled land out from Botn's river to
Kalman's river, and dwelt at Ferstikla. He married
Gunnvor, the daughter of Hrodgeir, the Sage.

Their children were Thorhalli, the father of Kolgrim,
the father of Stein, the father of Kvist, from whom the
Kvistlings are descended. The daughter of Kolgrim the
Old was Bergthora, whom Ref in Brynjudale married.

Early Christian Settlers.

CHAPTER XV. Two brothers settled the whole of
Akranes between Kalman's river and Char river; the
one was named Thormod, he had the land to the south of
Reymir, and dwelt at Holm; he was the father of Bersi
and Geirlaug, the mother of Tung-Odd. Ketil had Akranes to the west and to the north of Akrafell to the Char
river. His son was Jorund the Christian, who dwelt in
Gardar or the Garths,† which place was then named
Jorundholt. Jorund was the father of Kepp, the father
of Eimar, the father of Narfi and Harvar, the father of
Thorgeir. There was a man named Asolf, he was the
kinsman of Jorund, in Gardar or the Garths. He came
out into Osar, in the east country ‡; he was a good
christian, and refused to have any intercourse with

---

* Hersir is a chief or lord, the political name of the Norse chiefs of the earliest
age, especially before the time of Harald Fairhair and the settlement of
Iceland.

† Literally the "enclosures" or intakes. The word 'Garth' as place name is
in this acceptation often found in Lakeland. Gard, the original Icelandic word
here used, is often found in north English place names, and field names as
Gards, etc.

‡ Osar is literally "the river's mouth" as taking in all the land that bounded
the estuary.

heathen

[PART I, CHAPTER XV.]

heathen men, and would not accept meat from them. He made for himself a scale * under Eyjafell, which is now called Asolf's Scale, the easternmost.

Asolf did not hold converse with any other men, but when people pryed in to see what provisions he had, they saw in his scale a great store of fishes.

CHAPTER XVI. And when men went to that brook † which flowed near to his dwelling, they discovered it to be full of fish, so that men thought that no such marvel had ever been seen before ; but when the men of the neighbourhood got aware of this, they drove him away, and would not allow him to enjoy this blessing. Asolf moved his dwelling to Midscale ‡ and abode there ; then the fish vanished from the brook (at the eastern scale) when the people wanted to catch them, but when they came to Asolf then was the stream which flowed past his house full of fish. Then he was driven forth from thence and went to the scale which was farthest to the west, and all things again happened in the same manner. § And when he set out from thence to find out his kinsman Jorund, Jorund bade Asolf to abide with him, and Asolf said he had no mind to dwell with anyone else. Then Jorund caused a house to be made for him at Holm the innermost, and had his means of sustenance carried thither to him, and he continued there as long as he lived, and there he was buried. A church now stands where his tomb was, and he is deemed a most holy man.

---

* Skali, the Icelandic word, is a *hut* or *shed* put up for temporary use. This is the earliest Norse sense and it is still so used in Norway.

† The Icelandic word is Laekr=a brook or rivulet, and is in the Landnama very frequently compounded to form place names.

‡ Compare Cumberland Place Names—Scales, Sea Scale, Scale Hill, Nether Scales.

§ That is the fish were found in the same miraculous abundance in the stream that flowed past his scale or dwelling.

Bekan

[PART I, CHAPTER XVII.]

Bekan and other early Settlers.

CHAPTER XVII.   There was a man called Bekan, who
settled in the landtake of Ketil, from Berrydale's river to
Char river, and dwelt at Bekan Stead.   Finn the rich, the
son of Haldor, the son of Hogni, went from Stafanger to
Iceland, he married Thorvor, the daughter of Thorbjarn
from Mossfell, the son of Hradi, he settled to the south of
Salmon river all unto Kalman river, and dwelt at Midfell. ·
His son was Thorgeir, father of Jostein, the father of
Thorun, the mother of Gudrun, the mother of Sæmund,
the father of Brand the Bishop.

Skeggi in Skogar was the son of Thorun, and he was
the father of Spyrmir and Bolli in Skogar.   Hallkel, who
settled Hvilarsida (=side of the white river), dwelt first at
Akraness at Hallkellsted, before the sons of Bersi drove
them forth from thence.   But when he went back for his
cattle which had been going abroad there grazing unshep-
herded, he was slain, and was there howed=buried.
Haven-Ormr settled land about Melahverfi out to Char
river and Salmon river, and inward to Andakil's river, and
dwelt at Hofn.   His son was Thorgeir Cutcheek, father
of Thorun, the mother of Thorun, the mother of Jostein,
the father of Sigurd, the father of Bjornhedin.   Thorgeir
Cutcheek was of the body guard of King Hakon, the foster-
son of Adalstein ; he brought from Fitjar a wound in his
cheek and great renown.

· Two brothers settled in the landtake of Finn and Orm.
Hrodgeir the Sage in Saurby, and Oddgeir at Leira.*

Finn and Orm bought them out as they thought the
land there was too narrow for them.   Thereupon Hrodgeir and his brother took land in Floi, † the Rape ‡ of the

---

* Leira=Clarty Beck.
  † Floi=a mossy moor or expanse of mossy waste—occurs with the same
meaning as Flowe in Cumberland, e.g., Wedholme Flowe, Bowness Flowe,
Solway Flowe.   Compare Kelpies Flowe in Scott's " Bride of Lammermoor."
  ‡ Hreppr or Rape.   After the introduction of Christianity to Iceland it was all
divided into Hreppr or Poor Law districts, mostly, though not always coinciding
with the Sokn or parish.

                                                    Hraungernings

[PART I, CHAPTER XVII.]
Hraungerdings, and Hrodgeir dwelt at Hraungerdi,* and Oddgeir in Oddgeirsholar; he married the daughter of Ketil giofu.

Kveldulf's last voyage. His last words and death. The chest containing his dead body cast overboard. His companions find it cast ashore.

CHAPTER XVIII. There was a man named Ulf, the son of Brund-Bjalfi and Hallbera, the daughter of Ulf the Dauntless, from Hrafnista. Ulf was married to Salbjorg, the daughter of Berdlu-Kari; he was called Kveldulf † (=a wolf of the evening). Thorolf and Skallagrim were their sons. King Harald the Fairhaired caused Thorolf to be killed north in Alost at Sandness, through the slander of the son of Hildirid. King Harald would make no atonement for the murder.‡ Then Kveldulf and Grim arrayed a merchant ship and were minded to go to Iceland, because they had got news that Ingolf their friend was there. While they were lying sea-bound in Solund-isles they seized there the round § ship which King

---

*Gerdi as here used is a "place girded round," "a fenced field," "an enclosure." Hraun in volcanic Iceland means a lava field when cold. Hence in this meaning it is often applied to Icelandic place names, and in this Book of the Settlement the reader will find the following place names: Hraun, Hraundale, Hraun Firth, Hraun Holt or Wood, Hraun Haven.

† Kveldulf. This name of Kveldulf betokens that he was a berserk, otherwise *bearsark* or *bearcoat*, i.e., *a wild warrior or champion* of the heathen age. In battle the berserkers were subject to fits of frenzy called berserkgangr, when they howled like wild beasts, foamed at the mouth, and gnawed the iron rim of their shields. During those fits they were, according to popular belief, proof against steel and fire, and made great havoc in the ranks of the enemy. When the fever left them they were weak and tame. In the Icelandic poem, Hornklofi, there is a passage which speaks of the berserker as howling and bellowing and gnawing the iron of his shield.

‡ For a full account of this murder or massacre see Egil's Saga. It was really what is termed a "burning in" one of the most deadly and fatal recorded in Norse annals. It commenced a deadly feud which lasted for three generations between the families. The Egil's Saga is entirely occupied with the details of that feud.

§ The word translated round ship in the Icelandic is Knörr=a merchant ship, as distinguished from the langskip=the large ancient ship of war.

Harald

[PART I, CHAPTER XVIII.]

Harald had taken from Thorolf, when his men had just come back from England, and they slew there Hallvard the Hardy-farer and Sigtrygg the Swift-farer, who had brought that deed about (*i.e.* the seizure of Thorolf's ship). They also slew the sons of Guttorm,* son of Sigurd Hart, the first cousins of the King, and all their ship's crew, except two men whom they left to take the tidings to the King. Then they fitted up both the ships for a voyage to Iceland. They manned each vessel with thirty men, and Kveldulf steered the newly captured ship. Grim the Halogalander,† the son of Thorir, the son of Gunnlaug, the son of Hrolf, the son of Ketil Keelfarer was the second in command to Kvedulf in the ship which he steered. The two vessels kept each other in sight while at sea, but when they were far on the ocean Kveldulf fell ill, and commanded that if he should die they should make a chest (kist) for his body and bid them say to Grim his son that he should take up a dwelling in Iceland, the shortest way from the spot where his chest should come a-land, if such should be fated to it. After that Kveldulf died, and his chest was shot overboard. Then Grim ‡ held to the south, round the land, they having learned that Ingolf abode south in the country. They sailed to the west by Reykjanes and steered their course into the Firth, and then the ships separated so that neither knew aught of the other. Grim the Halogalander and his company sailed up through the whole Firth until they had passed all the rocks, and there they cast anchor. When the flood tide set in, they hove up into the mouth of the

---

* Guttorm was brother to Ragnhild, father of Harald Fairhair, consequently his sons were first cousins to the King.
† In Icelandic Haleski, *i.e.* from the land of the northern lights.
‡ When Kveldulf died then Grim the Halogalander took command and steered the ship. This Grim must be carefully distinguished from Grim otherwise Skallagrim the son of Kveldulf, who commanded and steered the other ship.

river

[PART I, CHAPTER XVIII.]
river and brought up their ship as far as it would
float ; that river is now called Gufa *; there they landed
their belongings. Exploring the country, they had gone
but a very short distance before they' discovered the
chest of Kveldulf cast ashore in a certain creek. They
bore it to a ness which was there, and raised over
it a heap of stones.

Borg the home of Kveldulf's descendants.

CHAPTER XIX. Skallagrim † came to land there at the
place now called Knararness in Myrar, afterwards he
surveyed the land.   There was much moorland and wide
woods and it was far there between fell and foreshore.
Then they went inwards along the Firth, and they came
to a ness where they found swans,‡ and they called the
place Swans' Ness. They did not stay in their course
until they had found Grim the Halogalander, who told
Skalla-grim all about their faring, as also of the words
that Kveldulf had left for his son Grim.
Skallagrim went to see where the chest had come
ashore ; it seemed to him that a short way from there
would be a good spot for a dwelling-stead. Skallagrim
remained there during the year in which he arrived from
the main, during which time he surveyed all the district,
and settled all the land from Seal Tarn and upwards to
Borghraun, and southwards to Haven Fells—a country as
broad as it shed widely waters to the sea. He raised his
dwelling near the creek where the chest of Kveldulf had
come ashore, and called it Borg, and so also he called all
that firth Borg Firth. There he settled all the county

---

* Gufa=*the steam or vapour river*, so called from the vapour of the water
from hot springs.
† Skallagrim the name by which Grim is afterwards known is really a nickname
meaning "Grim the bald headed."
‡ Alft=Swan, so the place is called Alftanes.

with

[PART I, CHAPTER XIX.]

with his companions, and many men afterwards took land
there by his advice.   Skallagrim gave land to Grim the
Halogalander on the south of the firth, between Andakil's
river and Grim's river, he dwelt at Hvanneyri.   His son
was named Ulf, father of Hrolf, in Geitland.

There was a man named Thorbjorn the Black, he
bought land from Haven-Orm, in from Selaeyri (=Seal
Island) and up to Fors * river ; he dwelt at Skeljabrekka,
his son was Thorvard, who married Thorun, the daughter
of Thorbjorn from Ornholt, their sons were Thorarin
the blind and Thorgil 'Orraskald,' who was with Olaf
Kvaran † in Dublin.   Skorri, the freedman of Ketil Gufu,
took Skorradale up above the water, and was slain there.

Bjorn the gullberi settled Reykjardale the Southernmost, and dwelt at Gulliberasted. ‡   His son was
Grimkell the Godi in Blaskogar,§ he married Signy, the
daughter of Valbrand, the son of Valthjof, their son was
Hord, who was the leader of the Holmesmen.   Bjorn the
gulliberi married Ljotun, the sister of Kolgrim the old,
Svarthofdi at Reydarfell was another of their sons ; he
married Thurid, the daughter of Tunga-Odd, their
daughter was Thordis, whom Gudlaug the Rich married.
Thjostolf was the third son of Bjorn, the fourth was
Geirmund.

Thorgeir Meldun ‖ accepted from Bjorn all land above
Grim's river.   He dwelt at Tungufell ; he married
Geirbjorg, daughter of Balki, from Rams-firth ; their son
was Veleif the old.

Fluki the thrall of Ketil Gufu settled Flokidale and was
slain there.

---

* Fors=Lakeland Force, as Airey Force, Stock Ghyll Force, &c.
† Kvaran=the nickname of this Norse King of Dublin.   Derivation of the
the word probably Gaelic.
‡ Literally the gold bearers' sted.
§ The black wood.
‖ Meldun is a nickname—a Gaelic word.

Other

[PART I, CHAPTER XX.]
Other Settlements round Borgarfirth. Slaughter by Torfi.

CHAPTER XX. There was a man of high degree named Oleif hilt, he came in his ship to Borgfirth* and was for the first winter with Skallagrim; he settled land by the advice of Skallagrim, between Grim's river and Geir's river, and dwelt at 'Varmalæk (=warm brook). His sons were Ragi in Laugardale, and Thoraninn, the lawspeaker, who married Thordis, the daughter of Oleif-Feilan† their daughter was Vigdis, who was married to Stein, the son of Thorfin. The son of Ragi was Gudthorm, father of Gunnvor, the mother of Thorny, the mother of Thorlak, the father of Runolf, the father of Thorlak the Bishop. Ketil slumber and Geir, his son, came to Iceland and were with Skallagrim the first winter. There Geir married Thorum, the daughter of Skallagrim. In the following spring Grim showed them land for settling, and they took land up from Flokadale's river to Reykjadale's river, and all the tongue of land up to Red Goll, and all Flokadale, above the slopes. Ketil dwelt at Thrand-holt, from him Blundsvatn (=Slumber water) derives its name; there he dwelt afterwards. Geir the rich, his son, dwelt in Geirshlid ‡ and had another dwelling at upper Reykir. His sons were Thorgeirr Slumber, and Slumber Ketill, and Svardkel in Eyri; the daughter of Geir was Bergdis, who was the wedded wife of Gnup at Hrisar,§ the son of Floki. Of that stock was Thorod Hrisablund (=Blund of Hrisar). Onund Breidskegg (=broad beard) was the son of Ulf, the son of Ulf " Fitjumskegga (=Beard o' Fitjar), the son of Thorir hlammandi-Clash. Onund settled all the tongue of land

---

* On the Map 'Borgarfjordr.'
† Feilan is a Gaelic nickname.
‡ Hlid=a slope or mountain side, found frequently in place names.
§ Hris is literally the Scrubs or Brushwood. In the dialect of Cumberland and Westmorland the most usual appelation of brushwood was ' Rice.'

between

[PART I, CHAPTER XX.]

between Hvit river and Reykjardale's river, and dwelt at Breidabolsted. He married Geirlaug, the daughter of Thormod, on Akraness, the sister of Beri; their son was Tungu-Odd, and their daughter was named Thorodda. She married Torfi, the son of Valbrand, the son of Valthjof, the son of Orlyg, from Esjuberg, and she had from home for a dowry * the half of Breidabolsteid with Halsaland. He gave to Signy, his sister, Signysted, and she dwelt there. Torfi slew the men of Kropp, twelve of them together. He also especially promoted the slaughter of the Holmesmen, and he was at Hellisfitar, with Illugi the black, and Sturla the Godi † when eighteen cavemen were slain there. They also burned, in his own house, Audun, the son of Smidkel, at Thorvardsted. The son of Torfi was Thorkel, at Skaney.

Tungu Odd married Jorunn, the daughter of Helgi; their children were these : Thorvald the ringleader in the burning of Blund Ketil, and Thorod, who married Jofrid, the daughter of Gunnar; their daughter was Hungerd, who was married to Sverking, the son of Hafrbjorn. Thurid was a daughter of Tungu-Odd, who was married to Svarthofdi, and Jofrid, whom Thorfinn, the son of Sellhoris, had for wife, and Hallgerd, the wife of Hallbjorn, the son of Odd from Kidjaberg. Kjolvor was the mother's sister of Tungi Odd, who dwelt at Kjolvorsted; she was the mother of Thorleif, (a daughter) who was the mother of Thurid, the mother of Gunnhild, owned of Kali and of Glum, the father of Thorarin, the father of Glum at Vatnlausu=waterless.

CHAPTER XXI. There was a man named Raud, he settled land up from Raudsgill to the Gills, and dwelt at Raudsgill; his sons were Ulf in Ulfsted, and Aud in

---

* The Icelandic phrase here is fylgði henni heiman, meaning literally "there followed her *from* home."

† Godi, see note at end of Part I.

Audsted,

[PART I, CHAPTER XXI.]

Audsted, to the north of the river, whom Hord slew; wherefrom takes its rise the Saga of Hord, the son of Grimkels, and of Geir. There was a man named Grim, he settled land further to the south, up from Gills to Grimsgill, and dwelt at Grimsgill, his sons were Thorgils auga at Augasted, and Hrani at Hranisted, the father of Grim, who was called Stafn Grim; he dwelt at Stafn-grimsted, this is now called Sigmundsted; opposite to this, north of the Hvit river, upon the bank of the river is his How, there he was slain.

Thorkell Kornamuli took the southern ridge up from Kolls læk to Deildgill, and dwelt at· As=the ridge. His son was Thorborg Kornamuli, who married Alof Ellidask-jold * the daughter of Ofeig and Asgerd, the sister of Thorgeir Gollnis; their children were Eysteinn and Hafthora, who married Eid Skeggison, who afterwards dwelt at As. There died Midfjordskeggi, and his How is there below the garth=enclosure. Another son of Skeggi was Koll, who dwelt at Kollslæk. The sons of Eid were Eystein and Illugi. Ulf was the son of Grim the Halogolander, and of Svanlaug, the daughter of Thormod from Akraness, the sister of Bersi. Ulf settled land between the Hvit river=white river, and the southern glaciers, and dwelt in Geitland. His sons were Hrolf the Rich, the father of Halldora, who was owned of Gizur the White; their daughter was Vilborg, who was wedded to Kjalti, the son of Skeggi. Another son of his was Hroald, the father of Hrolf the younger, who married Thurid the daughter of Valthjof, the son of Orlyg the old; their children were:—Kjallak at Lund in Sydradale=Southern dale, the father of Koll, the father of Bergthor; another was Solvi in Geitland, the father of

---

* This word has reference to the shield that was placed upon the poop of a ship.
† On Haugr or How.

Thord

[PART I, CHAPTER XXI.]

Thord in Reykjaholt, the father of Solvi, father of Thord, the father of Magnus, father of Thord, the father of Helga, the mother of Gudney, the mother of the Sturlasons : Sighvat, Thord and Snorri.* The son of Sighvat was Sturla, the father of Thurid, who married the knight Rafn, their children were Jon, Korpt, Hallkatla, Valgerd, and Thorgerd. The sons of Hallkatla and Jon Pereson were Sturla and Peter, and Steinum a daughter, who married Gudmund, the son of Thorstein, the son of Skeggi. The third son of Hrolf was Illugi, the Red, who first dwelt at Hraunas, he had then for wife Sigrid, daughter of Thorarin the evil, a sister of Musa-Bolverk ; that homestead (*i.e.* Hraunas) Illugi gave to Bolverk, while he, Illugi, went to keep house at Hofstead in Reykdale, because the Geitlanders had to uphold that Temple in equal halves with Tungu Odd. Afterwards Illugi dwelt at the Inner Holm on Akraness, because he exchanged with Holm-Starri both lands and wives and all chattels. Then Illugi married Jorun, the daughter of Thormod, the son of Thyjostar from Alftness, but Sigrid hanged herself in the Temple, because she would have nought to do with the exchange of husbands. Hrolf, the younger, gave Thorlaug Priestess, his daughter, to Oddi, son of Yr, thereupon Hrolf betook himself west to the Ball river and dwelt there long and was known by the name of Hrolf of the Ball river.

Note on the Godi and the Institution of the Althing A.D. 930.

The Norse chiefs who settled in Iceland finding the country uninhabited, solemnly took possession of the land, directing their landtake by the omens of the drifting ashore of the high seat pillars, &c., and then in

---

* Snorri Sturlason, the Historian, A.D. 1178 to 1241.

order

[PART I, CHAPTER XXI.]

order to found a community, they built a temple and called themselves by the name of goði * or hof goði =*temple-priest*, and thus the temple became the nucleus of a new community, which was calied goðorð. Many independent goðar and goðorð sprung np throughout all the country, until about the year 930 the Althing was erected where all the petty sovereign chiefs goðar entered into a kind of league, and formed a general government for the whole Island. In A.D. 964 the constitution was settled ; the number of goðorð being fixed at three in each thing (shire), and three things in each of the other three quarters, but four in the north ; thus the number of goðar came to be nominally thirty-nine, really thirty-six as the four in the north were reckoned out as three.†

SECOND PART.

Here begins the Landtake in the Quarter of the Western Firths, where many men of great degree have settled.

CHAPTER I. There was a man named Kalman, from Sodor=the Hebrides, by origin, he went to Iceland and came into Hvalfjord, and remained for the winter by Kalman's river. His two sons were drowned there in Hvalfjord. Afterwards he settled land all to the west of Hvit(=the white) river, between Fljot and Kalman's tongue, and so all to the east, up to the glaciers, as far as the grass grew, and dwelt at Kalman's tongue. He was drowned in the Hvit river when he had gone south to Hraun, to visit his sweetheart, and his How is at Hvitarbakka,‡ (=white river's bank), the southernmost. His son was Sturla the godi, who dwelt at Sturlastead,

---

* Goði plural Goðar.
† See division called þing in Map.
‡ Bakki. Bakka is a bank of a river, water, or chasm.

up under Tungafell, up from Skaldskelmis dale, and afterwards he abode in Kalman's tongue. His son was Bjarni,
who had a feud with Hrolf the younger and his sons
about the little Tongue. Then Bjarni made a vow to
embrace the Christian religion. After that the Hvit river
opened for itself the channel, in which it now flows, and
then Bjarni got for his own the little Tongue, and the
land out about Grindr and Solmundshofdi. The brother
of Kalman was named Kylan ; he dwelt down below
Kollshamar. His son was Kari, who had a strife with
Karli, the son of Konal, at Karlistead, the freedman of
Hrolf, from Geitland, about an ox which the event
showed to belong to Karli. Afterwards Kari incited his
thrall to slay Karli. The thrall * behaved as if he was
mad, and rushed to the south over the lava plain. Karli
was sitting upon his threshold, the thrall gave him his
death-wound. Kari afterwards slew the thrall. Thjodolf,
the son of Karli, slew Kylan, the son of Kari, at Kylan's-
holar; afterwards Thjodolf burned Kari in, in his house, in
the place that is now called Brenna=the burning. Bjarni
Sturlason received baptism and dwelt at Bjarnistead, in
the little Tongue, and there caused a church to be built.
There was a man of great worth named Thrand Nefja,
the father of Thorstein, who married Lopthæna, the
daughter of Arnbjorn hersir, from the Fjords (=The
Firths in Norway). The sister of Lopthæna was Arnthrud, who was the wife of Thorir the hersir, the son of
Hroald, and their son was Arinbjorn the hersir. The
mother of the two, Lopthæna and Arnthrud, was Astrid
Slækidreingr (=the sleek damsel?), the daughter of Bragi
the Skald, and Lopthæna, the daughter of Erp lutandi
(=the louting). The son of Thorstein and Lopthæna
was Hrosskel, who married Joreid, the daughter of Olvir,

---

* See note Part I, 18, on "Berserkr."

the

the son of Finn, the son of Mottul the King. Their son was named Hallkel.

Hrosskel fared to Iceland and entered the coast at Grunnfjord. He abode first at Akraness, there Ketil and his brother Thormod * dealt unneighbourly with him; afterwards he settled the white river side, between Kjarriver and Fljot, he dwelt at Hallkelstead, and Hall-kell his son after him, who had for wife Thurid dylla, the the daughter of Gunnlaug, from Thverarhlid (=cross river slope), and of Velaug, the daughter of Orlyg, from Esjaberg. Hrosskel gave land to Thorvard, the father of Smidkel, the father of Thorarin and Audun, who were the leaders of the Hellismen; † he dwelt at Thorvardstead, his two sons were both named Gisli. The children of Hallkel and Thurid were Thorarin and Finnvard, Tind, and Illugi the black, and Grima, whom Thorgil, the son of Ari, had for wife while he abode at Hraunsas. Musa Bolver slew Thorarin. Then he let rear there a fort, and he made a bed for Hvit-river through fellridge, while formerly it fell down through Metrakka-dale. Illugi and Tind set upon Bolverk in the fort.

Settlements by the Kjarr river and Hvit (white) river. The ancestors of those who fought in the Battle upon the Heath. Snorri of Melar.

CHAPTER II. Asbjorn the Rich, who was the son of Hord, bought land to the South of Kjarr ‡ River, up from Skeggjalæk to Hvitbjorg (=The white precipices or rocks); he dwelt at Asbjornstead, he married Thorbjorg, the daughter of Midfirth Skeggi; their daughter was

---

* See Pt. I, ch. xv, beg.
† Cavemen.
‡ Kjarr-p-Kjörr. Dan Kjaer—Copsewood or Brushwood. It is found very commonly with this meaning in Lakeland, as field names, *e.g.* Ellercar, Dillicars, Carr Cottage and Carr Lane.

Ingibjorg

[PART II, CHAPTER II.]
Ingibjorg, whom Illugi the Black married. There was
a man named Ornolf who settled Ornolf's dale and
Kjarrdale, northward up to Hvitbjorg. Ketil blund (=
slumber) bought land of Ornolf, all to the North of Cliff
(Klif), and dwelt at Ornolfsdale ; then Ornolf made his
dwelling up in Kjarrdale, that which is now called
Ornolfstead. Above the cliff the dale is named Kjarrdale,*
because there there was brushwood and copsewood.
Between Kjarr River and Cross River a dwelling might
not be set up there. Blund-Ketil was a man of mighty
wealth ; he let woods be cleared wide about and abodes
he reared there. The brother of Grim haleyski (=from
Halogoland in Norway) was named Hromund, the son
Thorir, the son of Gumlaug, the son of Hrolf, the son of
Ketil Kjolfari (=Keel farer *i.e.* the navigator). Hromond
brought his ship into the Hvit (white) river. He settled
Crossriverdale and Crossriverslope,† out to Hallmuli, and
forward to Cross River; he dwelt at Hromundstead, the
place which is now called Karlsbrekka. His son was
Gunnlaug Ormstunga *i.e.* serpent's tongue, who dwelt at
Gunnlaug*stead* to the south of the Cross River. He
married Velaugu, as was before written, the daughter of
Orlyg, from Esjuberg, their daughter was Thurid, the
mother of Illugi the black, the father of Hermund, the
father of Hrein, the father of Styrmer, the father of
Hrein, the father of Valdis, the mother of Snorri, of
Melar,‡ the father of Hallera, whom Markus, the son of
Thord, had for wife. A shipmate of Hromund was
named Hogni, he dwelt at Hognistead ; his son was

---

* Kjarr=Copsewood or Brushwood.

† Icelandic þverárdal ok þverárhlíð.

‡ Melr, pl. Melar, means, first, *bent grass*, second, a *sandhill* grown with
such grass, and third, a *sandbank*, whether overgrown or bare. Many Cumberland place names seem to come from it, e.g. Millom, Eskmeals, Mealsgate,
Mealo; see also discovery and description of Raudamel in Book II, Chapter V,
of this work.

Helgi

[PART II, CHAPTER II.]

Helgi, at Helgi's water, the father of Arngrim the godi, who was at the burning of Blundketil; Hogni was the brother of Finn the Rich. Isleif and Israud, two brothers, settled land a down from Skeggjalæk, between Ornolfdale's River, and the white river, and by the North down to Raudlæk, by the South down to Hordholar. Isleif dwelt in Isleifstead, and Israud in Israudstead ; he owned land towards the South, along the white river, he was the father of Thorbjorn, the father of Liot, at Veggir, who fell in the Battle upon the Heath.

One of the ship's crew of Hromond was named Asgeirr, who dwelt at Hamar up from Helgiwater ; he married Hild Stjarna=the Star, the daughter of Thorvald, the son of Thorgrim-brækir, their sons were Steinbjorn, the strong and hard hitter, and Thorvard the father of Mæfa, whom Krifla married, and the third was Thorstein, the fourth Helgi, the father of Thord, the father of Skaldhelgi.

Settlements of Arnbjorg, Thorbjorn, Geirmund, Orn, Rauda Bjorn, Karl, and the freedmen of Skallagrim.

CHAPTER III. There was a woman named Arnbjorg, she dwelt at Arnbjorg's-læk ; her sons were these : Eldgrim who dwelt on the Hals* or Neck up from Arnbjorg's-læk at Elgrimstead, and Thorgest who received his death wound when he fought against Hrani at the place which is now called Kranifall. Thorun was the name of a woman who abode at Thorunholt, she owned land down to Vidilæk, and up to where it joined the land of Thurid the sooth-sayer, her sister, who dwelt at Grof. From her the deep Thorun's-hyl† in Thvera derives its

---

* Used of the narrow mountain pass or neck connecting two valleys and cor-responding with the word Hause as used in Lakeland, e.g., Tarn Hause, Esk Hause, Seatoller Hause.

† Hyl is a hole or deep place in a river.

name

[PART II, CHAPTER III.]

name, and from her the dwellers of the Hamar are descended.   Thornbjorn the son of Arnbjorn, the son of
Oleif lang neck was the brother of Lyling in Vapnfirth.
Thornbjorn settled Stafaholtstongue between the north
river and cross river,* he dwelt in Arnholt, his son was
Teit in Stafaholt, the father of Einar.   Thorlborn Blesi
settled land in Northriverdale to the south of the river
(north river), up from Krok and all Hellirdale and dwelt
at Besistead, his son was Gisli of Melar in Hellisdale,
from him the Gisliswaters take their name, another son
of Blesi was Thorfin of Thorfinstead, the father of Thorgerd, the mother of Helgi at Lund—Geirmund the son of
Gunnbjorn goblin settled the tongue between the North
river and Sand river and dwelt at Tongue, his son was
Bruni, the father of Thorbjorm at Steinar, who fell at
the Battle upon the Heath.   Orn the Old settled Sanddale
and Mjovidale, and likewise Northriverdale, down from
Krok unto Arnarbæli and dwelt at Harekstead.

Raudi-Bjorn settled Bjornsdale and all the dales which
open out therefrom and had another dwelling down from
Mælifellsgill, and another lower down in the countryside
as is written.   Karl settled Karlsdale up from Hreda-
water, and dwelt under Karsfell, he possessed land out to
Jafnaskard until it marched with that of Grim.   Gris and
Grim were called two freedmen of Skallagrim, to them
he gave land up against the mountain—to Gris—Gris-
tongue, and to Grim—Grimsdale.

Settlement of Bersi godless and the freedmen of Grim.

CHAPTER IV.   There was a man named Bersi godless,
the son of Balki, the son of Blæing from Ramfirth, he

---

*This river name which occurs in the Book of Settlement very frequently, is
literally thwart river, i.e., side or tributary river, that is a tributary stream
flowing into another or main stream, and the land included between those rivers
as they bifurcate is termed a tongue or tungu.   This river name is given in the
original Icelandic at Page 30, Note 2.

                                                          took

[PART II, CHAPTER IV.]

took all Lang Valzdale * and dwelt there. His sister was:
Geirbjorg, who was married to Thorgeir in Tungufell,
their son was Veleif the old—Bersi the godless got for
wife Thordis the daughter of Thorhadd from Hitardale,
and received with her Holmsland, their son was Arngeir,
father of Bjorn, champion of the men of Hitdale. One
of the freedmen of Skallagrim was named Sigmund, he
gave him land between the Glufr river and the North
river, he dwelt at Haugar before he took himself to
Munadar-ness and from him Sigmundness takes its name.

Raudi-Bjorn bought land from Skallagrim between
Glufr-river † and Gufa-river, he dwelt at Raudabjornstead,
up from Eskiholt, his son was Thorkell Trefill in Skard
and Helgi in Hvamm ‡ and Gunnvald the father of
Thorkel, who married Helga, the daughter of Thorgeir of
Vidimyri.

Thorbjorn Krum and Thord Beigaldi were the names
of two brothers ; Skallagrim gave them land beyond the
Gufu river, and Thorbjorn dwelt at Holar, and Thord at:
Beigalda. Skallagrim gave land to Thorir Thuss and
Thorgeir Jardlang and Thorbjorg Staung, their sister, up
along Langriver, on the south of it. Thorir dwelt at
Thuss Stead, Thorgeir at Jardlangstead, and Thorbjorg
in Stangholt. There was a man named Ani to whom
Grim gave land between Lang river and Hafslæk ; he
dwelt at Annabrekka, his son was Onund Sjani the father
of Steinar, and Dalla, the mother of Kormak.

Thorfin the Strong was the name of the standard-
bearer of Thorolf, the son of Skallagrim. To him

---

* Valzdale = Waterdale ; compare Wasdale and Wasdale Head.

† Literally between the ravine river and the vapour river—Gljufr being a steep
chasm or descent within which the river flowed, and Guf being the vapour or
smoke ascending from a hot river.

‡ Hvamm—this as common Icelandic noun is the name of any grassy slope by
the side of a river. Hummer as found in Lakeland corresponds exactly with
inform and meaning.

Skallagrim

[PART II, CHAPTER IV.]

Skallagrim gave Sæunn his daughter and land beyond Lang river,* out to Leiralæk (=miry water), and upward to the mountain.   He dwelt at Foss; their daughter was Thordis, mother of Bjorn, the champion of the men of Hitdale.   There was a man named Ingvarr, father of Bera, whom Skallagrim had for wife.   Grim gave him land between Leiralæk and Straum firth, he dwelt at Alptaness.   Another daughter of his was Thordis, who was the wife of Thorger Lambi, at Lambistead, who was the father of Thord, whom the thralls of Ketill Gufa burnt in his house.   The son of Thord was Lambi the strong.   There was a man named Steinof who took to himself on both sides Hraundale (=Lava valley), all to Grjota (=gritty river), by the leave of Skallagrim; he was the father of Thorleif, from whom the Hraundalers are come.   The daughter of Steinolf was named Thorun, who was the wife of Thorbjorn, the son of Vifil, the father of Thorgerd, the mother of Asmund, father of Sveinbjorn, the father of Odd, the father of Gro, the nuther of Odd, of Alptaness.

Thorhadd was a son of Stein muchsailing, the son of Vigbjod, the son of Bodmod, from Bulkarum; he settled Hitdale, southward to Grjota river, and westward to Kalda (=the cold stream), and between Hita and Kalda (=the hot stream and the cold stream), down to the sea.   His son was Thorgeirr, the father of Hafthor, the father of Gudny, the mother of Thorlak the Rich, the father of Thorleif beiskaldi, the father of Thorleik, the father of Ketil, the father of Valgerd, the mother of the Narvisons, Thorlak and Thord, to wit.   The sons of Thorgeir were Grim in Skard, and Thorurin, Finnbogi, Eystein, Gest and Torfi.   Thorgils knappi, the freedman of Kolli, the son of Hroald, settled Knappidale; his sons were Ingjald

---

* Langa may be translated " Long Stream."

and

and Thorarin, and Thorir, who dwelt at Akrar, and got for his own land between Hita and Alpta (=the hot river and the swan river), and up until it joined the landtake of Steinolf,. The son of Thorarin was Thrand, who married Steinun, the daughter of Hrut, at Kambness. Their sons were Thorir and Skum, the father of Torfi, the father of Janni. His son was Hrut, who married Kolfinn, the daughter of Illugi the Black. Now have those men been recounted who settled in the landtake of Skallagrim.

Grim draws up a mereman (marmennil) while fishing which he compels to foretell place for settlement. First appearance of Volcano Eld-borg to Thorir his son in old age.

CHAPTER V.   There was a man nomed Grim, the son of Ingjald, the son of Hroald, from Haddingdale ; he was the brother of Asi, a hersir.   He went to Iceland to seek for settlement, and sailed by the north of the land ; he was for one winter in Grimsey, in Steingrimsfirth ; his wife was named Bergdis, and their son Thorir.   Grim went out to fish in the Autumn with his housecarles and the lad.   Thorir lay in the prow and was in a seal-bag which was drawn together at the neck.   Grim drew up a mereman and when he came up asked him " What do you foretell shall be our fortune, or where shall we settle in Iceland ?   The mereman answered, " No need to tell the fortune of you and your men, but rather of the lad that lays in the seal bag, he shall there settle and take land where Skalm your mare lays down under her load," and no more words got they from him.   Later in the winter Grim and his men rowed out, but the lad was upon land ; then the whole crew was lost.   Then Bergdis and Thorir went about spring-time from Grimsey, and westward over the Heath to Breidafjord (=Broadfirth) ; there Skalm went before them and never laid down.

Another

[PART II, CHAPTER V.]

Another winter they were at Skalmness, in Breidafjord, and in the summer after they turned south, then Skalm went before them until they came off the Heaths to Borgfjord, unto a spot where two red sandhills * stood before them. There Skalm laid down under the westernmost sand hill, under her load. There Thorir took land from the south of Gnupa to Kalda (or Coldstream), down below Knappadale, between fell and foreshore; he dwelt at Raudamel † the westernmost. He was a great Chieftain.

Then was Thorir old and blind, when once he went out late one evening and saw how a man rowed up from the offing into the mouth of Kalda (cold stream), in an iron tub, great and evil looking, and walked aland there up to the homestead called Hrip, and set to digging there in the gate of the milking-stead, and in that night there came earth-fire (volcanic eruption), and then the Borg lava was created by fire, and there stood the dwelling where now is the volcanic hill Eld-borg.‡

The son of Selthoris was Thorfin, who married Jofrid, the daughter of Tunga Odd, their sons were Thorkel and Thorgils, Stein and Galti, Orm and Thororm and Thorir. Steinn Thorfinson was the father of Arnoru, the mother of Hallbjorg, the mother of Oddnyj, the mother of Geirlaug, the mother of Snælang, the mother of Markus of Melar. The daughter of Thorfin was Thorbjorg, who married Thorbrand from Alptafirth. Selthorir and his heathen kindred died § into Thorisbjorg=Thorir's rocks. Thorkell and Thorgils, the sons of Thorfinn both married Um, the daughter of Alf of the Dales. Skalm, the mare

---

* Sand Melir tveir raudir.
† Or " The Red Sandhills " compare Cartmel Eskmeals, &c.
‡ Eld-borg. In the original Icelandic of the Landnama the name of this mountain is Borgarhraun or " The Fortress of Lava."
§ " Die into, into the rocks called by the name of Thoris," so as to dwell in them after death. See Part II, Chapter 12, for a like belief about Helgafell by the heathen descendants of Thorolf. A full explanation is given in the note upon that chapter.

of Thorir, died in Skalmkelda (Skalm's Ditch). Kolbein
Klakkhofdi, the son of Atli of Atley from Fjaler, went to
Iceland and bought all the land between Kalda and Hita,
or the cold river and the hot river, down below Sand-
brekka, and dwelt at Kolbeinstead ; his sons were
Finnbogi in Fagriskogr and Thord the Scald.

Note on Eldborg and Raudamel.

At the distance of two miles róse the grand circular
crater of Eld-borg, which is not only remarkable on
account of its singular configuration, but also because it
stands quite insulated in the middle of an extensive plain,
which it has almost entirely deluged with lava.

On our arrival at the base of the volcano, we could not
sufficiently admire the regularity with which it rose by a
gradual acclivity till within about eighty feet of the
summit, when the heath and every vestige of vegetation
ceased, and a wall of dark vitrified lava rose at once in
nearly a perpendicular direction, and terminated in a
rough and irregular top. From the perfect resemblance
of this wall to an immense artificial fortification, it has
obtained the name of Eld-borg, or "The Fortress of Fire."
When we reached the summit we were not a little alarmed
that we were only separated from a tremendous abyss by
a dome of lava, in many places not six inches thickness,
extremely loose in contexture and mouldering with age
into the crater, which opened like an immense basin
directly before us. It is not an entire circle, but some-
what oval ; its longitude stretching. east-south-east to
west-north-west. The crater measures 1800 feet in circumference, and consists of rugged cliffs amongst which
a number of ravens annually build their nests.

From the summit we had an extensive view of the
plain which the lava has inundated, and higher up the
opposite valley several red cones presented themselves,

which

which have also poured forth streams of melted sub-
stances, the largest of which are those situated in the
vicinity of *Raudamel.—Henderson's Travels.*

*Settlements by Straumfjord river. The Holmgang. Ancestors
of the Sturlungs of Hvamm. Hospitality of Thora. Story
of the interment of Asmund.*

CHAPTER VI. Thormod and Thord gnupa were the
sons of Odd the Rank, the son of Thorvid, the son of
the son Freyvid, the son of Alf from Vors; these brothers
went to Iceland and settled land from Gnupa to Straumfjord river. Thord had Gnupadale and dwelt there, his
son was Skapti, the father of Hjorleif the godi, and of
Tinna, who was married to Ref the Great, the father of
Steinunn, the mother of Hofgurd Rey. Thormod dwelt
at Raudkollstead; he was called Thormod the godi; he
married Gerd, the daughter of Kjallak the Old. Their
son was Gudlaug the Rich; he married Thordis, the
daughter of Svathofdi, the son of Bjorn Gullber (goldbearer), and of Thurid, the daughter of Tungu Odd, who,
at that time, dwelt in Horgsholt. Gudlaug the wealty
observed that the lands of Raudamel were better than
other lands south in that countryside. Then he challenged
Thorfinn for his land, and called him out to the Holmgang.* They both fell on the Holm, but Thurid, the
daughter of Tungu Odd, healed them both of their
wounds and reconciled them. Gudlaug afterwards settled
land from Straumfjord river to Furu, between fell and
foreshore, and dwelt at Borgholt; from him are the
Straumfirthings come. His son was Gudleif, who had a
ship of his own, while another of his own had Thorolf,

---

* Holmgang. This was the Norse wager of battle and was so called from the
fact that the intending combatants in the duel went alone to an Island (Holm),
and there fought to the death. The survivor usually retained the name Holmgang as a nickname.

the

[PART II, CHAPTER VI.]

the son of Lopt the Old, when they fought with Earl Gyrd, the son of Sigvaldi. Another son of Gudlaug was Thorfin, the father of Gudlaug, the father of Thordis, the mother of Thord, the father of Sturla, in Hvamm. A daughter of Gudlaug the Rich was named Valgerd. One of the body guard of Harald the Fairhaired was named Vali the Strong; he wrought a manslaughter in a hallowed place and was outlawed. He went to the Hebrides or Sodor, and took up his abode there, but his three sons went to Iceland. Hlif hestageldir was their mother. One was named Atli, another Alfarin, and the third Audun Stoli, They all went to Iceland. Atli, the son of Vali, and Asmund, his son, settled land from Fura to Lysa. Asmund dwelt in Langholt, at Thoratofts, he had for wife Thora, of Langholt. Then Asmund as he grew old dwelt at Oxl, but Thora dwelt there after (at Langholt), and had her Scale built right across the highway, and there she sat upon a stool, and invited as guests there whoever would eat meat. Asmund was howed (interred) in Asmund's how, and laid in his ship, and his thrall or slave was laid beside him.* A man heard the following ditty sung within his howe (gravemound) as he passed by it :

> In stony stead,[1] on Atal's Raven,[2]
> I have the prow-room to myself,
> Nor is the deck with thanes [3] o'ercrowded,
> The timbers' steed [4] is my abode.
> But better to one skilled in battle,
> In empty space than evil suite,[5]
> Yet longer [6] people may remember
> I'm master here of my own ship.

---

* In another copy of the Landnama (the Melabok) it is said that the thrall committed suicide through grief at his master's death.
(1) The stone-walled tomb.
(2) Atall, a sea king of fame, his raven=ship.
(3) =men, warriors.
(4) =vessel.
(5) i.e. the fellowship of the thrall buried with him.
(6) i.e. longer than the fact that a thrall was left to disgrace and annoy him in death.

After

⌊PART II, CHAPTER VI.⌋

After that they made for the How, and the thrall was taken out from the ship. Hrolf the Stout, son of Eyvind Oak Crook, brother of Illugi, Fells-godi east from Sida, settled land from Lysa to Hraum haven; his son was Helgi, in Hofgarth, father of Finnbogi and Bjorn, and Hrolf Bjorn was the father of Gest, the father of Skald Reef.

Deadly conflict between the party of Laugarbrekka-Einar and the party of Lon-Einar about alleged witchcraft. Einar's grave mound.

CHAPTER VII. There was a man named Solvi who settled land between Hellir and Hraun Haven (Lava Haven). He dwelt at Brenning and afterwards at Solvahamar, because he thought that there it would be more gainsome * to him to be.

Sigmund, the son of Ketil Thistle, who had settled Thistilfjord in the north, had for wife Hildigun; he settled land between Hellishraum (cavern-lava) and Beruvikrhraun (Berewick lava); he dwelt at Laugarbrekka, and there he is howed.† He had three sons, one was Einar, who afterwards dwelt at Laugarbrekka. Father and son sold Lonland to Einar, who afterwards dwelt there; he was called Lon-Einar. After Sigmund died Einar went to Laugarbrekka with seven men, and summoned Hildigun for witchcraft, when Einar her son was not at home. He returned home just after Lon-Einar was gone forth.‡ Hilidigun told him these tidings and brought him a kirtle new-made. Einar took his shield and sword and work-horse, and rode after them. He rode his horse to death in Thufubjorg, but got up with them at Mannafallsbrekka

---

* The Icelandic word is ' gagnsamari ' meaning ' to be of benefit.'
† Heygŏr.
‡ Nyfarinn a braut.

Mannfall

[PART II, CHAPTER VII.]

(Mannfall-brink); thére they fought and thére fell four
men of the party of Lon-Einar, but two thralls of his ran
away from him. The two namesakes fought long until
the breeks' girdle* of Lon-Einar tore asunder, and as Einar
laid hold of it, his namesake gave him his death blow.†
A thrall of Laugarbrekka-Einar was named Hreidar,—he
rushed after them, saw from Thufubjorg where the thralls
of Lon-Eimar ran away, and he ran after them and slew
them both in Thrallwick. In return for that Einar gave
him his freedom and land as much as he was able to
encircle in three days—that is called Heidarsgarth ‡ where
he dwelt afterwards. Einar at Laugarbrekka married
Unni the daughter of Thorir, the brother of Aslak in
Langdale. Their daughter was Hallveig whom Thorbjorn
the son of Vifil had for wife. Another son of Sigmund
was named Breid, he was brother to Einar; he had for
wife Gunnhild the daughter of Aslak from Langdale.
Their son was Thormod who had for wife Helga the
daughter of Onund, and sister of Skald Hrafn; their
daughter was Herthrud whom Simon had for wife; their
daughter was Gunnhild whom Thorgils had for wife;
their daughter was Valgerd the mother of Finnbogi the
Strong, the son of Geir. The third son of Sigmund
was named Thorkell, he was married to Joreid the
daughter of Tind the son of Hallkel. Laugarbrekka-Einar
was howed § (interred) a short way from the How of

---

* The Icelandic word for girdle here is bróklindi, and signifies that which keeps
up the brók, plural brækr=breeches. This word brók is of Celtic origin and is
identical with the Gaelic bræcan=tartan. It means in its *first* sense *tartan* or
party coloured cloth; *secondly breeches* or *breeks*. The famous mythical
Danish King Ragnar Loobrok, had his name hence—lod-brok=hairy breeches.
An Icelandic proverb runs thus : barnid vex, en bróken ekki=*the bairn waxes
but the breeches not*, meaning, give your children plenty of room in their first
breeches.
† Icelandic banahögg.
‡ Garth is enclosure. Many parallels occur in North English Place Names
and Field Names, e.g. Loppergarth, Hall Garth, Garth Nook, Applegarth,
Garth House, The Garths.
§ Heygðr,

Sigmund

[PART II, CHAPTER VII.]

Sigmund (his father). His grave* is ever green, winter and summer. The son of Lon Einar was named Thorkel; he married Grimu, the daughter of Hallkel, before she was wedded by Thorgils, the son of Ari; their son was Finnvard. Another daughter of Laugarbrekka-Einar was Arnora, who was the wife of Thorgeir, the son of Vifil. Their daughter was Ingveld, whom Thorstein, the son of Snorri the godi, had for wife. Their daughter was Ingud, who was married to Asbjorn, the son of Arnor.

Settlements of the descendents of Grimkell. Thorarin Korni the hamramr mjök, i.e., the great wizard who could change his shape.

CHAPTER VIII. There was a man called Grimkel, the son of Ulf Crow, the son of Heidar, the brother of Gunnbjorn, after whom the Gunnbjornskeries are named; he settled land from Beruvikhraun† to Neshraun† and out onward over the ness, and dwelt at Saxihvoli. He drove out thence Saxi, the sou of Alfarin, the son of Vali, and he dwelt afterwards in Hraun,† at Saxihvoli. Grimkel married Thorgerd, daughter of Valthjof the Old; their son was Thorarin Korni, he was of exeeding great strength, and lies in Kornis How. Thorsteinn Korni married Jorunn, the daughter of Einar, in Stafaholt; their daughter was Jarngerd, who was married to Ulf, the son of Uggi. There was another son of Grimkel named Klæng, he married Oddfrid, the daughter of Helgi, from Hvanneyri, their son was Kolli, who married Thurid, the daughter of Asband, from Kamb. Their son was Skeggi, the father of Thorkatla, who was the wife of Illugi, the son of Thorvald, the son of Find; Illugi was the father of Gils, who slew Gjafvald. Another son of Kolli was

---

* How or Haugr.
† Both these names from Hraun = Lava.

named

[PART II, CHAPTER VIII.]

named Bord; he married Valgerd, the daughter of Vidar; their daughter was Vigdis, who was married to Thorbjorn the Stout; their daughter was Thordis, who was the wife of Thorbrand at Olvus-water. Thorir was their son and Bjarni in Breidabolstead, and Torfi, but their daughter was Valgerd, who married Runolf, the son of the Bishop, *i.e.* Bishop Ketil. Another daughter of Bard was named Asdis; she was first married to Thorbjorn, the son of Thorvald, the brother of Mana Ljot, of the same mother; their daughter was Thurid, who was married to Thorgrim, the son of Odd; their children were Geirmund in Mafahlid and fourteen others. Asdis was married a second time to Skuli, the son of Jorund. Valgerd, from Mossfell, was their daughter. Alfarinn, the son of Vali, had first settled the ness between Bervikhraun and Enni; his sons were Hoskuld, who dwelt at Hoskuld's river, and Ingjald, who dwelt in Ingjaldshvol, and Got at Gotilæk, and Holm Kell at Fors,* by Holmkel's river. There was a man named Olaf the Bellows who settled land inward from Enni to Frodis river, and abode in Olaf's Vik.

Geirvid accused of witchcraft. Her trial by Duradóm is broken up by a free fight. Settlement of Herjolf. Slays a wood-bear.

CHAPTER IX. There was a man named Orm the Slender who brought his ship to the mouth of Frodis river, and dwelt at Brimilsvellir for a while. He drove away Olaf Bellows and settled the whole Vik or Bay between Enni and Hofdi, and dwelt then at Frodis water. His son was Thorbjorn the Stout; he married first Thurid, daughter of Asbrand from Kamb, and their children were Ketil Kappi, Hallstein and Gunnlaug, and Thorgerd, who was the wife of Onund Sjoni. Thorbjorn

---

* Force or Waterfall.

afterwards

[PART II, CHAPTER IX.]

:afterwards married Thurid, the daughter of Bork the ·Stout, and Thordis, the daughter of Sur.   Thorbjorn the ·Stout summoned Geirvid, the daughter of Bægifot, for :witchcraft after that Gunnlaug his son died of that ill-·ness which he had caught when he went to learn the art .of magic from Geirvid.   She was the mother of Thorarin ,in Mafahlid.   In this action Arnkell the godi was challenged for a verdict of twelve neighbours, and he declared Geirvid not guilty because Thorarin took the ,oath upon the altar ring, and so caused the action to collapse.   After that some studhorses of Thorbjorn were lost upon the fell; he charged Thorarin with that and went to Mafahlid and set up a door-doom (ok setti dura-dóm).*   They were twelve together, but Thorarin and his were seven in the house before them, to wit, Alfgeir from the Hebrides, and Nagli and Bjorn the Eastman, and three house-karles ; they broke up the court and fought in the inclosure (tūn), near the house.   Aud the wife of Thorarin called upon the women to separate them ; one man fell of the party of Thorarin, and two of the party of Thorbjorn.   Thorbjorn then went away and bound up their wounds by the stackgarth on the Vogar.   The hand of Aud was found in the enclosure.   Therefore went Thorarin after them and found then by the stackgarth. Nagi ran weeping (greeting) past them, and so rushed forth upon the fell.   There Thorarin slew Thorbjorn and wounded Hallsteinn to death.   Five men fell there of the party of Thorbjorn.   Arnkell and Vermund gave aid to Thorarin, and sat together at Arnkel's house.   Snorri the godi took up the blood-suite after Thorbjorn and at the Thorsness Thing made them all guilty who had taken part in the fight.   Afterwards he burnt the ship of Algeir and his companions at the mouth of the salt eyr † river.

---

* Dyradómr=a court at the door of the defendant.
† Eyrr or Eyri is the name of the gravelly bank of a river or of the small tongue of land that adjoins the river's mouth.

Arnkel

[PART II, CHAPTER IX.]

Arnkel purchased a ship for them in Dogurdarness, and saw them off until they had cleared all islands; hence hostilities broke out between Arnkel and Snorri the godi. Ketil Kappi was at that time abroad; he was the father of Hrodny, the wife of Thorstein, the son of Vig-Styr. Sigurd Svinhofdi was a great warrior, he dwelt at Kvern- ·vogastrand. Herjolf, his son, was there eight winters, when he slew a wood-bear for tearing to pieces a goat of his. Respecting this fact there were these verses:

> Bruin bottom-singéd
> Bit a goat for Herjolf,
> But Herjolf hulky-bottomed
> Avenged his goat on Bruin.

Herjolf was twelve winters old when he avenged the death of his father. He was a man most mighty of his ·hands. Herjolf went to Iceland in his old age and settled the land between Bulandshofdi and Kirkfirth, or Kirkjufjordr. His son was Thorstein Kolskegg, the father of Thorolf, the father of Thorarin the Black, the Mafh- liding (or of Mafahlid), and Gudny, whom Vermund the Slender married; their son was Brand the Bounteous, and their daughter was Thorfinna, whom Thorstein Kaggason ·had for wife. Vestar, the son of Thorolf Blodruskalli, or Bladderpate, married Svand, the daughter of Herrod; their son was Asgeir. Vestar went to Iceland with his father in his extreme old age, and settled Eyrland * and ·Kirkfirth; he dwelt at Ondurd-Eyr. Vestar and Thorolf were howed both of them at Skallaness. Asgeir, the son of Vestar, married Helga, the daughter of Kjarlak; their son was Thorlak, and the sons of him and Thurid, the daughter of Audun Stoffi, were Steinthorr and Thord Blig, who married Ottkatla, the daughter of Thorvald, the

---

* See meaning of Eyrr above.

son

son of Thormod the godi; a third son was Thormod, who married Thorgerd, the daughter of Thorbrand, from Alpta fiord (Swan firth); a fourth son was Bergthor, who fell at Vigrfirth; their sister was Helga, whom Asmund, the son of Thorgest, had to wife. Steinthor had to wife Thurid, the daughter of Thorgils, the son of Ari; Gunlaug was their son, who had to wife Thurid the Sage, the daughter of Snorri the godi.

Settlements upon the lava plains. Appearances of a mysterious horse.

CHAPTER X. There was a man named Kol who settled land from the west from Firthhorn, east to Trollhals (Troll's Neck or Hause), and out about Berserk's eyr to Hraunfjord (Lava Firth), his sons were Thorarin and Thorgrim from whom the Kolsons' Fell received its name. Father and son dwelt at Kolgrafir (Kolsgraves), from them the Kolgreflings are descended. Audun Stoti, son of Vali the strong, settled all the land of Lava Firth up above the lava, between Swine water or Svinavatn and Trolls' Hause; he dwelt in Lava Firth and was a mighty man of his hands; from him are the Lava firthers descended. Audun married Myruna, the daughter of Maddad, King of the Irish. Audun saw about Autumn how a dapple grey horse ran down from Herdwater to his stud, and knocked under the stallion. Then Audun caught the dappled grey horse, and yoked it to a two-ox sledge, and carted in with it all the hay of his field. Until mid-day the horse was workable, but as the day wore, it sunk with its hoofs into the ground up to the fetlock, and after sunset it broke all the harness to pieces, and went to the lake, and was seen never afterwards. The son of Audun was Stein, the father of Helga, who married An of Hraun (the Lava); their son was Mar, the father of Gudrid, the

mother

[PART II, CHAPTER X.]
mother of Kjartan and An of Kirkfell. Another son of
Audun was named Asbjorn, the third Svarthofdi, and a
daughter he had, Thurid, who married Thorlak, the son
of Asgeir of Eyr.

*Descendants of Ketil Flatnose. Dispute with Harald Fairhair.
Hrolf the Ganger.*

CHAPTER XI.   There was a man named Bjorn, the son
of Ketil Flatnose, and Yngvild, the daughter of Ketil
Wether, a hersir of Hringriki.   Bjorn remained at home
in the possessions of his father, when Ketil went to the
Hebrides or Sodor.   But when Ketil withheld the tribute
due to King Harald Fairhair, then the King drove Bjorn
from his father's estates, and took them under himself.
Then Bjorn went west over the sea, but would not settle
there ; thence he was called Bjorn the Easterner ; he
married Gjaflaug, the daughter of Kjallak, the sister of
Bjorn the Strong.   Bjorn the Easterner went to Iceland
and settled land between Lava Firth and Staff river, and
dwelt in Bjorn Haven, at Borgholt, and he had a pasture
dairy (Sel) up at Sel, and kept a lordly house.   He died
at Bjorn Haven and was howed at Borglæk, because he
was the only unbaptised son of Ketil Flatnose.
The son of Bjorn and Gjaflaug was called Kjallak the
Old ; he dwelt at Bjorn Haven after his father, together
with Ottar, the father of Bjorn, the father of Vigfus, in
Drapahlid, whom Snorri the godi caused to be slain.
Another son of Ottar was Helgi ; he harried Scotland, and
took thence captives, Midbjorg, the daughter of Bjolan the
King, and Kadlin, the daughter of Gaungu Hrolf or
Rolf the Ganger ; he married her, and their son was
Osvif the Sage, and Einar Skalaglam who was drowned
in Einar's Skerry, in Selasund (Sealsound), and his shield
came ashore in Skjaldey or Shield Island, and his cloak
·at

[PART II, CHAPTER XI.]

at Feldar Holm or Cloak Holm. Einar was the father of Thorgerd, the mother of Herdis, the mother of Stein the Skald. Osvif married Thordis, daughter of Thjodolf, from Haven; their children were Ospak, father of Ulf the Marshal, the father of Ion at Rowan-wall (Reyrvöll), father of Erlend Himaldi, the father of Eystein the the Archbishop, and Thorolf, Torrad, Einar, Thorbjorn and Thorkel; they were outlawed on account of the slaughter of Kjartan, the son of Olaf. A daughter of Osvif was Gudrun, the mother of Gellir and Bolli and Florleik and Thord Cat. The son of Bjorn the Easterner was named Vilgeirr. Kjallak the Old married Astrid the daughter of Hrolf, a hersir, and of Ondott, the sister of Olvir Bairnkarl; their son was Thorgrim the godi, he married Thorhlid, the daughter of Thord the Yeller; their sons were Viga Styrr and Vermand the Slender, and Brand, the father of Thorleik. The daughters of Kjallak the Old were: Gerd, whom Thormod the godi had to wife, and Helga, the wedded wife of Asgeirr at Eyri.

Settlement of Thorolf Mostbeard, A.D. 884. His high seat posts come to land in Broadfirth. He finds them at Temple Stead on Holy Fell. Temple set up there and District Assembly. Fight and consequent feud between the men of Thorsness and the followers of Kiallak the Old, A.D. 932 to 934.

CHAPTER XII. Thorolf,* son of Ornolf=fishdriver, dwelt in Most Isle. He was called Mostbeard; he was

---

*Respecting Thorolf's early history, I have translated and condensed the following from the Eyrbyggja Saga — Thorolf (originally Rolf) lived in Most, an island of Hordarland, in Norway. He changed his name from Rolf to Thorolf on account of his devotion to Thor. He was a mighty chieftain of great strength and stature. His flowing beard and the place of his abode obtained for him the nickname of Mostbeard. For affording shelter to Biorn Ketilson, son of Ketil Flatnose, named in chapter XI, made an outlaw by King Harald, Thorolf was himself made an outlaw, and followed the fortunes of his friend Ingolf, the first settler in Iceland. Before setting out, Thorolf pulled down the temple of Thor, and took with him most of the timbers that were therein, and the mould from under the seat where Thor sat.

much

[PART II, CHAPTER XII.]

much devoted to offering up sacrifices and believed in
Thor. He emigrated to Iceland on account of the
tyranny of Harald Fairhair, and sailed by the southern
part of the land; but when he came west, off Broadfirth,
he threw overboard the high seat posts, whereon Thor
was carved. And he prayed, thus over them that Thor
as he called the posts or pillars might there come to land
where the God wished him to settle, and he promised
that he would dedicate all the land of his settlement
(landnàm sitt) to Thor, and name it after him. Thorolf
then sailed into the Firth, and gave a name to the Firth,
and called it Broadfirth (Breiðafjörd). He settled land
on the south side, near the middle of the Firth. There
he found Thor cast aland, upon a point of land which is
now called Thorsness (Thorsnes), on that account. They
landed further up the ness in the Bay, which is now
called Temple Bay (Hofsvåg). There he reared his home
and there he built a large temple, and consecrated it to
Thor,* and now the place is called Temple Stead
(Hofstadir). Before his time the Firth had been very
sparsely settled, or probably had not been settled at all.
Thorolf settled land (*nam* land) from Staff river (Stafa),
inwards to Thors river (Thorsar), and called all that part
Thorsness (Thorsnes). He had so great a reverence for
that fell which stands on the ness, and which he called
Helgafell † (=Holy Fell), that he enjoined that thither

---

* The site of the Temple is still shown close to the hamlet Hofstead, on the
west side of the Peninsula. For description of Thorolf's Temple see note at the
end of this chaptsr.

† Helgafell. About noon I arrived at the western base of Helgafell, a low
mountain, consisting of trapp, cr an irregular kind of basalt, perpendicular on
the north and east sides, but accessible from the west and south sides where it is for
the most part covered with grass. Helgafell was the abode of Snorri Godi, priest
of Thor, and one of the most powerful chiefs in the west of Iceland. The
Eyrbyggja Saga is almost wholly taken up with a detail of his intrigues, his
prosecutions and his cruelties. One of the first churchcs was built here on the
public adoption of the Christian religion, and in A.D. 1183 the monastery of
Flatey was transferred to this place. It became one of the richest in Iceland,
and at the time of the reformation possessed ninety-six farms, when it was
secularized and its lands were added to the Danish Crown.—*Henderson's Travels.*

should

[PART II, CHAPTER XII.]

should no man unwashen look, and there was so great place hallowedness (sanctuary) that nothing should be destroyed on the mountain, neither cattle nor people, unless they should go away on their own accord.

That was the belief of them (Thorolf and his kinsmen), that *they should die into the mountain.* There on the ness where Thorr (=Thor's Pillar or High Seat Post, carved with Thor's image), came ashore, Thorolf had all the Dooms (=law courts), and there was set up the District Assembly (legislative) by the advice of all the men of the countryside, *i.e.* the dependants of Thorolf, who formed his Temple Parish, as it were, he being their Temple Priest. But while men were at the Thing, easements should surely not be made on land (*i.e.* it was strictly forbjdden for men to go on nature's errands on the land), and for that purpose was set apart that skerry (seacliff) which is called Dirt Skerry (Dritsker), for they should not defile such a Holy place as this was. But when Thorolf was dead and Thorstein his son still young, then they (to wit, Thorgrim, son of Kallak the Old, and Asgeir, his son-in-law and their party), would not go into the skerry upon their errands (easements). This the Thoressings would not allow, that they should defile so Holy a spot, therefore they fought (to wit, Thorstein Codbiter and Thorgeir Staple), against those (to wit, against Thorgrim and Asgeir), there at the Thing about the Skerry, and certain men fell there and many more were wounded before they could be parted. Thord the Yeller (Thord Geller) appeased them, and whereas neither side would yield, and the Holy Place had been defiled by the blood of the deadly feud (heipt=implacable or mortal hostility), this counsel was taken to remove the Thing away therefrom, and take it up into the ness, where it now is. There was there then a place of great hallowed.

ness

[PART II, CHAPTER XII.]

ness (sanctity), and there still stands the stone of Thor,[*] over which they broke those men whom they sacrificed, and close to this was that Doom Ring (dómhríngr), where people were doomed or condemned to sacrifice.

There also Thord the Yeller [†] placed the quarter Parliament, by the counsel of all the men in the quarter.

The son of Thorolf Mostbeard was Hallstein, Priest of the men of Codfirth (Thorskafjardargodi), father of Thorstein the Black, a Seer. Osk was the mother of Thorstein the Black, and daughter of Thorstein the Red.

Another son of Thorolf was Thorstein Codbiter. He had to wife Thora, the daughter of Olaf Feilan, sister of Thord the Yeller. Their son was Thorgrim, father of Snorri the Priest, and Bork the Big, father of Sam, whom Asgir slew.

Note upon The High Seat Pillar, öndvegis sula.

The derivation of this word is from sula=a post or pillar, and from önd-vegi, which is the common form. The derivation of the word is not quite settled yet. But the most probable derivation is from önd=*porch, doorway,* and vegr *way.* Önd-vegis sæti is probably the original expression : the seat that faced the way along which arrivals to the hall made their progress up to the chief's presence. It is a noteworthy fact, that no pillars or high seat posts are mentioned dedicated to any other god but Thor. In the main, the pillars were emblems of tribal chieftainship, in its two principal aspects : *martial* leadership and *priestly* authority.

---

[*] For " The Stone of Thor " and " Doom Ring," see note at the end of this chapter.

[†] Thord Yeller instituted courts called Quarter Courts in A.D. 964. The land was politically divided into Quarters called the East, West, North, and South Quarters. Each Quarter had a Court called the Quarter Court. At a later date a fifth High Court, called Fimtar-domr=Fifth Court, was erected about A.D. 1004.

Literally

[PART II, CHAPTER XII.]

Literally an *opposite seat,* or *high seat* ; so called because two seats were placed opposite to one another. In ancient timbered halls the benches were placed long ways, running along the walls of the halls, with the two seats of honour in the middle, facing one another; the nothern bench facing the sun, was called *öndvegi it ærdra : the higher or first high seat;* the opposite or southern bench being *it uædra* the *lower or second high seat.* The two high seats were the most honoured places in the Hall, and a chief guest used to be placed in the southern high seat. In England the master and mistress sitting opposite to each other at each end of the table may be a remnant of this old Scandinavian custom. The sides of·the high seats were ornamented with uprights (öndvegis sula), carved with figures, almost invariably a head of Thor. These posts were regarded with religious reverence ; many of the settlers of Iceland took those high seats with them, as in the case of Ingolf, before mentioned, and Thorolf, as mentioned in the preceeding chapter. When near Iceland they threw them overboard to drift ashore, and where they found them there they took up their abode. When a man of rank died, the son, after all rights performed, solemnly seated himself in his father's seat, as a token of succession, and there is a case in which the sons sat not in the father's seat till they had avenged his death. In the Heimskingla it is said that in Norway, in Sweden, and in Denmark that the King's High Seat was in the middle of the long bench at feasts, with the Queen on the left hand and that this was called the King's High Seat (Konungs öndvegi).

The Holy Hill or Helga Fell on Snæfellness. The earthly Paradise of Thorolf and his descendants who settled around Broadfirth (Breiðafjörð.

The sacred character of the mountain where Thorolf

first

[PART II, CHAPTER XII.]

first landed, and its connection with the religious belief
of the Norseman is well marked by a passage in this
chapter. " Thorolf settled land from Staffriver inward to
Thorsriver, and called all that part Thorsness. He had
so great reverence for that fell which stands upon the
ness and which is called Helga Fell=The Holy Fell, that
he ordained that thither should no man unwashen look,
and there was so great a place hallowedness=sanctuary
that nothing should be destroyed upon the mountain,
either of cattle or people, unless it should go away of its
own accord." The Holy Fell therefore, where Thor's
Pillar or High Seat came ashore, was consecrated as a
place of sanctuary or refuge. Moreover it was the
entrance to Valhalla or the Northern Hades. " *It was
the belief of Thorolf and his descendants that they should die
into the mountain*," *i.e.*, that they should dwell within the
mountain after their death.

It is an advantage to rightly understanding this passage
that the Eyrbyggja Saga in its first twelve chapters deals
almost exclusively with Thorolf, his landing, his form of
religious worship and his descendants. It seems to be a
perfectly independent testimony to the history of Thorolf
and his Settlement. The Landnama's account certainly
has not been derived from it, neither has it, so far as I am
able to judge, been taken from the Landnama. Chapter
XI of the Erybyggja Saga, when describing the death of
Thorstein, the son of Thorolf Mostbeard, the original
settler, gives a graphic account of what is meant by *die
into the mountain*, which is as follows: "That same
harvest Thorstein went out to Hoskuld's Island to lay in
stores of fish, and it chanced that one evening in that
harvest that a shepherd of Thorstein went to look after
his flock to the north of the Holy Fell He observed that
the fell opened out towards the north end, and within the
fell (Helgafell) he saw mighty fires and could hear a great

noise

[PART II, CHAPTER XII.]

noise there, and the clanging of drinking horns. And he
listened to hear if he could catch any distinct words, and
he heard that they were greeting Thorstein and his
seafaring companions, and bidding him sit in the high
seat over against his father (Thorolf Mostbeard). This
forewarning the shepherd told to Thora, the wife of
Thorstein, in the evening. She spake little about it, but
said that it might be the foreboding * of heavier tidings.
The morning after men came out from Hoskuld's Island
and told these tidings that Thorstein Codbiter had been
drowned while fishing, and men regarded this as a great
disaster."

Note on Thorolf's Temple at Templestead.

" There he built a Temple and a mighty house it was.
Within the door of the Temple stood the pillars of the
High Seat (High Seat Posts), and nails were therein;
they were called the Gods nails. But off the innermost
house there was another house, of that position whereof
now is the choir of the Church, and there stood a stall in
the midst of the floor of the fashion of an altar, whereon
lay a ring without a join which weighed twenty ounces,
and on this men were bound to sware all oaths taken at
the court ; and that ring must the Chief have on his arm
at all man-motes. Upon this stall stood the blood-bowl,
and therein was the blood-rod like unto a sprinkler by
which was sprinkled from the bowl that blood which was
called " Hlaut " which was the blood which flowed from
those beasts which had been offered in sacrifice to the
gods, and around the stall were the gods arranged in the
Holy Place.

All men in the district were bound to pay toll to that
temple, and were bound to follow as liegemen the Temple

---

* What was known as a *foreboding* or *forewarning* of death is well known
amongst the old local superstitions of Cumberland.

Priest

[PART II, CHAPTER XII.]
Priest in all his goings. And the Chief, *i.e.*, Temple
Priest, was bound to uphold the Temple and keep it in
repair, and also to provide therein the sacrificial festivals.
—*Eyrbyggja Saga*, Chapter IV.

*Note on the Stone of Thor, Blot-steinn or Stone of Sacrifice.
From Henderson's Travels in Iceland.*

"It was some time before we could find the place. A
little to the south of the cottage we fell in with an
immense number of small square heights, which are
evidently the ruins of the booths used by this people at
the Public Assembly. We here instituted a strict search
after the Blot-stein or Stone of Sacrifice, otherwise called
the Stone of Thor, on which human victims were immo-
lated to Thor; but sought it in vain in the immediate
vicinity of the Booths, none of the stones in that quarter
answering to the description which had been given of it.
At last we discovered a large stone in the middle of a
morass at some distance, which, though rough and un-
shapen, was determined to be the identical "Stone of Fear"
"by the horrid circle of Brumo" in the centre of which
it is situate. The stones which form the circular ring
appear also to be of a considerable size; but as thay are
now almost entirely covered by the morass, it is impossible
to ascertain their depth, except by digging. The circle
itself is about 12 yards in diameter, and the stones are
situated at short distances from each other. The *blot-
steinn* is of an oblong shape, with a sharp summit, on
which the backs of the victims were broken that were
offered as expiating sacrifices in order to appease the
wrath of the offended Deity, and purge the community
from the obnoxiousness of guilt. Within the circle called
in Iceland *domhringr*, sat the judges before whom the
accused, with their advocates and witnesses were convened,
while

[PART II, CHAPTER XII.]

while the spectators crowded around the outside of the range in order to hear the trial. The remains of these forensic and sacrificial circles are still found in great abundance throughout Scandinavia, and it is more than probable that many of the circles of stones discovered in different parts of Great Britain, especially Scotland, were used for similar purposes, and owe their existence to the Picts, or the intercourse which, in ancient times, was maintained between the northern nations and the coasts of our Islands."

Settlement of Geirrod and Ulfar. Hospitality of Geirrid his sister. Duel at the Holmgang between Thorolf and Ulfar. Death of Ulfar. Settlements in the Eyri. Origin of the community whose history is related in the Eyrbyggja Saga.

CHAPTER XIII. There was a man named Geirrod who went to Iceland, and with him went Finngeirr, son of Thorstein Snow Shoes (öndurs), and Ulfar Kappi (or the champion); they went from Halogaland to Iceland. Geirrod settled land in from the Thor's river to Langdale river. He dwelt at Eyri. Geirrod gave to his shipmate Ulfar land upon each side of Ulfar's mountain, until this side of the mountain. Geirrod gave Finngeirr land up to about Alptafjörd (Swan's Firth): he dwelt in the place which is now called Karstead. Finngeirr was the father of Thorfinn, father of Thorbrand, in Alptafirth, who married Thorbjorgu, the daughter of Thorfinn, the son of Selthor. The sister of Geirrod was named Geirrid, who had been married to Bjorn, the son of Bolverk, blindingatronju=blinding snout). Their son was named Thorolf. They (to wit, Geirrid and Thorolf) went to Iceland after the death of Bjorn, and they were for the first winter at Eyri.

In

[PART II, CHAPTER XIII.]

In the spring Geirrod gave his sister a homestead at Borgdale, when Thorolf went abroad upon a plundering expedition. Geirrid spared not meat to men. She caused them to make her scale right across the hihgway, and she sat upon a stool and invited in guests, and within a table stood already ready and meat upon it.

Thorolf came to Iceland after the death of Geirrid. He challenged Ulfar for his land and proposed the contest of the Holmgang. Ulfar was then old and childless; he fell in the Holm and Thorolf was wounded in the leg, and walked lame ever after; hence he was nicknamed maimed-foot.

After Ulfar, Thorolf took some of his land, and some of it took Thorfinn in Swanfirth; Thorfinn established on his share of the land his freed-men Ulvar and Orlyg. Geirrod in Eyri was the father of Thorgeir Kenty (=Staple) who moved the homestead from the Eyri* up to the fell; he was the father of Thord, the father of Atli.

Thorolf Maimed-foot was the father of Arnkel the godi, and of Geirrid, who had for wife Thorolf in Mafvahlid. The sons of Thorbrand in Swanfirth were Thorolf Kimbi and Thorod, Snorri, Thorfinn, Illugi, Thormod; they quarrelled with Arnkel about the inheritance of their freedmen, and were abroad with Snorri the Godi at the slaying of him at Orlygstead. After that Thorleif Kimbi went; then Arnbjorn, son of Asbrand, from Broadwick, struck him with a porridge ladle or porridge stick (=thivel). Kimbi took it in jest. Thord Blig reproached him with this at the Thorsness thing, when he sued for

---

*Eyrr or Eyri was a gravelly bank as either of the banks of a river or also used of small tongues of land running into the sea. The Eyrr-byggjar were the buildings upon the Eyrrar gravelly beach, and the Eyrbyggjia Saga, literally the Saga of the Eyrri builders, was the history of those men who had builded or settled there.

the

[PART II, CHAPTER XIII.]

the hand of Helga, his sister; then Kimbi caused Blig to be smitten with a sand sod. From this arose the quarrel between the Eyrbyggjar and the sons of Thorbrand and Snorri the godi. They fought in Swanfirth, and upon Vigrafirth.

There was a man named Thorberg; he went from Stelifirth, in Norway, to Iceland, and settled both * the Langdales, and dwelt in the outer; his son was Aslakr, who had for wife Arnleif, daughter of Thord the Yeller; their children were these: Illugi the Mighty, and Gunnhild, whom Breid married first, and afterwards Halldor, of Holmlatr. Illugi the Mighty married Gudleif, daughter of Ketil Smithy Log=anvil stock; their sons were Eyjolf and Endridi, Koll and Gellir; their daughters were: Herthrud, whom Thorgrim, the son of Vermund, had for wife, and Fridgerd, whom Odd, the son of Drafla, had for wife; and Gudrid, whom Bergthor, the son of Thormod, the son of Thorlak, married first, and afterwards Jorund, in Skorradale, further, Jodis, who married Mar, the son of Illugi, the son of Ari, and Arnleif, who married Koll, the son of Thord Blig. From Illugi are the Langdalers come. Stein the Much-Sailing, the son of Vigbjod, the brother of Thorir Harvest-Mirk, settled Shawstrand, till it marched or met with the settlement of Thorberg, and up to the Salmon river; he dwelt at Breidabolstead. His son was Thorhadd, in Hitriverdale, and Thorgest, who married Arnora, the daughter of Thord the Yeller; their sons were: Stein the Lawspeaker and Asmund, and Haflidi and Thorhadd.

Discovery, A.D. 982, and settlement, A.D. 986, of Greenland by Eirek the Red.

CHAPTER XIV. Thorvald, the son of Asvald, the son

---

* Hvarntveggja Langdale=both the Langdales, *i.e.*, the outer and the inner. Compare the Langdales in Westmorland, implying two dales: Little Langdale and Great Langdale.

of

[PART II, CHAPTER XIV.]

of Ulf, the son of Ox-Thorir, and Eirek the Red, his
son, went from Jadar * for the sake of manslaughters,
and settled land on the Hornstrands, and built at
Drangar, where Thorvald died. Eirek married, when
there, Thjodhild, the daughter of Jorund, the son of Atli,
and of Thorbjorg knarrarbringu=the ship's breast,
whom at this time Thorbjorn of Hauksdale had for wife;
Eirek then went from the north and cleared land † in
Hawkdale, he dwelt at Eirekstead, near Vatnshorn.
There the thralls of Eirek let fall a rock-slip upon the
dwelling of Valthjof, at Valthjofstead, but Eyjolf Saur,
his kinsman, slew the thralls at Skeidsbrekka, up from
Vatnshorn. For that sake Eirek slew Eyjolf Saur; he
also slew Holmgang-Hrafn at Leik-Scales. Geirstein
and Odd, at Jorvi, the kinsmen of Eyjolf, took up the
blood-suit after him; then was Eirek exiled from Hawkdale; he then settled Brokey and Oxey, and dwelt at
Tradir, in the Southey, the first winter. Then he left
seat-beams of his house with Thorgest; afterwards Eirek
went to Oxey, and dwelt at Eirekstead; then he claimed
his seat-beams, and could not obtain them; Eirek took
the seat-beams from Breidabolstead, and Thorgest went
after him; they fought a short distance from the fence
at Drangar, there fell two sons of Thorgest, and some
other men besides; thereupon both sides sat at home,
amidst an armed company. Styrr sided with Eirek, and
Eyjolf from Sviney, and the sons of Thorbrand from
Swanfirth, and Thorbjorn, the son of Vifil; and with
Thorgest sided the sons of Thord the Yeller, and Thorgeir
from Hitriverdale, Aslak from Langdale, and Illugi, his
son. Eirek and his party were outlawed at the Thorsness
Thing. Then he fitted out a ship in Eireksvag, but

---

* Jardarr, the local name of a district in Norway, literally "The Borderland."
† The Norse word is ruddi=to clear, and this word is still used with the same
meaning of *clearing a wood* in Lakeland.

Eyjolf

⌊PART II, CHAPTER XIV.⌋

Eyjolf hid him in Dimunvag, while Thorgest and his party were seeking him about the islands. Thorbjorn and Eyjolf and Styr followed Eirek out beyond the islands; he told them that he purposed to seek that land which Gunnbjorn, the son of Ulf Crow, saw when being driven west, beyond Iceland (by a storm), he found there Gunnbjorn's skerries. Eirek said that if he discovered land he would afterwards re-visit his friends. Eirek sailed from off Snæfellness, and he came out at Midjokul, at the place which is now called Blueserk; he went thence to the south, along the land, to see if that it could be settled. He was the first winter in Eirek's Island, nigh to the middle of the western settlement, and the next spring he went to Eireks-firth, and took there for himself a dwelling. He went that summer into the western wastes, and wide about there he assigned names to places. He was the next winter at Eireksholmes, near to Hvarfsgnipa. But the third summer he went north as far as Snæfell, and came to Hrafnsfirth. Then he felt sure he had got round the extremity of Eireksfirth; he sailed from thence back, and was the third winter in Eirek's Island, at the opening of Eireksfirth. Later in the summer, he went to Iceland, and came to Broadfirth; he was for that winter at Holmlatr with Ingolf. In spring Thorgest and Eirek engaged in battle, and Eirek had the worst of it; after that they were reconciled. That summer Eirek went to settle that land which he had found, and which he called Greenland,* for he said that

---

* Greenland, an extensive region stretching, so far as we know, from 59 45′ to 83½° north lat., and from 17° to 73° west long.; its north-western extremity, however, being not yet accurately defined. It is an island of almost continental size, surrounded by smaller islands. Its area may be estimated at 512,000 or at 320,000 square miles, according as it takes in or leaves out islands and fjords running inland which average 60 miles in length. It was first discovered, as noted above, by Eirek the Red, one of the earliest settlers of Iceland, after having been before sighted by Gunnbjorn. After having explored it, Eirek founded there in the year 986 two colonies—Osterbygd and Westerbygd=Eastern and Western Settlements. The colonies afterwards came under the dominion of

many

[PART II, CHAPTER XIV.]

many men would desire to visit it if he gave the land a good name.

So men of lore say that that summer twenty-five ships went to Greenland from Broadfirth and Borgfirth, and that fourteen got through to the west, that certain of them were driven back, and some were lost. This took place fifteen years before Christian faith was made law in Iceland.

There was a man named Herjolf, the son of Bard, the son of Herjolf, the friend of Ingolf the Settler. Ingolf gave land to Herjolf and his between Vag and Reykjanes. Herjolf the younger went to Greenland, when Eirek the Red settled the land. With him in the ship was a man from the Hebrides, a Christian. He composed the poem called 'Hafgerdingadrapa' in which the following verse occurs:

> This the harm-free[1] monks' controller[2]
> Pray I, that he speed my journey;
> Let the Lord of earth's high hall-roof,[3]
> Hold o'er me the stall of falcon![5]

Herjolf settled Herjolfsfirth and dwelt at Herjolfness. He was a most noble man.

Norway, but were neglected and suffered from disaster and privation. Finally the Westerbygd was attacked and destroyed by the Eskimo intruders from the north, some years after 1340. Subsequently the connection with Europe gradually grew less and less, until, according to obscure accounts, it wholly ceased after 1448, and Greenland almost passed into oblivion. When discovered in 1585 the Eskimo were its only inhabitants. Corroborating, however, the above passage in the Landnama, remarkable ruins of undoubted Scandinavian origin were early discovered on two points of the west coast, one in the present district of Juliane-haub, between 60 and 61° north lat., and the other in Godthaab, between 64 and 65°. In each case the ruins lay scattered over an area of some hundred square miles, occupying small, flat and fertile spots round the heads of the fjords. The southern group contains about 100 such spots, each with ruins of from two or three up to thirty houses; the northern group is much poorer. For latest information see Nansen's account of his expedition across Greenland in 1888.

(1) Good, full of mercy.
(2) Christ, as head of his Church.
(3) Lord of heaven, God.
(4) The falcon's stall, or the perch whereon it sits.

Eirek

[PART II, CHAPTER XIV.]

Eirek afterwards settled Eireksfirth and dwelt in Brattahlid, and Leif, his son after him. These men took land
in Greenland who had gone out then with Eirek, namely,
Herjolf, Herjolfsfirth: he dwelt at Herjolfsness; Ketil,
Ketilsfirth: Hrafn, Hrafnfirth: Solvi, Solvisdale: Snorri,
the son of Thorbrand, Swanfirth, Thorbjorn Glora,
Siglufirth: Einar, Einarfirth: Hafgrim, Hafgrimsfirth
and Vatnahverfi: Arnlaug, Arnlaugsfirth: but certain went
to the western settlement.

There was a man named Thorkell Farserk, the sister son
of Eirek the Red; he went to Greenland with Eirek, he
settled Hvalseyfirth, and most places between Eireksfirth
and Einarsfirth, and dwelt at Hvalseyfirth; from him the
Hvalseyfirthers are descended. He was of exceeding
strength. He swam out to Hvalsey=Whale Island, after
an old ox, and brought it from the island on his back,
when he wanted to give good cheer to his kinsman, Eirek,
and there was not a seaworthy vessel at hand; that was
a distance of half a sea knot or mile=vika.* Thorkell was
interred in the (tun) enclosure at Hvalseyfirth, and his
ghost has ever since haunted the place.

*Olave the White King of Dublin marries Aud, daughter of
  Ketil Flatnose. Thorstein their son and Sigurd conquer
  more than half of Scotland. Thorstein falls in battle.*

CHAPTER XV. Ingolf the strong settled land in from
the Salmon river to Skraumuhlaups river, and dwelt
at Holmlatr. His brother was Thorvald, the father of
Thorleif, who dwelt there afterwards.

Oleif the White was the name of a war-lord, he was the

---

* Vika. This word meant a sea knot or mile, or what would now be called a
geographical mile, and corresponded to a röst on land. The term seems to have
been derived from vik, a *small bay*, denoting the distance from ness to ness, and
referring to a time when ships coasted along the sea shore. The word is still
in almost exclusive use in Iceland.

son

[PART II, CHAPTER XV.]
son of King Ingald, the son of Helgi, the son of Olaf, the son of Gudraud, the son of Halfdan Whiteleg, the King of the Uplanders.   Olave the White harried in the West-viking,* and conquered Dublin in Ireland, and Dublinshire, and was made King over it.   He married Aud the Deep-minded, the daughter of Ketil Flatnose. Thorstein the Red was their son.   Oleif fell in battle in Ireland, and Aud and Thorstein went thence to Sodor, or the Hebrides; there Thorstein married Thurid, the daughter of Eyvind the Easterner, and sister of Helgi the Lean; they had many children.   Their son was named Olaf Feilan, and their daughters, Groa and Alof, Osk, and Thorhild, Thorgerd and Vigdis.   Thorstein became a war-lord; he entered partnership with Sigurd the Mighty, the son of Eystein Glumra; they conquered Caithness, Sutherland, Ross and Murray, and more than half Scotland, and Thorstein became King thereover, until the Scots betrayed him, and he fell there in battle.   Aud was then in Caithness, when she heard of the fall of Thorstein; she caused a merchant ship to be made in a wood, in secret, and when it was ready she held out to the Orkneys; there she gave in marriage Gro, the daughter of Thorstein the Red.   She was the mother of Grelad, whom Thorfinn Skullcleaver had in marriage.   After that Aud went to seek Iceland; she had with her in the ships twenty free men.

Queen Aud settles all the Dale-lands, A.D. 892.

CHAPTER XVI.   There was a man named Koll, the son of Vedrar (Wether) Grim, the son of Asi a hersir; he had the management of the affairs of Aud, and was most honoured by her.   Koll married Thorgerd, daughter of Thorstein the Red.   A freedman of Aud's was named Erp; he was the son of Melldun, an Earl in Scotland, even he who fell before Earl Sigurd the Mighty.   The

---

* Viking raids on Western or British Islands.

mother

[PART II, CHAPTER XVI.]

mother of Erp was Myrgjol, the daughter of Gljomal, King of the Irish. Earl Sigurd took them (Erp and Myrgjol), captives in war, and enslaved them. Myrgjol was the handmaid of the wife of the Earl, and served her faithfully; she was skilled in many arts; she took charge of a charmed child of the Earl's lady, whilst she was at the bath. After that Aud bought her for a great price, and promised her freedom if she would serve Thurid, the wife of Thorstein the Red, as she had served the Earl's lady. Myrgjol and Erp her son went to Iceland with Aud. Aud held first to the Faroe Islands * and there gave in marriage Alof, the daughter of Thorstein the Red; thence are the Gotuskeggjar=the Gatebeards descended. Afterwards she went to seek Iceland. She came to Veikarskeid, and there was shipwrecked. She went thence to Keelness to Helga Bjola, her brother, who offered her a lodging there with half of her companions, which she thinking a mean offer, said that he would always be a manikin. She then went west to Broadfirth, to her brother Bjorn, who, knowing the liberal and generous character of his sister, went to meet her, accompanied by all his domestics, and asked her to stay with him, and also offered to provide for all her retinue. She accepted his offer. Afterwards in spring Aud went to seek a settlement (landaleit) up the Broadfirth, accompanied by her liegemen. They ate their Dögurð †=

---

* Faroe Islands, literally Sheep Islands. A Danish group of Islands, twenty-two in number, of which 17 are uninhabited, lying between the Shetlands and Iceland, 200 miles north-west of the Shetlands, from 61 25° to 62 25° north-east, and 6 19° to 7 40° west long. Area 513 square miles. Population in 1880 was 11,220. They are volcanic, rocky mountains attaining the maximum height of 2,502 feet and 2,895 feet.

Currents amongst the islands, strong and stormy, and whirlwinds frequent. The largest islands are Strömö, 28 miles long by 8 broad. Österö, Sandö, and Suderö. Capital, Thorshaven, in Strömö, with 984 inhabitants. The inhabitants are of Norse descent, and speak an old Norse dialect.

† The Dögurd or Daymeal was the chief meal of the old Scandinavians, and was taken in the forenoon, corresponding with breakfast, and was so distinguished from the night meal or other principal meal of which they partook.

day

[PART II, CHAPTER XVI.]

day meal in the south of Broadfirth, at the place which is now called Dogurdarness=Daymeal ness ; afterwards they passed through Eyjasund=Island sound. They came ashore at that ness where Aud lost her comb, which they called from that circumstance Kambness=Combe Ness.*

Queen Aud settled all the territory of the Dale lands to the inner firth from Daymeal-river to Skraumhlaups river. She dwelt at Hvamm, at the mouth of the Char river, there the place is called Aud's tofts. She had her prayer station at Cross-Knolls; there she caused them to raise crosses because she was baptized and was a true believer. Her kinsfolk had great faith in those Knolls. There they made a temple † and there they sacrificed, and it was the firm belief of them that they should die into that mound, and Thord the Yeller was led thither before he took over his lordship of a Godi, as is related in his saga.

Queen Aud gives lands for settlement to her shipmates and freedmen.

CHAPTER XVII. Aud gave lands to her shipmates and freed-men. Ketil was the name of the man to whom she gave land from Skraumuhlaups-river to Hord-dale river ; he lived at Ketil-stead ; he was the father of Vestlidi and Einar, the father of Kleppjarn and Thorbjorn, whom Styr slew, and of Thordis, the mother of Thorgest.

Hord was the name of a shipmate of Aud's, to whom she gave Hord-dale ; his son was Asbjorn, who had for

---

* Compare Black Combe in the south-west of Cumberland.
† The word for temple here is Hörg=a heathen temple, as distinguished from Hof, the Christian temple. The use of Hörg in this passage is very significant as showing that the descendants of Aud were relapsing again into heathen worship. There is a very marked difference between the two. Hof was *a house of timber*, while Hörg was *an altar of stone* erected on high places, or a sacrificial cairn. It is retained in Icelandic Place Names in Landnama and elsewhere as Hörg-à and Högar-dalr ; in the north, Hörga-eyrr ; in the west, Hörgs-hylr.

wife

wife Thorbjorg, the daughter of Midfirth-Skeggi; their children were: Hnaki, who had for wife Thorgerd, the daughter of Thorgeir Cutcheek, and Ingibjorg, whom Illugi the Black had for wife.

Vivil was the name of a freed-man of Aud; he asked her why it was that she gave him no place of abidance, as she did to other men; she said it mattered not, he would be accounted a noble man wheresoever he came; but she gave to him Vivils-dale, and there he took up his abode, and had quarrels with Hord. The son of Vivil was Thorbjorn, the father of Gudrid, whom Thorstein, the son of Eirek the Red, had for wife, but later she was the wife of Thorfinn Karlsefni. From her and Thorfinn are come these bishops: Bjorn, Thorlak, Brand; another son of Vivil was Thorgeir, who had for wife Arnora, the daughter of Bath-brink-Einar (Laugar-brekku-Einarr), and their daughter was Yngvild, whom Thorstein, the son of Snorri the godi, had for wife.

Hundi was the name of a freed-man of Aud's, Scotch by kin, to whom she gave Hundi-dale, where he abode for a long time.

Sokkolf was yet a freed-man of Aud's; she gave to him Sokkolfs-dale, and he lived at Breidabol-stead, and from him many folk have sprung.¹

To Erp, the son of Earl Melldun, who has been mentioned before, Aud gave freedom and therewith the the land of Sheepfell; from him are sprung the Erplings. One son of Erp was called Orm; another, Gunnbjorn, the father of Arnora, whom Kolbein, the son of Thord, had for wife; a third son of his was Asgeir, father to Thorarna, whom Sumarlid, the son of Hrapp, had for wife; a daughter of Erp was Halldis, whom Alf o' Dales had for wife; one more son of Erp's was Dufnall, the father of Thorkel, the father of Hjalti, the father of Beinir; and still a son of Erp was Skati, the father of Thord, the father of Gisli, the father of Thorgerd.

There

[PART II, CHAPTER XVII.]

There was a man named Thorbjorn, who lived at Vatn
(water) in Hawkdale; he had for wife   , and their
daughter was Hallfrid, whom Hoskuld, in Salmonriver-
dale, had for wife; they had many children; Bard was a
son of theirs, and .Thorleik, the father of Bolli, who had
for wife Gudrun, the daughter of Osvif; their sons were:
Thorleik and Hoskuld, Surt and Bolli; their daughters:
Herdis and Thorgerd. Before being the wife of Bolli,
Gudrun had been the wife of Thord, the son of Ingun,
and their children were Thord Cat and Arnkatla. The
last, who had Gudrun for wife, was Thorkel, the son of
Eyolf, and their children were: Gellir and Rjupa. Bard,
the son of Hoskuld, was father of Hallbjorg, whom Hall,
the son of Fight-Styr, had for wife; the daughters of
Hoskuld were: Hallgerd Turn-breeks, Thorgerd and
Thurid.

Other settlements made by Queen Aud's followers.

CHAPTER XVIII. Koll took to himself the whole of
Salmonriver-dale, all unto Hawkdale-river; he was called
Koll o' Dales; he had for wife Thorgerd, the daughter of
Thorstein the Red; their children were Hoskuld and
Groa, whom Veleif the Old had for wife; also Thorkatla,
whom Thorgeir the godi had for wife. Hoskuld had for
wife Hallfrid, the daughter of Thorbjorn, from Vatn;
.their son was Thorleik, who had for wife Thurid, the
daughter of Arnbjorn, the son of ' Sléttu'-Bjorn; their
son was Bolli.

Hoskuld bought Melkorka, the daughter of Myrkjartan,
a king of the Irish; their sons were Olaf Peacock and
Helgi; but the daughters of Hoskuld were Thurid and
Thorgerd, and Halgerd Turn-breeks. Olaf had for wife
Thorgerd, the daughter of Egil Skallagrim's son; their
sons were: Kjartan and Halldor, Steinthor and Thorberg:

[PART II, CHAPTER XVIII.]

berg; the daughters of Olaf: Thurid, Thorbjorg the Big and Bergthora. Kjartan had for wife Hrefna, the daughter of Asgeir Madpate; their sons: Asgeir and Skum.

Herjolf, the son of Eyvind 'Eld,' was the second husband of Thorgerd, the daughter of Thorstein the Red; their son was Hrut, to whom Hoskuld paid into his mother's inheritance the land of Combeness between Hawkdale-river and that ridge which there runs down from the mountains into the sea. Hrut abode at Hrutstead; he had for wife Hallveig, who was the daughter of Thorgrim of Thickshaw, and a sister of Armod the Old. They had many children. Their son was Thorhall, the father of Haldora, who was the mother of Gudlaug, the father of Thordis, who was the mother of Thord, the father of Sturla, of Hvamm. Grim, also, was a son of Hrut, as well as these: Mar, Endridi and Stein, Thorljot and Jorund, Thorkel, Steingrim, Thorberg, Atli, Arnor, Ivar, Kar, Kugaldi; and these were his daughters: Bergthora, Steinun, Rjupa, Finna, Astrid.

Aud gave Thorhild, the daughter of Thorstein the Red, in marriage to Eystein 'Meinfret,' the son of Alf, in Osta; their son was Thord, the father of Kolbein, the father of Thord the Skald; also Alf o' Dales, who had for wife Halldis, the daughter of Erp, whose son was Snorri, the father of Thorgils, the son of Halla. The daughters of Alf o' Dales were these: Thorgerd, whom Ari, the son of Mar, had for wife, and Thorelf, whom Havar, the son of Einar, the son of Klepp, had for wife; their son was Thorgeir. Thorolf Fox was also a son of Eystein's; he fell at Thingness-Thing, out of the band of Thord the Yeller, when he and Tongue-Odd fought. Hrapp was the name of a fourth son of Eystein's.

Aud gave Osk, the daughter of Thorstein (the Red), in marriage to Hallstein the godi; their son was Thorstein the

[PART II, CHAPTER XVIII.]
the Swart. Vigdis, the daughter of Thorstein (the Red)
Aud gave away to Kamp-Grim; their daughter was
Arnbjorg, whom Asolf 'Flosi,' of Head (-land), had for
wife; their children were Odd and Vigdis, whom Thorgeir, son of Kadal, had for wife.

*Death of Queen Aud. Her Arval Feast and Burial within
the Sea Shore.*

CHAPTER XIX. Aud brought up Olaf Feilan, the son
of Thorstein the Red; he got for wife Alfais, of Barra, the
daughter of Konal, the son of Steinmod, the son of Olvir
Bairn-carle. The son of Konal was Steinmod, the father
of Halldora, whom Eilif, the son of Ketil the Onehanded,
had for wife. The children of Olaf Feilan and Alfdis
were Thord the Yeller and Thora, the mother of Thorgrim, the father of Snorri godi. Thora was also mother
of Bork the Stout, and of Mar, the son of Hallward.
Ingjald and Grani were sons of Olaf Feilan, and Vigdis
was the name of a daughter of Olaf Feilan A third
daughter of Olaf Feilan was called Helga, whom Gunnar,
the son of Hlifar, had for wife; their daughter was Jofrid,
whom Thorodd, the son of Tongue Odd, had for wife first,
and who afterwards was the wife of Thorstein, the son of
Egil. Another daughter of Gunnar was Thorun, whom
Herstein, the son of Blund-Ketil, had for wife; Raud and
Hoggvandil were the sons of Gunnar. A fourth daughter
of Olaf Feilan was called Thordis, whom Thorarin
'Ragis-brother' had for wife; their daughter was Vigdis,
whom Stein, of Redmell, the son of Thorfinn, had for
wife.

*Aud was a great lady of state; when she was weary
with old age, she asked to her her kinsmen and affinity,
and arrayed a most stately feast; and whenas the feast
had stood on for three nights, she bestowed gifts upon

---

* This passage is given in original on next page.

her

[PART II, CHAPTER XIX.]
her friends, and gave them wholesome counsels, saying, even then, that the feast should stand on for still another three nights, and giving to understand that this would be her arval-feast (funeral feast). The next night she died, and was buried on the shore, between high and low water mark, even as she herself had ordered, for this reason, that she would not lie in unhallowed earth, being baptized. After that the belief of her kindred grew corrupt. *

Note on the Arval Feast of Queen Aud.

In the original Icelandic of the above passage there are so many words bearing such a strong affinity to our Cumberland and Westmorland dialect, that I have thought it well to subjoin it in full:

Auðr var vegskona *mikil;* þá er húm var ellimód, *bauð* hún til sím *frændum* sinum ok mágun ok *bjó* dyalega veizlu; en er þrjar *Nætr* hafdi veizlan staðit, þá valdi hún *gjafir* vinum sínum ok rèð þeim *heilrædi*; sagdi hún at þá skyldi *standi* veizlan enn iij *Nætr*; hún *kvad* þat vera skyldu *erfi* sitt; þá *nótt eptir* anðaðist hún, ok var grafin í *flæ*ðarmáli, sem hún hafði fyrir sagt, þvìat hún vildi eigi *liggja* í óvígðri *moldu,* er hún var skírð.

I may here add the following note on Arvals and Arval in their Cumberland acceptation (Ice *erfi*). It is given also in my volume on " Lakeland and Iceland," published by the English Dialect Society. " Arvals is used of meat and drink supplied at funerals. Arval is anything connected with heirship or inheritance; used chiefly in reference to funerals. The friends and neighbours of the family of deceased were invited to dinner on the day of the interment, and this was called the Arval dinner, a solemn festival to exculpate the heir and those entitled to the possessions of deceased from the mulets or fines to the lord of the manor, and from all accusation of having

* See Part V., 15.

used

[PART II, CHAPTER XIX.]

used violence. In later times the word acquired a wider application, and was used to designate the meals provided at funerals generally.*"

Note on the voyages and settlements of Queen Aud.

The history of Queen Aud and her settlements end with the passage given above. It may be well, therefore, to note in this immediate connexion how close seems to have been her relationship to the early Norse settlers of Iceland on the one hand, and to the Norsemen who settled the British Islands on the other. Descended from one of the most distinguished families in Norway, she was the widow of Oleif, the White King of Dublin, the founder of a dynasty which long ruled there.*

, After the death of her husband, Oleif (see Book of Settlement, II, 15), slain possibly in a rising of the Irish against their conquerers, she left Ireland, taking with her one grandson and six granddaughters. She was followed by a large company of her kinsfolk and dependents, Irish and Norse. They took with them their families, their cattle, and such means of cultivation as at that time they possessed. It may be noted here that Christianity was the form of religion she had adopted when she left the British Islands. Whether she was a baptized Christian when she left Ireland, or whether in Scotland she embraced the faith first preached there by St. Columba, the monk of Iona, does not appear. She held this belief, however, firmly to the last, and it is worthy of note, as appears from the Landnama, that Ingolf, Kveldulf and

---

* As we approach Dublin the numerous Norse names along the coast—Lambay Island, Ireland's eye (Norse ey or eyja=Island), the Skerries, the Hill of Howth, Leixlip=Salmon Leap on the Liffy—prepare us to learn that the Scandinavians in Dublin were governed by their own laws till the thirteenth century, and that in Oxmanton(=Eastmanstown) they had their own separate quarter of the city, guarded by walls and gates.

other

[PART II, CHAPTER XIX.]

other settlers who came directly from Norway, were all devoted worshippers of Thor, while those who came from the British Islands were mostly professers of the Christian faith.　She went first to the Hebrides, called also Sodor, which is the Latin translation of Sudreyjar,* =the Southern Islands of the Landnama.

Thence she went to Scotland, where her son Thorstein, in partnership with Sigurd the Mighty, subdued Caithness, Sutherland,† Ross and Murray, and in all, more than half of that kingdom, of which he was made King.　The Scots, however, betrayed him, and he fell in battle. Again, then, Aud set forth on her voyage of settlement, and stayed and left some of her descendants in the Orkneys and some also in the Faroe Islands.　Afterwards she went to seek Iceland and (A.D. 892) she settled the Dale lands, being the dales that shed their waters into, the innermost part of Hvamm firth (on the map Hvammsfjördr), all round the head of the Bay, and out to Daymeal water running from the North into the bay a few miles of west Hvamm or Hvammr.

This Bay, it will be seen, opens inland from the Southern portion of Broadfirth (Breidifjordr).　The islands which almost block up the entrance will sufficiently account for the name, Eyjasund or Island Sound.　Her brother-in-law, Helgi the Lean, went to the North of Iceland and occupied large claims in Eyjafirth, while Ketil Fiflski, her sister's son, settled in the East, her brother Helgi Biolan in the South; Biorn, another brother, in the West.　From this powerful kindred of

---

*These islands include, under the name Hebrides, all the islands, about five hundred in number, on the West coast of Scotland, including Bute and Arran, and to the same group were anciently assigned the peninsula of Cantyre, the Island of Rathlin, and the Isle of Man.

†Sutherland is Norse, meaning land to the *south* of the Orkney earldom. Here as well as in Caithness we find numerous Norwegian names, such as Brora, Thurso, Wick, Skeroar, Loch Skerrow, and Sandwich Bay, Loch Laxford.

Queen

Queen Aud sprung the most distinguished Icelandic
families. All that is great and noble in its early history
seems closely connected with her by marriage or by birth.

*Settlement of Kjallak. His blood-feud. Births of Hamund
and Geirmund, sons of King Hjor. Bragi's prophecy
concerning them. Battle in Hafursfirth, A.D. 885.
Settlement of Geirmund in Broadfirth.*

Kjallak was the name of a man, the son of Bjorn the
Strong, who was the brother of Gjaflang, that Bjorn the
Easterner had for wife. Kjallak went to Iceland and
settled land from Daymeal river to ' Klofningar,' and
abode at Kjallakstead; his sons were : Helgi Roe and
Thorgrim Tanglestalk ' under Fell ' (=of Fell), Eilif the
Proud, Asbjorn Muscle of Orristead, Bjorn Whalemaw
at Towngarth, Thorstein Thinning, Gizur the Glad, of
Score-wick, Thorbjorn Scurvy at Ketilstead. A daughter
of Kjallak was Æsa, in Swiney, who was the mother of
Tinforni. There was a man, Ljotolf by name, to whom
Kjallak alloted an abode at Ljotolf-stead, up from ' Kalda-
kinn ' (Coldcheek); his sons were Thorstein and Bjorn
and Hrafsi. Ljotolf was of giant blood by his mother's
kindred; he was a smith in iron; he and his sons betook
themselves to Ljotolfstead, out in Fell-woods. Thorun,
of Thorun's Tofts, was mother of Oddmar, and foster-
mother of Kjallak, the son of Bjorn Whalemaw. Alof,
the daughter of Thorgrim ' under Fell,' was seized with
frenzy, and folk would have it that Hrafsi was the cause
thereof; he laid hands on Oddmar beside her bed and
said that he himself was indeed the cause of the disorder;
then Thorgrim gave to him Deild-isle. Hrafsi vowed he
would cut down Oddmar in the very face of Bjorn unless
he atoned for him. Kjallak was not willing to let go the
island. Hrafsi took some live-stock of theirs out of a
boat-shed built of turf, and the sons of Kjallak gave chase,
but

but failed to catch him.   After this Eilif and Hrafsi made
a rush off for the island ; an arrow struck the intestine of
Eilif Grisly, and he became a shape-changer * ; Bjorn
Whalemaw took the life of Bjorn, the son of Ljotolf at
sports, and Ljotolf and his made a bargain with Oddmar
that he should bring Bjorn where they might have a
chance of him; Kjallak the Young ran after him, but
before they could overcome him they (Bjorn and his) took
the lad and slaughtered him at Kjallaks-knoll, he being
then seven winters old.   After this the sons of Kjallak
set upon Ljotolf and Thorstein in a certain under-ground
chamber at Fellwoods, and Eilif found the other outlet
of it and got in at the back of them and slew them both.
Hrafsi walked into the house of Orristead, when there
was an entertainment forward, and was dressed in
woman's clothes ; Kjallak sat on the daïs with a shield ;
Hrafsi dealt a deathwound at Asbjorn and walked out
through the wall; Thord Vivil's son told Hrafsi that his
oxen were lying in a ditch; he bore his shield; he,
Hrafsi, hurled it over a cliff, when he saw the sons of
Kjallak, and they could not overcome him until they
felled timbers about him.   Eilif sat by while they made
the onset on him.

Hjorleif, king of the Hordlanders, had for wife Asa
the Light ; their son was Otrygg, the father of Oblaud,
the father of Hogni the White, the father of Ulf the
Squinter.   Another son of Hjorleif was Half, who was
the captain of 'Halfsrekkar'; his mother was Hild the
Slender, the daughter of Hogni, of Niord-isle.   King
Half was father of King Hjor, him who avenged his
father in company with Solvi, the son of Hogni.   Hjor
made a harrying raid on Bjarmland,† and took captive

---

* Hamadist=to change the shape, and so to become subject to fits of fury.
See note on Berserks, page 19.
† Bjarm is the "beaming or radiance of light." Bjarm was the name of a
people or tribe of the Russian Empire, the Perms of the present day.

there

[PART II, CHAPTER XIX.]

there in war Ljufvina, the daughter of the King of the Bjarms; she was left behind in Rogaland when King Hjor went out to the wars, and then she gave birth to two sons, one was named Geirmund, the other Hamund, and very swarthy of hue they were; at that time her bond-maid also gave birth to a son, and he was called Leif, being the son of Lodhott, a thrall. Leif was light of hue, and therefore the queen exchanged her boys with the bondmaid, and took Leif to her as her own son. But when the King came home, he took a dislike to Leif, saying that he looked like to be a manikin. Next time when the King went out on viking raids, the Queen asked to her house Bragi the Bard, and bade him look heedfully at the boys, being then three winters old; she shut the lads up with Bragi in one chamber and hid herself under the daïs. Bragi then sang this:

Two are inside here,	But Leif the third,
I trust well both,	The son of Lodhott,
Hamund and Geirmund,	Rear him not Queen,
Hjor's own offspring.	Few will prove worse!

And he smote his staff on the daïs wherein the Queen hid. So when the king came home, the queen told him of this, and showed him the lads, and he vowed he had never seen such ' hell-skins,' and therefore were both brothers so named ever afterwards. Geirmund Hellskin was a king of war-hosts, and harried in the viking-raids of the west, but had the dominion he ruled over in Rogaland. But when he came back, after having been away for a long time, King Harald had fought in Hafurs-firth* with Eirek, King of the Hordlanders, and with

---

* Battle of Hafursfirth, A.D. 885. This great sea fight affected the Settlement of Iceland more perhaps than any other event. It was the great crisis of the resistance of the Jarls or Kinglets of Norway to their conquest by Harald Fair-hair. The song of Hornklofi says "The high born King fought with Kjotvi the wealthy; ships came from the west with gaping dragon's heads and curved beaks.

Sulki,

[PART II, CHAPTER XIX.]

Sulki, King of Rogaland, and with Kjotvi the Wealthy, and gained the day. By then he had laid under his sway the whole of Rogaland, and bereft many men there of their freehold lands, so Geirmund saw no other choice at hand for him but to betake himself away, for there he could get no beseeming redress. So he made up his mind to seek for Iceland. To this journey there betook themselves with him these: Ulf the Squinter, his kinsman, and Steinolf the Low, who was the son of 'hersir' Hrolf of Adgir, and of Ondott, the sister of Olvir Bairncarle. Geirmund and his fellow-farers sailed, having inkling of each other (all the way), each steering his own ship until they made Broadfirth, and came to anchor by Ellidis-isle. Then they learnt that the bay was settled on the southern side, but on the western, slightly so, or not at all. So Geirmund made for Middlefell-strand, and took to himself land from Fabeins-river to Clove-stones; he laid his ship into Geirmunds-creek, but spent the first winter in Booth-dale. Steinolf took land east, away from Clove-stones, but Ulf took land on the western side of the firth, as soon will be told. Geirmund found his land-take too narrow, in that he kept a house of state and a household so large that he had eighty freed-men; he dwelt at Geirmund-stead 'under Skard.'

There was a man called Thrand Spindle-shanks, who went to Iceland with Geirmund Hellskin; he had his kindred about Agdir (in Norway); he took to himself the

---

They were laden with warriors and white shields, *Western* spears and *Welsh* swords. The Bearserks yelled with war in their hearts. They joined battle with valiant king of the Eastmen who put them to flight." At last the Vikings turned their warships and fled across the North Sea. The king Harald, hot content with this crushing blow, followed it up relentlessly, and made a great expedition to the Orkneys, then the focus of the Viking movement, to strike at the root of the influence which he dreaded. There was now no further choice; the Norsemen in the western (British) Islands were forced to bow to the King, or to fly to lands beyond his sway. These lands were generally in Iceland, and in the Landnama many a man is recorded as having fought at Hafursfirth and having fled hence to Iceland.—Preface to Sturlunga Saga. References to Hafursfirth in Book of Settlement at I, 6; II, 19. 29, 32 twice; III, 2; V, 11, 13.

islands

[PART II, CHAPTER XIX.]
islands west of ' Bjarneyjaflói ' (=the Bjorn-isles-Broads)
and abode in Flatey; he had for wife the daughter
of Gils ' Skeid' neb (Skeið=fast sailing man of war);
their son was Hergils ' Hnapprar,' who dwelt in Hergilsisle; the daughter of Hergils was Thorkatta, whom Mar
of Reek-knolls had 'for wife, but Hergils had for wife
Thorarna, the daughter of Ketil Broad-sole. Their son
was Ingjald, who dwelt in Hergilsisle, and was a backer-
up of Gisli Surson, wherefore Bork the Stout had him
bereft of the ownership of the islands; and then he
bought Hlid (Slope), in Codfirth; his son was Thorarin,
who had for wife Thorgerd, the daughter of Glum,
the son of Geiri; their son was ' Helgu'-Steinar;
Thorarin was in the company of Kjarton, in Swine-dale,
when he fell. Thrand Spindle-shanks abode in Flatey at
the time when Odd the Gaudy and his son, Thorir, came
out to Iceland; they took up land in Codfirth, Odd
abiding at ' Skogar ' (The Woods), while Thorir went
abroad and took to warring; he came by a great store
of gold in Finmark; in fellowship with him were the sons
of Hall of Hof-(=Temple-) stead, and when they came to
Iceland, Hall laid claim to the gold, which led to great
quarrels, out of which sprang the Saga of the Codfirthers.
Gold-Thorir dwelt at Thorirs-stead and had for wife
Ingibjorg, the daughter of Gils ' Skeid '-neb, and a son of
theirs was Gudmund. Thorir was a man most exceedingly mighty of his hands.

Settlements wealth and retainers, of Geirmund " Hellskin."

CHAPTER XX. Geirmund went west to the Strands
and took there land from ' Ryt' or Peak, west of Horn, and
thence away east to Stream-ness (Straum-ness); there he
set up four manors: one in ' Adal '-wick, under the care
of his steward; another in ' Kjarans '-wick, looked after
by

[PART II, CHAPTER XX.]

by his thrall, Kjaran; a third on West-Common, under the care of Bjorn, his thrall, who, after Geirmund's days, became guilty of sheep-lifting; * by the money he paid as fine the commons were secured.   A fourth manor of Geirmunds was in Bard-wick, and was taken care of by his thrall Atli, who had fourteen thralls serving under him.   When Geirmund went from one to the other of his manors he wonld have a following of eighty men.   He was amazingly wealthy of chattels, and had exceeding plenty of live-stock; the tale goes that his swine pastured on Swine-ness, and his sheep on Herdness, while he kept up a pasture-dairy in ' Bitra.' Some say that he also had a manor at Geirmundstead, in ' Sel '-river-dale, off Steingrimsfirth   So wise men say that he was the noblest of all 'land-take-men' (land-náms-menn=original settlers) in Iceland.   In quarrels with men here he had but little share, and he came out a man on in years withal.   He and Kjallak strove about the piece of land which lay between ' Klofningar ' and ' Fabeins '-river, and fought on the fields west of ' Klof-ningar, where both wanted to sow the land; in that strife Geirmund got the better of it.   Bjorn the Easterner and Vestar of Eyri brought about peace between them; on going to this peace-meeting Vestar landed at Vestars-ness.   Geirmund hid a great treasure of his own in Duck-Ditch (Andar kelda), beneath Skard; he had for wife Herrid, the daughter of Gaut, son of Gautrek; their daughter was Ufri; later he had for wife Thorkatla, the daughter of Ofeig, the son of Thorolf, and their children were Geirrid and   . Geirmund died at Geirmund-stead, and he is laid in a ship there in the wood away from the fence-wall.

---

* The question of sheep-marking and their ownership generally is dealt with under Part V., 5.

Settlements

[PART II, CHAPTER XXI.]
Settlements of Steinolf, Slettu-Bjorn, Olaf Belg, and Gisl Skeid-neb.

CHAPTER XXI. Steinolf the Low, the son of 'hersir' Hrolf from Adgir, took land up from Clove-Stones to Grit-mead-Mull (Grjótvallar-mùli), and abode at Steinolfs-Hill, in Fairdale; he walked inland up to the top of the mountain, and saw to the landward a broad dale all over-grown with wood; a glen he found in the dale, and there he let rear a homestead, which he called Saurby (Sowerby), by reason of the much bogland that was there; the same name he gave to all the dale; now the spot is named Turfness, where the home-stead was planted. Steinolf had for wife Erny, the daughter of Thidrandi; their son was Thorstein the Bonder, but their daughter Arndis the Wealthy, the mother of Thord, the father of Thorgerd, whom Odd had for wife; the son of these was Hrafn the Limerick-trader, who had for wife Vigdis, the daughter of Thorarin 'Fylsenni.' Their son was Smart, the father of Jodis, whom Eyolf, the son of Hallbjorn, had for wife; their daughter was Halla, whom Atli, the son of Tami, had for wife, and the daughter of these was Yngvild, whom Snorri, the son of Hunbogi, had for wife. Steinolf missed three swine, which two winters afterwards were found in Swinedale, there being then thirty swine. Steinolf also took to himself Steinolfs-dale in Crook-firth.

'Sléttu'-Bjorn was the name of a man who had for wife Thurid, the daughter of Steinolf the Low; by the counsel of Steinolf he settled the western side of the valley of Saurby; he abode at 'Sléttu'-Bjorns-stead, up from Thwartfell; his own son was Thjodrek, who had for wife Arngerd, the daughter of Thorbjorn, the son of Shield-Bjorn; their sons were Fight-Sturla, who built the homestead of Stead-Knoll, and Knott, the father of Asgeir, and of Thorbjorn and of Thjodrek, by whom the
'burgh'

[PART II, CHAPTER XXI.]

'burgh' (volcanic peak) on Kollfirth-heath is named. Thjodrek, son of 'Sléttu'-Bjorn, found the lands of Saurby too narrow, and therefore he betook himself to Icefirth. There is laid the Saga of Thorbjorn and Howard the Halt.

Olaf 'Belg,' whom Orm the Slender drove away out of Olafs-wick, took for himself Belg-dale, and abode at Belg-stead, until Thjodrek, he and· his, drove him away; then he settled land in from Gritmead-mull, and abode in Olafsdale; his son was Thorvald, who handselled to Ogmund, the son of 'Völu'-Stein, a lawsuit against Thorarin the Yelling for sheep-lifting; for that cause Thorarin slew Ogmund at the Codfirth-Thing.

Gisl 'Skeid'-neb settled Gilsfirth, between Olafsdale and Crookfirth-mull, and lived at the Cliffs; his son was Hedin, the father of Haldor the godi, of Garps-dale, who was the father of Thorvald, of Garpsdale, who had Gudrnu, the daughter of Osvif, for wife.

Settlements of Thorarin Crook, Ketil Broad-sole and Ulf the Squinter. Ari is drifted over the ocean to Whitemen's land or Ireland the Great, conjectured to be South America.

CHAPTER XXII. Thorarin Crook settled Crooksfirth from Crookfirth-ness to Goatfell; he strove with Steinolf the Low about Steinolfs-dale, and rowed with nine men after him, when he went home from an outlying pasture-dairy with six men; they fought on the shingle shore by Fairdaleriver-mouth, and from a neighbouring house there came men to the help of Steinolf; there Thorarin Crook fell together with four others, and on Steinolf's side there fell seven; their barrows are on the spot.

Ketil Broad-sole settled Bearfirth; he was the son of Thorbjorn 'Talkni'; his daughter was Thorarna, whom Hergils 'Hnappraz,' the son of Thrand Spindle-shanks,

had

[PART II, CHAPTER XXII.]

had for wife ; their son was named Ingjald, who was the father of Thorarin, who had for wife Thorgerd, the daughter of Glum, the son of Geiri; their son was 'Helgu'-Steinar. Thrand Spindle-shanks had for wife the daughter of Gils 'Skeid'-neb, and their daughter was Thorarna, whom Hrolf, the son of Helgi the Lean, had for wife. Thorbjorg 'Knarrarbingu' was another daughter of Gils 'Skeid'-neb; a son of his was Herfid, who dwelt at Crooksfirth.

Ulf the Squinter, son of Hogni the White, took the whole of Reekness between Codfirth and Goatfell; he had for wife Bjorg, the daughter of Eyvind Eastman, and sister to Helgi the Lean ; their son was Atli the Red, who had for wife Thorbjorg, the sister of Steinolf the Low ; their son was Mar of (Reek-)Knolls, who had for wife Thorkatla, the daughter of Hergils 'Hnappraz'; their son was Ari, who was drifted over the ocean to Whitemens'-land, which some call Ireland the Great,* and lies west away in the ocean anigh to Vineland the Good ; thither men hold that there is six days' sailing from Ireland due west. Ari could not get back from this country and there he was christened. This tale was first told by Hrafn the Limerick trader who had spent a long time in Limerick in Ireland. Thorkel, the son of Gellir said that Icelanders, who had heard Earl Thorfin of Orkney tell the tale, avowed that Ari had been recognised in Whitemens'-land, and that he had not been able to get away from there, and was held there in much honour. Ari had for wife Thorgerd, the daughter of Alf o' Dales, and their sons were Thorgils and Gudleif and Illugi ; this is the race of the Reeknessings. Jorund was the name of a son of Ulf the Squinter, he had for wife

---

* Whiteman's land or Ireland the Great—to which Ari was drifted over the ocean, is supposed to have been South America as being nigh to Vineland the Good, or North America.

Thorbjorg

[PART II, CHAPTER XXII.]

Thorbjorg ' Knarrarbringa,' and their daughter was
Thjodhild, whom Eirek the Red had for wife, and their
son was Leif the Lucky of Greenland. A son of Atli the
Red was named Jorund, he had for wife Thordis the
daughter of Thorgeir ' Suða ' (Seething ? or Humming ?)
and their daughter was Otkatla, whom Thorgils, the son
of Koll, had for wife. Jorund was also father to Snorri.

Hallstein settles Codfirth; makes High-seat posts from drift-
wood. Thorbjorn ". Loki" settles Deepfirth to Steamfirth.
Ketil " Gufa " comes from Viking raids in Ireland and
settles Gufuscales and Gufuness. Flight and feuds of his
thralls. " Burning in," by thralls at Lambistead. The
burning in is avenged.

CHAPTER XXIII. Hallstein, the son of Thorolf Mostbeard settled Codfirth, and abode at Hallstein's-ness ; he
made a blood-offering to the end, that Thor would send
him high-seat posts; after that a tree drifted aland sixty-
three ells long, with a span of two fathoms in thickness.
This was used for high-seat posts, and out of it are made
high-seat posts well-nigh at every homestead throughout
the cross-firths (the smaller firths that cut into the land
off the main bay); the ness where the tree came ashore is
now called Spruceness (Grenitrés-nes). Hallstein had
harried Scotland and taken there the thralls which he
brought out with him ; these he sent for salt-making out
into ' Svefn '-isles . . . * Hallstein had for wife Osk,
the daughter of Thorstein the Red ; their son was
Thorstein Swart who found out the ' summer-eke.' †

---

* A sentence of seven words here, incomprehensible.
† Sumar auki = the summer-eke = the intercalary week, an Icelandic calendar
term ; the ancient heathen year consisted of 364 days, or 12 months of 30 days
each, plus 4 days which were the auka nætr, or eke nights—the remaining day
and a fraction was inserted every sixth or seventh year at the end of summer,
which in such years was 191 days long; the summer-eke was introduced by
Thorstein the Wise, in the middle of the tenth century, and is still observed in
Iceland.

Thorstein

[PART II, CHAPTER XXIII.]

Thorstein Swart had for wife . . . . , their son was
Thorarin and their daughters were Thordis, whom
Thorkel 'Trefill' had for wife, and Osk, whom Stein
Muchsailing had in wedlock, their son was named Thorstein the White; a bastard son of Thorstein the Red was
called Sam, he who quarrelled with 'Trefill' about the
inheritance after Thorstein, which he (Sam) wanted to
secure for the children of Thorarin (the son of Thorstein).

Thorbjorn 'Loki' was the name of a man who was the
son of Bodmod from Skut. He went to Iceland, and
settled Deepfirth and Groness on to Steamfirth; his son
was Thorgils of Thorgilsstead in Deepfirth, the father of
Koll, who had for wife Thurid, the daughter of Thorir,
the son of Earl Hallad, the son of Rognvald, the Earl of
Mæri (in Norway). The son of Koll and Thurid was
Thorgils, who had for wife Ottkatla, the daughter of
Jorund, the son of Atli the Red; their son was Jorund,
who had for wife Hallveig, the daughter of Oddi, who
was the son of Yr and Ketil 'Gufa.' A son of Jorund
was Snorri, who had for wife Asny, the daughter of
Fight-Sturla; their son was Gils, who had for wife
Thordis, the daughter of Gudlaug and of Thorkatta, the
daughter of Haldor, the son of Snorri godi; but the son
of Gils was Thord who had for wife Vigdis, the daughter
of Sverting, and their son was Sturla of Hvamm.

There was a man called Ketil 'Gufa,' a son of Orlyg,
the son of Bodvar, the son of Vigsterk; Orlyg had for
wife Signy, the daughter of Obland, and sister of Hogni
the White. Ketil, their son, came out to Iceland late in
the 'land-take-tide'; he had been on Viking raids in the
west, and brought with him out of the west-roving some
Irish thralls; one called Thormod, another Floki, a third
Kori, fourth Swart, and two by the name of Skorri.
Ketil took to himself Whalerus-ness and sat out the first
winter at 'Gufu'-Scales, but in the spring he flitted
further

further east up the Nesses, and sat the next winter at
' Gufu '-ness.   Then Skorri the older and Floki ran away
from him with two women and a deal of goods.   They
kept in hiding in Skorris-holt within Skorris-dale, but
they were slain in Flokisdale and Skorris-dale.   Ketil
had got no settled abiding place about the Nesses, so he
went up into Burgfirth and sat a third winter at ' Gufu '-
Scales by Steamriver ; but early next spring he went west
to Broadfirth to look out lands for himself ; there he
stayed at Geirmundsstead and wooed Yr the daughter of
Geirmund and got her for wife.   Geirmund pointed out
lands to Ketil on the west side of the firth.   But while
Ketil was in the west, his thralls ran away and came by
night down upon Lambistead where, at that time, there
dwelt Thord, the son of Thorgeir Lumbi and of Thordis,
the daughter of Yngrar ; and Thordis was the sister of
the mother of Egil Skallagrimsson.   The thralls bore fire
against the house and burnt in his home Thord and all
his household ; they broke there open a store-house and
took away many goods and chattels, whereupon they
drove home horses and loaded them and set off on their
way to Swanness.   That morning Lambi the Strong, the
son of Thord, came home from the Thing, when they
were off and on their way already ; he set off after them,
and men flocked to him from the homesteads in the
neighbourhood, and when the thralls saw this, they all
bolted each his own way.   They laid hands on Kori
in Korisness, but some of the thralls plunged out
a-swimming ; Swart they caught in Swartskerry ; and
Skorri in Skorrisey off the Moors, and Thormod out in
Thormodskerry being a sea mile out away from the
land.   But when Ketil ' Gufa ' came back (from the west)
to fetch his belongings, he set off westward again passing
the Moors, and spent the fourth winter at ' Gufu '-Scales
on Snowfellness.   After this he settled ' Gufu '-firth and
Scaleness

[PART II, CHAPTER XXIII.]
Scaleness even unto Kollfirith. Ketil and Yr had two
sons, one being Thorhall, the father of Hallvor, whom for
wife had Bork, the son of Thormod, the son of Thjost ;
the other was Oddi, who had for wife Thorlang, the
daughter of Hrolf of 'Ballara' and of Thorid, the daughter
of Valthjof, the son of Orlyg from Esjaberg.

Koll, Knjuk, Geirstein, Geirleif and sundry other settlers.

CHAPTER XXV.   Koll, the son of Hrvald, settled
Kollfirth and Kvigand-ness and Kvigand-firth and sold to
sundry people from his landtake.

Knjuk was the name of a son of Thorolf Sparrow, he
came out to Iceland with Orlyg, and was called Ness-
Knjuk, he took for himself all the nesses from Kvigand-
firth to Bardistrand.   Another son of Knjuk was Einar,
the father of Steinolf, the father of Salgerd, the mother
of Bard the Swart.   A daughter of Knjuk's was called
Thora, whom for wife had Thorvald, the son of Thord,
the son of Viking, and their son was Moor-Knjuk, the
father of Steinolf, the father of Halla, the mother of
Steinun, the mother of Hrafn of Eyri and of Herdis,
whom the Speaker-at-law, Gizur, the son of Hall, had for
wife.   The daughter of Rafn was Steinun, the mother of
Rafn, a knight, and of Halla and Herdis, whom Svarthofti,
the son of Dugfus, had for wife, their son being Oli, who
had for wife Salgerd, the daughter of Jon ; their daughter
was Steinun, whom Hawk the son of Erlend had for wife.
Knjuk had in marriage Ey, the daughter of Ingjald, the
son of Helgi the Lean ; their son was Eyolf, the father
of Thorgrim (called) Katla's son.   Glum had Katla to
wife before (Thorgram had her) and their daughter was
Thorbjorg Coalbrow, about whom Thormod sang his
songs.   A son of Thorgrim's was named Steingrim, who

was

⌈PART II, CHAPTER XXV.⌉

was the father of Yngvild, whom Ulfhestin of Willow-
moor had for wife.

Geirstein ' Kjalki' settled ' Kjalka '-firth and Herdness,
by the counsel of Knjuk. He was the son of Thorgils,
who had for wife Thora, the daughter of Vestar of Eyri;
their son was Stein the Danish, who had for wife Hallgerd, the daughter of Ornolf, the son of Armod the Red.
Ornolf had for wife Vigdis, the daughter of Thorgils.
The name of a daughter of Stein the Danish and Hallgerd
was Vigdis, whom Illugi Steinbjornson had for wife;
their daughter was Thorun, the mother of Thorgeir
Longhead.

Geirleif, the son of Eirek, the son of Hogni the White,
settled Bardistand, between Waterfirth and ' Berghliðar,'
he was the father of Oddlief and Helgi Skarf. Oddleif
was the father of Gest the Sage as well as of Thorstein
and of Æsa whom Thorgils, the son of Grim from Grimsness had for wife; their sons were Jorund of Miding
(Midmead) and Thorarin of Bowerfell. Gest had for
wife . . . . . ; their children were Thord and Halla,
whom Snorri, the son of Alf o' Dales, had for wife; their
son was Thorgils. Another daughter of Gests was
Thorey, whom Thorgils had for wife; their son was
Thorarin the father of Jodis, the mother of Illugi, the
father of Birna, the mother of Illugi and Arnor, and
Eyvind the father of Steingrim, the father of Helga, the
mother Jorun, the mother of Hawk, son of Erlend. Helgi
Skarf was father to Thorbjorg ' Katla ' whom Thorstein
the son of Salmund, had for wife; their sons were Ref
in ' Brynja '-dale and Thord, the father of Illugi, the father
of Hrodny, whom Thorgrim 'Sviði' (singer) had for wife.
Thordis was the name of another daughter of Helgi Skarf,
she was the wife of Thorstein, the son of Asbjorn, from
Kirkby in the East; their son was Surth, the father of
Sighvat, the Speaker-at-law. Geirleif had for wife Jora,
the

[PART II, CHAPTER XXV.]
the daughter of Helgi. Thorfin was the name of a third son of Geirleif; he had for wife Gudrun, the daughter of Asolf; their son was named Asmund and he had for wife Hallkatla, the daughter of Bjorn, the son of Mar, the son of Asmund. The son of Asmund and Hallkatla was called Hlenni, he had for wife Ægileif, the daughter of Thorstein, the son of Krafla ; their son was called Thorfid, who was the father of Thorgeir Longhead; Thorstein the son of Oddlief was the father of Isgerd, whom Bolverk, the son of Eyolf the Grey, had for wife ; their son was Gellir the Speaker-at-law; still another daughter of Thorstein was Vèny, the mother of Thord Crowneb, from whom the Crowneblings are sprung.

Settlements of Armod, Thorolf Sparrow, Ketil Broadsole, and Orn. An Redfell harries Ireland in a Viking-raid to the west, afterwards settles in Iceland with his relations.

CHAPTER XXVI. Armod the Red, son of Thorbjorn and foster-brother of Geirleif, took for himself Redsand ; his sons were Ornolf and Thorbjorn, the father of Hrolf the Redsander.

Thorolf Sparrow came out with Orlyg, and took to himself the western side of Patreksfirth and the Wicks west of Bard, except Kollswick; there Koll the foster-brother of Orlyg abode. Thorolf also took to him Logwick (Keflavik) to the south of Bard, and dwelt at Whale-'làtr.' These were the sons of Thorolf Sparrow : Ness-Knjuk, and Ingolf the Stark, and Geirthjof. A daughter of Ingolf's was Thorarna, whom Thorstein, son of Oddlief, had for wife.

Thorbjorn 'Talkni' and Thorbjorn 'Skuma,' the sons of Bodvar Bladderpate, came out with Orlyg, they settled one half of Patreksfirth and the whole of Talkni's-firth unto ' Kopa '-ness.

Ketil

[PART II, CHAPTER XXVI.]

Ketil Broadsole, son of Thorbjorn 'Talkni,' took to
him all the dales from 'Kopa'-ness unto Dufans-dale;
he gave Thorarna, his daughter, in marriage to Hergils
'Hnappraz'; whereupon he betook himself south to
Broadfirth, and settled Bearfirth by Reekness.

Orn was the name of a man most worthy, a kinsman of
Geirmund Hellskin, who had to leave Rogaland before
the tyranny of King Harald Fairhair; he took for himself
land in Ornfirth as wide as it liked him, and sat the
winter out in Tentness, because the sun did not vanish
there through the shortest days.

An Redfell, the son of Grim Shaggy-cheek from
Hrafnista and of Helga, the daughter of An Bow-swayer,
fell into disfavour with King Harald Fairhair and for that
reason left the land for Viking-raiding in the west; he
harried in Ireland and got for wife there Grelad the
daughter of Earl Bjartmar; they went to Iceland and
came into Ornfirth a winter later than Orn. An spent
the first winter in Dunfansdale, where Grelad deemed the
earth smelt of ill fragrance. Orn heard of his kinsman,
Hamund Hellskin, that he was north in Eyja-firth, and
he was taken by a longing to go thither. Therefore he sold
to An Redfell all the land between Langness and 'Stapi.'
An set up a manor at 'Eyri' and there Grelad deemed
the herbage gave out a honeyed fragrance. A freedman
of An was Dufan; he abode behind in Dufans-dale. A
son of An was Bjartmar who was the father of two sons
of the name of Vegest and also of Helgi, the father of
Thurid 'Arnkatla' whom Hergils had for wife; their
daughter was Thurid 'Arnkatla' whom Helgi, the son of
Eythjof, had for wife. A daughter of Bjartmar was
Thorhild whom Vestein, the son of Vigeir had for wife;
their children were Vestein and Aud. A freed-man of An
was Hjallkar; his son was Bjorn, who was a thrall of
Bjartmar; he gave freedom to Bjorn, who thereupon
gathered

[PART II, CHAPTER XXVI.]

gathered wealth together; but Vegest made a-do thereover and thrust Bjorn through with a spear while (at the same time) Bjorn smote him unto death with a hoe.

Geirthjof the son of Vathhjof took land in Ormfirth: Forcefirth, to wit and Reekfirth, Trostansfirth and Geirthjofsfirth, and dwelt at Geirthjofsfirth; he had for wife Valgerd the daughter of Ulf the Squinter; their son was Hogni, who had for wife Aud, the daughter of Olaf 'Jafnakollr' and of Thora, the daughter of Gunstein. Their son was Atli, who had for wife Thurid the daughter of Thorleif, the son of Eyvind Knee and of Thorun Bedsow. Thorleif had for wife Gro, the daughter of Thorolf 'Brækir.' A son of Atli was named Hoskuld, the father of Atli, the father of Bard the Swart, the father of Sveinbjorn, the father of Rafn, the father of Steinun, the mother of Rafn the Knight.

Eirek settles Ditch Dale. Vestein and Dyra settle Dyrafith. Thord son of Harald Fairhair and his connections.

CHAPTER XXVII. There was a man named Eirek, who settled Ditch-dale south of Dyrafirth as well as 'Slétta'-ness all unto 'Stapi' and to the outer Neck in Dyrafirth; he was the father of Thorkel, the father of Thord, the father of Thorkel, the father of Steinolf, the father of Thord, the father of Thorleif, the mother of Thorgerd, the mother of Thora, the mother of Gudmund Pig, who got for wife Solveig, the daughter of Jon Loptson and by whom he had these children; Magnus the godi, and Thorlak, the father of Bishop Arni, and Thora, the mother of Earl Gizur.—Thorleif was the mother of Lina, the mother of Cecilia, the mother of Bard and of Thorgerd, whom Bjorn the English had for wife; their children were Arnis the abbot, and Thora whom Amundi, the son of Thorberg had for wife.

Vestein,

[PART II, CHAPTER XXVII.]

Vestein, the son of Vegeir, and brother to Vebjorn, the champion of Sogn-folk took to him land between the Necks in Dyrafirth and abode at Hawkdale; he had for wife Thorild, the daughter of Bjartmar, and their children were Vestein and Aud. Thorbjorn Sour came out when the land was all settled, and to him Vestein gave one-half of Hawkdale; the sons of Thorbjorn were Gisli, Thorkel and Ari; his daughter was Thordis whom Thorgrim had for wife and their son was Snorri godi. Later on Bork the Stout had Thordis for wife, and their daughter was Thurid who in her first wedlock was the wife of Thorbjorn the Stout, in her second of Thorod 'Skattkaupandi,' and their son was Kjartan of Frodis-river.

There was a man of great worth, named Dyri who, by the counsel of Earl Rognvald, and yet in truth by reason of the tyranny of Harald Fairhair, went away from south-'Mæri' to Iceland. Dyri settled Dyrafirth and abode at Necks; his son was Hrafn of 'Ketilseyri,' the father of Thurid, whom Vestein the son of Vestein had for for wife; their sons were Berg and Helgi.

, Thord was the name of a man, the son of Viking, or of king Harald Fairhair; he fared to Iceland and took to him land between 'Thufa' (Hummock) on Hillness and Landslip-gill; he had house in 'Alvidra' (Allweather-spot). Thord had for wife Thiodhild, the daughter of Eyvind Eastman and sister to Helgi the Lean. Their son was Thorkel the Wealthy, the champion of 'Alvidra.' He had for wife . . . . and one of their sons was named Thord, another Eyolf, the father of Gisli who had for wife Hallgerd the daughter of Vermund the Slender, and their son was Brand, the father of Gudmund priest of Herdholt, but their daughter was Thora, whom Brand, the son of Thorhad, had for wife; their daughter was Steinvor, the mother of Ranveig, the mother of Sæhild whom Gizur had for wife. Another son of Eyolf was named Helgi,

and

[PART II, CHAPTER XXVII.]

and his children were Olaf and Gudleif, whom ' Fjarska '-
Finn had for wife. Another son of Thord Vikingson was
named Thorvald the White; he had for wife Thora, the
daughter of Ness-Knjuk, their son was ' Myra '-Knjuk,
the father of Thorgant, the father of Steinolf who had for
wife Herdis the daughter of Tind; their children were
these : Thorkell of ' Myrar ' and Halla whom Thord, the
son of Oddleif, had for wife. Another son of Thorvald
the White was Thord the Lefthanded, who had for wife
Asdis, the daughter of Thorgrim, the son of Hard-Ref.
The mother of Asdis was Ranveig, the daughter of
Grjosgard, Earl of Ladir. Asdis was the mother of Ulf
the Marshal but she was sister to Ljot the Sage and to
Halldis, whom Thorbjorn, the son of Thjodrek, had for
wife. A daughter of Thord Lefthanded and Asdis was
Ottkatla whom Hurla Thjodrekson had for wife; their
son was Thord, who had for wife Hallbera a daughter of
Snorri the Godi; their daughter was Thurid, whom
Haflidi, the son of Mar had for wife. A son of Thord,
the son of Sturla, was Snorri, who had for wife Oddbjorg,
the daughter of Grim, the son of Lodmund; and their
children were ' Flugu '-Grim and Hallbera, whom ' Mag '-
Snorri had for wife. The daughters of Sturla were six
together: one was Asny, whom Snorri, son of Jorund,
had for wife; their daughter was Thordis, the mother of
Hoskuld the leech, who was the father of Margret the
mother of Thorfinn the Abbot. A son of Snorri and
Asny was Gils, the father of Thord, the father of Sturla
of Hvamm.

Settlements of Ingjald and Ljot the Sage. Gest foretells the
death of Ljot. The sons of Grim " Kogr " fulfil the
prophecy. *

---

* The tragic event narrated herein forms the historic basis for the Saga of
Howard the Halt.

CHAPTER

⌊PART II, CHAPTER XXVIII.]

CHAPTER XXVIII.   Ingjald, the son of Bruni, took to
himself Ingjaldsand between Hillness and 'Ofæra'; he
was the father of Hard-Ref, the father of Thorgrim, the
father of Ljot the Sage and his sisters as is written
afore.

Ljot the Sage, the son of Thorgrim the son of Hard-
Ref, his mother being Ranveig the daughter of Earl
Grjotgard, dwelt at Ingjaldsand.   Thorgrim Cur (Dog)
was a son of Ljots.   A sister of Ljots, Halldis, Thorbjorn,
son of Thjodrek, had for wife, while Ospak, the son of
Osvif, carried off Asdis, another sister of Ljot's.   For
that misdeed Ljot brought a lawsuit unto outlawry
against Ospak.   Ulf was named the son of Ospak and
Asdis, and he was brought up at Ljot's.   Grim 'Kögar'
dwelt at Brink, and his sons were Sigurd and Thorkel,
little men and small.   A foster-son of Ljot's was named
Thorarin.   Ljot bought meat of Grim to the worth of
twenty hundreds, and paid for it a brook that ran between
their lands and was called 'Osómi' (Mischief).   Grim
turned the brook on his meadows (for irrigation) and
dug the land belonging to Ljot, and he held Grim
guilty of a breach of a breach of the law therein, and
therefore they had but little to do with one another.
Ljot met a Norwegian in 'Vadill' and took him in, and
he fell in love with Asdis.   Gest the son of Oddleif, being
bidden, came to an autumn feast at Ljot's; at that time
there came thither Egill, the son of 'Volu'-Stein, and
prayed Gest to give some counsel to the end that his
father might get some ease from the grief unto death
that he strove with for the loss of his son Ogmund.
Gest then composed the beginning of Ogmund's-'drapa.'

Ljot asked Gest, what kind of a man Thorgrim Cur
would turn out.   Gest said that Thorarin, his foster-son,
would be the more renowned of the two, and bade Thorarin
look to it, lest that hair which lay on his tongue should
                                                       twist

[PART II, CHAPTER XXVIII.]

twist around his head. This Ljot took as a slight, and asked, the next morning, what might be in store for Thorgrim. Gest said, his sister's son, Ulf, would be the more renowned of the two. Then Ljot grew wroth; still he rode out a-way with Gest to see him off, and asked: "What will it be that brings about my death?" Gest said, he could not see his fate, but bade him stand well with his neighbours. Ljot asked: "Will the earth-lice, the sons of Grim 'Kogr,' bring about my death?" "Sore stings a starving louse," quoth Gest. "Where will it happen then?" quoth Ljot. "Near here," quoth Gest. The Norwegian road with Gest up unto the heath, and steadied him on horse-back when his nag stumbled under him. Then spake Gest: "Good hap sought thee now, and soon another will; look thou to it, that it may not be a mishap to thee!" The Norwegian found buried silver, when he returned home, and took for himself twenty pennies thereof, being minded that he would find his way to it later on; but when he made the search he found it not; but Ljot got him caught, when he was digging (for the treasure) and made him pay three hundred for every penny (of the twenty he had first taken). That autumn was slain Thorbjorn the son of Thjodrek. In the spring Ljot sat on a certain hillrise looking after his thralls; he had over him a cape the hood of which was tied round the neck, and a one-sleeved cape it was. The sons of 'Kogr' rushed upon the hill and hewed at him both at once and therewith Thorkel swiftly turned the hood over his head. Ljot bade them behave in a kind neighbourly manner but they all tumbled down from the hill unto the road where Gest had ridden, there Ljot came by his death. The sons of Grim went to Howard the Halt. Eyolf the Grey and Steingrim his son gave them all his aid.

Settlements

Settlements of Onund, Hallward Soughing, Thurid Soundfiller, Helgi son of Hrolf, Eyvind Knee, Vebjorn, Gunnstein and Haldor.

CHAPTER XXIX. Onund Vikingson, the brother of Thord in 'Alvidra' took Onund-firth and abode at 'Eyri.'

Hallward Soughing fought in the battle of Hafursfirth against King Harald; on account of that war he went to Iceland and took to him Soughings-firth and Scalewick unto Stile (Stigi) and abode there.

Thurid Sound-filler and 'Völu'-Stein, her son, fared from Halogaland to Iceland and took for themselves Bolung-wick and kept house at Waterness. For this was she called Sound-filler, that in a hard year in Halogaland she brought it about by wizardry that every sound was filled with fish; she also settled where should be the fishing point of 'Kviarmið' on Icefirth-Deep, and bespoke for herself in return a polled ewe from every good-man throughout Icefirth. The sons of 'Völu'-Stein were Ogmund and Egil.

Helgi was the name of a son of Hrolf from Gnup-fell; he was begotten in the east (Norway) and was an Uplander by his mother's kindred. Helgi went to Iceland to look up his kinsmen and came into Ey-firth where by that time all land was settled; after that he betook himself abroad, and was driven back by stress of into Soughing's-firth, and was through the winter with Hallward; but in the spring he went to look out for a place of abidance and he came upon a certain firth where, on the foreshore he found a 'skutill' (harpoon) and called the firth 'Skutils'-firth (Harpoon-firth), and there he abode afterwards. His son was Thorstein Evil-luck, who went abroad and slew one of the body-guard of Earl Hakon, the son of Grjotguard, but Eyvind, the counsellor

of

[PART II, CHAPTER XXIX.]

of the Earl, sent Thorstein unto Vebjorn, Sognfolk-trusty
(=Champion of Sogn-folk above, and below), and he
took Thorstein in, notwithstanding that Vedis, his sister
warned him against it. For this reason Vebjorn sold
his lands and went to Iceland when he mistrusted himself of the power of keeping the man safe.

Thorolf ' Brækir ' took some part of ' Skutils '-firth and
Scale-wick, and abode there.

Eyvind Knee went out from Agdir to Iceland together
with Thurid Bedsow, his wife. They took for themselves
Swanfirth and ' Seydis '-firth, and abode there. Their
son was Thorleif, who was mentioned before, and another,
Valbrand, the father of Hallgrim and Gunnar and Bjargey
whom Howard the Halt had for wife and whose son was
Olaf.

Geir was the name of a man of exceeding worth in
Sogn, he was called Vegeir, in that he was a great man
of blood-offerings ; he had many children : Vebjorn the
Champion of Sogn-folk was the oldest of his sons, these,
to wit: Vestein, Vethorm, Vemund, Vegest, and Vethorn ;
Vedis being a daughter. After the death of Vegeir,
Vebjorn fell into unfriendly ways with Earl Hakon, as
was said before, and therefore brother and sister (Vebjorn and Vedis) went to Iceland. They had a sea-faring
hard and long and made Barn-wick (Hlðu-vik) west of
Horn-head in the autumn. Then Vebjorn arranged a
great blood-offering ; and that day, he said, Earl Hakon
was making a sacrifice for the undoing of them. Now,
whenas he was in the midst of the ceremony, his brothers
egged him to put off (speedily), so he heeded not the
offering, and they put out to sea ; that day, in foul
weather, they wrecked their ship beneath huge crags,
and there they got up with much trouble, Vebjorn
leading ; that is now called Sogn-man's cliff. But
through the winter they were all taken in by Atli of
Fleet,

[PART II, CHAPTER XXIX.]

Fleet, the thrall of Geirmund Hellskin. And when Geirmund knew this ready deed of Atli's, he gave him freedom, and therewithal the manor which he had to look after; later on Atli became a great man. In the following spring Vebjorn took to himself land between Scate-firth and Horsefirth, as wide as he might walk round in a day, with so much more to boot as he called ' Foal-foot.' Vebjorn was a great man of fights, and there goes a great Saga of him. He gave Vedis in wedlock to Grimolf in Delight-dale (Unaðsdalr); they (afterwards) fell foul of each other, and Vebjorn slew Grimolf at Grimolf's-waters and for this Vebjorn was slain at a Quarter-court Thing on Thorness and three men beside.

Gunnstein and Haldor were the names of the sons of Gunnbjorn, the son of Ulf Crow, from whom the Gunn-bjornskerris take their name; they settled Scate-firth and ' Laugar '-dale and ' Ogr '-wick unto Narrowfirth. The son of Haldor was Bersi, the father of Thormod Coal-brow-skald. There, in ' Laugar '-dale abode afterwards Thorbjorn Thjodrekson, who slew Olaf, the son of Howard the Halt and of Bjargey, the daughter of Val-brand. Therefrom sprung the Saga of the Icefirthers and the slaughter of Thorbjorn.

Settlements of Snæbjorn brother of Helgi the Lean. Terrible blood feud between Snæbjorn and Hallbjorn on account of the murder of Hallgerd, Hallbjorn's wife.

CHAPTER XXX. Snæbjorn, the son of Eyvind East-man, and brother to Helgi the Lean, took up land between Narrowfirth and Langdale-river, and abode in Waterfirth; his son was Holmstein, the father of Snæ-bjorn Hog; but the mother of Snæbjorn was Kjalvor, and he and Tongue-Odd were sisters'-sous. Snæbjorn

was

[PART II, CHAPTER XXX.]

was fostered at Thingness in Thorodd's house, but at times
he would be staying with Tongue-Odd or with his mother.
Hallbjorn, the son of Odd of Kidberg who was the son
of Hallkel, the brother of Ketilbjorn the Old, got for wife
Hallgerd, the daughter of Tongue-Odd ; they stayed the
first winter (of their married life) with Odd, where Snæbjorn
the Hog was also staying. Between the newly married
couple there was but little love lost. At the flitting days in
spring Hallbjorn got ready to leave the house, and while
he was arranging matters for his departure, Odd left the
house and went to the hot spring at Reikholt, where his
sheep-pens stood. He did not want to be near when
Hallbjorn left, for it misdoubted him whether Hallgerd
would be willing to leave with him. Odd had always
sought to mend matters between them. Now when
Hallbjorn had saddled their horses, he went to the bower
where Hallgerd was seated on the dais combing her hair,
the hair covered her all down to the floor and of all
women in Iceland she and Hallgerd Turn-breeches have
been the most fair haired. Hallbjorn called upon her to
stand up and come away, but she sat and said nought ;
then he caught hold of her, yet no more did she rise
therefore; and so it went three times. So Hallbjorn
stood before her and sang :

> The Lofn of brimmed ale-beakers [1]
> Bedraped in linen, lets me
> Hand playing at her head-stern : [2]
> Thus the arms'-oak [3] repells me.
> That grief will ne'er be bettered
> Which for that bride I harbour ;
> Sore sorrow smites my heart's-root ;
> I'm wan with baleful trouble.

, (1) Lofn, one of the Asgarth goddesses, a goddess ; a goddess of ale-beakers =
a cup-bearer made in the image of a goddess = woman.
(2) Head-stern = the back of the head : she turns her back upon me begging
and praying her to come.
(3) Arms' oak, a kenning, circumlocution for woman.

After

[PART II, CHAPTER XXX.]

After this he twisted her hair round his hand and wanted to pull her down from the dais, but she sat and budged nowhither. Thereupon he drew his sword and cut off her head, walked out and rode away, they being three together with two pack-horses. There were but few people at home and forthwith a man was sent to Odd to tell him the news. Snæbjorn happened to be at Kjalvorstead, and Odd sent a man to him begging him to see to the pursuit ; but he said the himself should stir nowhere. Snæbjorn rode after them with eleven men, and when Hallbjorn and his saw the pursuit his companions begged him to ride off, but he would not. Snæbjorn and his men came up with them at the hills which now are called Hallbjorn's-Beacons. Hallbjorn and his went to the top of one of the hills and defended themselves there ; there three of Snæbjorn's men fell and both Hallbjorn's companions ; next Snæbjorn cut off the foot of Hallbjorn at the anckle joint, whereupon he limped to the southermost hill and slew there yet two men of Snæbjorn's and there Hallbjorn fell· withal ; therefore there are three beacons on that hill but five on the other. After this Snæbjorn returned. Snæbjorn owned a ship which was lying in Grim's-river-mouth, one half of which Hrolf the Redsander bought ; and Snæbjorn and Hrolf manned it each with twelve shipmates. In Snæbjorn's company were Thorkel and Sumarlid, sons of Thorstein the Red, the son of Einar the Staffholting. Snæbjorn also took on board Thorodd from Thingness, his foster-father, together with his wife, but Hrolf took on board Styrbjorn who after a dream he had had, sang this :

> The bane I see
> Of both of us,
> Noisome all things
> North-east at sea,

> Frost and cold,
> Fearful wonders,
> Such things tell of
> Snæbjorn slaughtered.

They

[PART II, CHAPTER XXX.]

They went in search of Gunnbjorn-skerries and they found a land, where Snæbjorn would not they should go ashore by night. Styrbjorn left the ship, and found treasure in a barrow and kept it hidden. Snæbjorn smote him with an axe and the treasure tumbled down. They made a scale for themselves which soon was snowed up. Thorkel the son of Red found that there was water on a forked pole which stood out in the scale window; and this was in the month of 'goi'; then they dug themselves out. Snæbjorn was busy mending the ship; but Thorodd and his wife were on his behalf home at the scale, while on behalf of Hrolf there were at the scale Styrbjorn and Hrolf himself; the others were out hunting. Styrbjorn slew Thorodd, but both of them together, Hrolf and Styrbjorn slew Snæbjorn. The sons of Red and all the rest of them swore oaths (to Hrolf) for the saving of their lives. They made at last Halogaland and fared thence to Iceland and hove in at 'Vadill.' Thorstein 'Trefill' guessed rightly what had happened to the sons of Red. Hrolf made for himself a fort upon Strandheath and 'Trefill' sent Sveinung to take his life. He first went to Hermund of 'Myrr,' then to Olaf of 'Drangar,' then to Gest at Hawe (Hagi*), and Gest sent him to Hrolf, his friend. Sveinung slew both, Hrolf and Styrbjorn and then went back to Hawe. Gest exchanged with him a sword and an axe for two grays with black manes, and sent a man on horseback round 'Vadil,' all the way to Kollfirth, bidding Thorbjorn the strong to claim the horses; and he slew Sveinung at 'Sveinung-seyrr,' because the sword (of Sveinung) broke right under the hilt. From this 'Trefill' boasted to Gest, when their wits were compared together, that he had so out-witted Gest as to make him send himself a man to take the life of his own friend.

---

* Hagi is a *pasture*, thus in Cumberland we have fields called "The Haggs."

Settlements

[PART II, CHAPTER XXXI.]

Settlements of Olaf ' Jafnakollr,' Orlyg son of Bodvar and Eirek Snare. The Landtakes of Geirmund in their order.

CHAPTER XXXI.   Olaf 'Jafnakollr' took land from Langdale-river to 'Sandeyrar'-river and dwelt in Delight-dale; he had for wife Thora, the daughter of Gunnstein, and their son Grimolf had for wife Vedis the sister of Vebjorn.

Thorolf Fastholder was the name of a man of high worth in Sogn; he fell into unfriendly dealings with Earl Hakon the son of Grjotgard and went to Iceland by the counsel of King Harald. He took land from 'Sandeyrar'-river to Trollspoor-river in 'Raven'-firth and dwelt at Snowfells. His son was Ofeig, who had for wife Ottkatla.

Orlyg the son of Bodvar, the son of Vigsterk, went to Iceland driven by the tyranny of King Harald Fairhair, and was the first winter with Geirmund Hellskin, but the next spring Geirmund gave him his manor in 'Adal'-wick and the land thereto belonging, Orlyg had for wife Signy, the daughter of Oblaud, Signy being the sister of Hogni the White; their son was Ketil 'Gufa,' who had for wife Yri, the daughter of Geirmund.

Here follow in order the landtakes of Geirmund, which are already written down above, all the way to Streamness east of Horn.

Orlyg got for his own 'Slétta' and Glacier-firths.

'Hella'-Bjorn, the son of Herfin and Halla, was a great Viking; he was ever a foe to King Harald; he went to Iceland and came in a ship all beset with shields into Bjornfirth, whence he was called Shield-Bjorn ever after; he took land from Streamness unto 'Drangar' and abode in Shieldbjorn's-wick, but had another home at Bjorn's-ness where the tofts of his great scale are still seen. His

son

[PART II, CHAPTER XXXI.]

son was Thorbjorn, the father of Arngerd, whom Thjodrek the son of 'Slettu'-Bjorn had for wife, their sons were Thorbjorn and Sturla and Thjodrek.

There was a man named Geirolf, who wrecked his ship against Geirolf's-Peak ; afterwards, by the counsel of Bjorn, he abode there beneath the peak.

Thorvald, the son of Asvald, the son of Ulf, the son of Ox-Thorir took 'Drangaland' and 'Drangavik' unto 'Eingines' and abode at 'Drangar' all his life. His son was Eirek the Red, who settled Greenland, as was said before.

Herradd Whitesky was a man of high worth ; he was slain at the bidding of King Harald, but his three sons went to Iceland and took up lands on the Strands ; Eyvind taking Eyvind-firth, Ofeig Ofeig's-firth, Ingolf Ingolf,s-firth, and there they all abode afterwards.

Eirek Snare was the name of a man who took land from Ingolf's-firth unto' Veiðilausa,' and abode in 'Trekyllis'-wick ; he had for wife Alof, the daughter of Ingolf of Ingolf's-firth, their son was Flosi who abode at Wick, when some Eastmen (Norwegians) broke there their ship and made of the wreck that ship, which they called 'Trekyllir' ; in that ship Flose started on a foreign voyage but was driven back into Axefirth. Therefrom sprang the Saga of Bodmod 'Gerpir' and Grimolf.

Settlements of Onund Treefoot, Bjorn, Steingrim, Koll, Thorbjorn 'Bitra,' Balki, and Arndis.

CHAPTER XXXII. Onund Treefoot, the son of Ofeig Clubfoot, the son of Ivar 'Beytil,' fought against King Harald in Hafursfirth and there lost his leg ; thereupon he went to Iceland and took land from Cliffs unto 'Ofæra' : Coldback's-wick, Kolbein's-wick, Byrgir's-wick to wit and abode at Coldback to old age ; he was the brother

brother of Gudbjorg, the mother of Gudbrand 'Kula,' the father of Asta, who was the mother of King Olaf (the Holy). Onund had four sons, one called Grettir, another Thorgeir Bottleback, the third Asgeir Madpate, the father of Kalf and Hrefna whom Kjartan had for wife and of Thurid whom Thorkel Ketch had for wife and whom Steinthor, son of Olaf, took to wife afterwards; the fourth son of Onund was Thorgrim Hoaryhead, the father of Grettir the strong.

Bjorn was the name of a man who settled Bjornfirth and had for wife a woman called Ljufa, their son was Svan who abode at Svan's-knoll.

Steingrim took to him the whole of Steingrims-firth and abode at Troll-Tongue; his son was Thorir, the father of Haldor, the father of Thorvald 'Orgodi,' the father of 'Bitru'-Oddi, the father of Steindor, the father of Odd, the father of 'Ha'-Snorri, the father of Odd the monk and Thorolf and Thorarin Ruffian.

Koll was named a man who settled Kollfirth and 'Skridnisenni' and dwelt 'under Fell' all his life.

Thorbjorn 'Bitra' was the name of a man, a Viking and a scoundrel; he went to Iceland with his kinsfolk, and settled the firth now is called Bitra and abode there. Some time afterwards Gudlaug, the brother of Gils 'Skeid'-neb wrecked his ship against that headland which now is called Gudlaug's-Head. Gudlaug got aland with his wife and daughter but the rest of the crew perished; then there came upon them Thorbjorn 'Bitra' and murdered man and wife, but took the maiden and brought her up. But when Gils 'Skeid'-neb was aware of this he set out and avenged his brother, slaying Thorbjorn 'Bitra' and sundry men besides. From Gudlaug Gudlaug's-wick takes its name.

There was a man named Balki, who was the son of Blæing, the son of Soti of Sotisness; he fought against

King

[PART II, CHAPTER XXXII.]

King Harald in Hafursfirth whence he went, to Iceland and took to himself the whole of Ram-firth, he abode at both homesteads called Balkistead, but last he dwelt at By * and died there. His son was Bersi the Godless, who at first abode at Bersistead in Ramfirth; but later he settled Langwaterdale and had another household there, this happening before he took for wife Thordis the daughter of Thorhadd from Hitriverdale and with her, for dowry, Holmesland. Their son was Arngeir the father of Bjorn the Champion of the Hitdalemen. A daughter of Balki was Geirbjorg, the mother of Veleif the Old.

Arndis the Wealthy, the daughter of Steinolf the Low took as time wore on land in Ramfirth out away from Board-'Eyrr' and dwelt at By; her son was Thord who formerly had dwelt at Mull † in Saurby.

Hromund the Halt and his sons Thorbjorn, Thorleif, and Hestein settle at Fairbrink. They summon Helgi and his clan of Viking Eastmen for horse stealing. Hromund and his sons are made wardens of the district. A poem relating the terrible and fatal conflict between Hromund and the Eastern Vikings, their final discomfiture and flight, names of chief settlers in Westfirth. Census.

CHAPTER XXXIII. Throst and Grenjud, the sons of

---

* By is Bæ in the Icelandic and derived from the verb *bua*=to *dwell*, so it means dwelling. "By" is identical with *by* that occurs as termination of the names of many villages in the North of England. The Cumberland Poet, Anderson, says :—

"There's Harraby an Tarraby,
And Wigganby beside,
There's Oughterby and Soughterby,
And 'bys' beath far an weyde."

† Icelandic Múli, meaning properly a *muzzle*, *snout*, whence the *mouth* of beasts—then as here a *jutting crag*, between two dales, fiórds or the like; in Scotland, Mull; in the Shetlands, Mule; Fjalls-múli in Landnama=a *mountain peak*, as Digri-muli, Seljalands-muli, as also in numberless place-names, as Múli, Múla-fjall, Múla-eyjar, Mula-sveit. See map. So also the Mull of Cantire, Mull of Galloway, Mullhead in the Orkneys, and the Island of Mull, names first given by the Norsemen, whence Mylskr=a man of Mull.

Hermund

[PART II, CHAPTER XXXIII.]

Hermund the Stooping, took up land in Ramfirth up from
Board-'Eyrr' and abode at 'Melar.'   From Grenjad
was sprung Horse-Gellir the Priest, but Orm was come
down from Throst.   A son of Throst, too, was Thorkel
of 'Kerseyrr,' the father of Gudrun, whom Thorbjorn
'Thyna,' the son of Hromund the Halt, had for wife ;
they (Hromund and Thorbjorn dwelt at Fairbrink.
Thorleif Hromund's fosterson was the son of Thorbjorn
Thyna and Gudrun.   Yet another son of Hromund was
called Hastein.   They (Hromund and his sons) had all
things in common.   A son of Thorkel the son of Throst
was Thorir and he abode at 'Melar' ; a daughter of his
was named Helga.   About this time there came out to
Board-'Eyrr' 'Sleitu'-Helgi and with him Jorund his
brother.   They were Vikings ; with them there were
twelve free men besides servants ; they all betook themselves to 'Melar.'   Then Helgi got for wife Helga the
daughter of Thorir.   Hromund and his sons lost some
stud-horses and held Helgi guilty of the deed and Midfirth-Skeggi summoned Helgi and his for horse-stealing
to the Althing, but Hromund and his sons were set to
keep order in the countryside and they had a trusty fort
at Brink (Fairbrink).   The Eastman arrayed their ship
for sea.   One morning a raven perched on the luffer* at
Brink and croaked loudly, then Hromund sang :

> 'Tis early morn, yet outside†
> I hear the black-skinned swan of
> The wound-thorn's sweat[1] a-croaking :
> The stout bird scents his quarry ;

---

* The Icelandic word which has been rendered 'luffer' is ljori = *an opening in
the roof* of ancient halls for the smoke to escape by, and also for admitting light,
as the walls of such dwellings had no windows.   The men who kept watch
used to sit at the ljori or luffer.

† The original Icelandic of this verse is given in a note at the end of the
chapter.

(1) Wound-thorn = sword, the sweat of it = blood, the black-skinned swan
thereof = black bird of prey = raven.

So

[PART II, CHAPTER XXXIII.]

So cried the hawk of battle [1]
Of yore. whenas the cuckoos
Of Gaut's ado [2] gave warning
Of coming doom of warriors.

Then Thorbjorn sang:

The mew of corpse-heaps' billow [3]
Clacks, hail-sprent, [4] as he comes to
The corpse-sea: [5] Now all eager
His morning prey he craveth;
So crowed the gawk of carrion [6]
Out from the tree of ages
Of yore, whenas the wound-hawks [7]
For warriors ' oath '-mead [8] lusted.

At this nick of time the Eastmen entered the fort, because the men at work there had not closed it. The brothers (Halstein and Thorbjorn 'Thyna' went out (to fight them), but the women said that Hromund was too old and Thorleif too young to go out (to fight), he was then but fifteen winters old. Then Hromund sang:

Stem of the flat-grounds circles! [9]
My death was not predestined
For *either* this *or* that day, [10]
So I shall face Ilms uproar; [11]

---

(1) Hawk of battle=raven.
(2) Gaut=Odin, his ' ado '=battle, the battle cuckoo=raven.
(3) Corpse-heaps' billow=blood, the mew of that billow or sea=carrion bird, raven.
(4) With the hoar-frost of the night still on his fell.
(5) As, by instinct, he feels that bloodshed is at hand.
(6) Gawk of carrion=raven.
(7) Wound-hawks=ravens.
(8) =blood; perhaps so-called because of the ancient custom of blending blood and tasting it, when solemn engagements were undertaken.
(9) =shields brimmed round with iron. Apostrophe to someone present.
(10) *i.e.* " Fate has no ' either ' ' or ' in its determination of the day of death: if I am not destined by it to die to-day, I shall not die to-day."
(11) Ilm (Ilmr) a goddess of Asgarth, must here stand for a Valkyrja, her uproar=battle.

[PART II, CHAPTER XXXIII.]

> I care not if the paint-wand
> Of Hedin's weeds [1] shall play on
> The red shields : at the outset
> My days' span was determined.

Six of the Eastmen fell in the fort, but the remaining
six bolted off. When Thorbjorn was about shutting up
the fort, he was shot through with a bill; but he took
the bill out of the wound and drove it in between the
shoulders of Jörund so that it went out into the chest;
but Helgi slung him on his back and so ran off. Hromund lay fallen and Thorleif grievously wounded.
Hastein followed up the pursuit of them until Helgi
dropped Jörund dead, whereat he returned. The women
asked for tidings, and Hastein sang :

> Six wound-rod-sweeping Njordungs, [2]
> Asleep with none to mourn them,
> Have found their death by weapons
> Outside here on the flagstones ;
> Methinks of these lawbreakers
> One half behind lie fallen,
> But edge-cut wounds full smarting
> To the run-aways I meeted.

The women asked how many they were (Hallstein and
his) ; Hastein sang :

> We, kinsmen, stood but four there
> Before their purposed onslaught,
> With no more men I carried
> To the fight the strap-path's-fire. [3]

---

(1) Hedin, a war lord, Snor. Edda I, 432, his weeds=coat of mail, the paint-
wand thereof=the wand that paints it=stains it red with blood, a sword.

(2) Niordungs, Niord's kin, gods; wound-rod=sword; wound-rod-sweeping
Niordungs=warriors.

(3) Strap=τελαμών, sword-strap going over the shoulder; its path is the
coat of mail over which it goes; the fire of the coat of mail=sword: I went
weaponed into the fight with only four companions.

While

[PART II, CHAPTER XXXIII.]

> While from the steed of Gylvi [1]
> Twelve frisky stems of Gunn-Thing, [2]
> Who *would* hie to our meeting,
> Came our cold glaves to redden. [3]

The women asked how many were fallen of the Vikings;
Hastein sang:

> Here seven of gods a-seeking
> For Svolnir's wall [4] have dipped down
> To earth their nose ; [5] o'er warriors
> Streamed warm blood, dew of corpses.
> Not more fir-stems of meetings
> Of Fjolnir [6] will take outward
> O'er Ekkils paths [7] the steed of
> Jalk's mere, [8] than took it hither.

> Here may be seen the signs of
> The deal-tongue's [9] precious day's-work :
> What deed by four boast-burdocks
> Of sword-din [10] now's effected.
> But, swinger of Gunn's roof's firebrand, [11]
> Methinks to those peace-breakers
> We gave a peace but scanty—
> The raven tore feed from corpses.

---

(1) Gylvi, a sea-king, his steed=ship.
(2) Gunn (Gunnr) a Valkyrja, her Thing=meeting, assembly=battle; the stems of battle=warriors.
(3) Observe the double meaning in ' to *redden* cold glaves.'
(4) Svolnir=Odin; his wall=shield; gods a-seeking for it=warriors.
(5) Have bitten the dust.
(6) Fjolnir=Odin; his meetings=battles, the fir-stem of battles=warriors, men.
(7) Ekkill, a sea king; his paths=ocean.
(8) Jalk, a name of Odin, must here stand for that of a sea-king; the sea-king's mere=ocean; his steed thereof=ship; here the ship in which the Vikings came to Iceland.—NOTE: ' Not more '=fewer; the Viking's number having gone down from 12 to 5.
(9) Deal=deal-wood=bow; the tongue of it=the tongue that holds it, the hand; ' the day's work of our hand is preceious.'
(10) Burdock (' bŏrr ') of sword-din=warrior; a ' boast-burdock' thereof=the warrior, who may boast of victory by means of it.
(11) Gunn, a Valkyrja, her roof=a shield, the fire-brand of the shield=the gleaming, flashing sword. This line is an apostrophe to someone present.

Upon

[PART II, CHAPTER XXXIII.]

Unto these men of ravage
We got their fight-shirts reddened.
My sword is keen.   We were all
Right hard at work while fighting.
Men valiant kept the hanging
Hild's boarding's fire-tongues [1] ready   ·
Beneath their shields.   The falcons
Of corpses [2] lost their hunger.

At a loud roar we started
A fierce burst of stone-throwing;
Gray clothes of Thund, [3] midst singing
Of swords, were rent asunder :
Or e'er the stems of weapons [4]
Gave way, their respite seeking,
When still more found their death-day—
Shields with fight-squall were smitten.

Hark, how the wound-swan [5] yelleth
O'er corpses, where lie fallen
The stems of vict'ry's altars ; [6]
Wound-mew [7] drink blood-tide's billow.
Its swill then gat the eagle
When guilt-rich ' Sleitu '-Helgi
Had his red coif: [8] the talons
Of the ern [9] are clogged with carrion.

Up from the steed, most goodly,
Of oars [10] the elm-Thing's urgers [11]
Came, wearing *polished* helmets,
To have a meeting with us.

---

(1) Hild (Hildr) a Valkyrja ; her hanging board or boarding=a shield ; the fire-tongue thereof=a sword.
(2) =ravens.
(3) Thund (þundr) one of Odin's names ; his gray clothes=byrny, or coat of mail.
(4) =warriors.
(5) =raven
(6) Victory's altars= shields ; the stems=up-beearers thereof, warriors, men.
(7) =raven.
(8) =had his head covered with blood.
(9) =eagle.
(10) Steed of oars=ship.
(11) Elm=bow (the elm-wood being used for that weapon of attack); the bow's Thing or asembly=battle, the urgers thereof=warriors. men.

· But

[PART II, CHAPTER XXXIII.]

> But off they went, a-wearing
> *Red* hair,[1] these earth-chain's oxen [2]
> Commanders, god-forsaken,
> Unto their boat—what sword-stems![3]

Helgi and his companions put off to sea the same day and were all lost on Helgi-skerry of 'Skridins-enni.' Thorleif was healed of his wound, and abode at (Fair) Brink; but Hastein went abroad and fell aboard the Long-Worm* (Olaf Tryggvison's ship, in the battle of Svold.)

Now are written down most of the land-takes in the Westfirthers' Quarter, according as men of lore have told of them. And now it must have been heard, that many great men have taken up their abode in that Quarter and that from them many noble families have sprung, even as we have now heard.†

These are the noblest 'land-take-men' (landnàmsmenn) in the Westfirthers' Quarter: Hrosskel, Skallagrim, 'Sel'-Thorir, Bjorn the Easterner, Thorolf Mostbeard, Aud the Deep-minded, Geirmund Hellskin, Ulf the Squinter, Thord Vikingson, though in some families male lines maintain themselves longer (than in those of this Quarter.) When the good men of Iceland were counted, there were nine hundred (=9 by 120=1080) good men in this Quarter.

---

(1) Note the contrast between *polished* helms on arrival and *red*, i.e., blood covered hair on departing.

(2) Earth-chain=the earth surrounding ocean, sea; its ox=the ship, ploughing it.

(3) Said in scorn=what pitiable wielders of a sword.

* The story of the battle of Svold, A.D. 1000, in which 'The Long Serpent' engaged, and the clearing of the ship and mysterious disappearance of Olaf Tryggvison is told in the "Heimskringla," or Story of the Kings of Norway. See Translation by Morris and Magnusson, Chapter cxiv to the end.

† These words seem unmistakably to point back to the *first* secession of 'Landnama,' as being due to oral tradition for this Quarter.

Note

[PART II, CHAPTER XXXIII.]

Note to Chapter XXXIII.

' The following is the first stanza in the original Icelandic of the remarkable poem that occurs here :

> út heyri ek svan sveita
> sara þorns er mornar,
> braỏ vekr broginmóỏa,
> blắfjallaỏan gjalla ;
> svắ gól fyrr, þa er feigir
> fólknắrúngar vắru
> gunnar haukr, er gắukar
> Gauts bragdắ spắ sagdu.

It will be seen that this, probably the earliest specimen
of Norse poetry committed to writing, runs in stanzas of
eight verses each, that the lines are alliterative, that is,
two words commence with the same letter in one line and
one word with that letter in the next line—*e.g.* 1st line,
svan sveita ; 2nd line, sara &c. The various epithets
applied in those verses to the raven shows how highly
figurative the poetry is, and the mythology of the old
Norse gods, which characterizes it throughout, proves it
to belong to the old heathen age.

Third Part.

*Now begins the Landnam in the Northern Quarter, which has
been the most thickly settled of all Iceland and wherein
the greatest events have happened both in old times and
new, as further on will be set forth and as experience
bears witness to.*

*Eysteinn ' Meinfret' settles the Dales. Thoradd settles Rams-
firth and dwells at Thoroddstead. Fur Bjorn settles
Midfirth. Midfirth Skeggi his son and his exploits.
Harald Ring settles Waterness. Audun Skokil, grandson of Ragnar Lodbrog, settles at Audunstead. His
connexions and their Settlements.*

CHAPTER

[PART III, CHAPTER I.]

CHAPTER I. Eysteinn 'Meinfret,' son of Alf from Osta, settled the eastern Ramfirth Strand next to Balki and dwelt there some winters before he married Thorhild, the daughter of Thorstein the Red ; then he betook himself from the north to the dales and settled there. Their sons were Alf, in the dales, Thord and Thorolf Fox, and Hrapp.

There was a man named Thorodd, who settled land in Ramsfirth, and dwelt at Thoroddstead. His son was Arnorr 'hynef,' who married Gerd, the daughter of Bodvar from Bodvar's-knolls ; their sons were Thorbjorn, whom Grettir slew, and Thorod dràpustufr, * the father of Valgera, who was the wife of Skeggi Skammhondungr (or shorthanded), the son of Gamli, the son of Thord, the son of Eyjolf, the son of Eyjar, the son of Thorhrolf 'fasthaldi' or fastholder from Snæfell. The son of Skeggi 'Skammhondung' was Gamli, the father of Alfdis, the mother of Odd the Monk.

There was a man of great renown in Norway named Skutadar-Skeggi, his son was Bjorn, who was called Skin or Fur-Bjorn, because he used to go to Holmgard, *i.e.* Novgorod in Russia ; and when he tired of trading journeys he went to Iceland and settled Midfirth and Linakradale (Flaxfielddale), his son was Midfirth-Skeggi ; he was a great bravo and a sea-farer ; he harried in Easternway, *i.e.* in the Baltic, and lay in Denmark at Sjoland (Sealand), when he went from the east ; there he made a raid on the land and broke into the Howe or Burial Mound of King Hrolf Kraki, and seized there Skofnung, the sword of King Hrolf and the ax of Hjalti, and much treasure besides, but he could not possess himself of Laufi (the sword of Bodvar Biarki.)

Skeggi dwelt at Reykir in Midfirth and married Hall-

---

* Dràpustufr is in Icelandic a rhymer or poetaster.

[PART III, CHAPTER I.]

bera, the daughter of Grim ; their children were Eid, who
married Hafthora, the daughter of Thorberg Kornmull
and of Alof 'Ellida-shield,' the sister of Thorgeir 'gollnir'; .
they had many children. Another son of Skeggi was
Koll, the father of Kalldor, the father of Thorkatla and
of Thordis, whom Skhald-Helga married. The daughters
of Skeggi were Hrodny, whom Thord Yeller married, and
Thorbjorg, whom Aslejord the wealthy married, the son
of Hord ; their daughter was Ingibjorg, whom Illugi the
Black had to wife ; their sons were Gunnlaug Ormstunga
or serpent's tongue, Hermund and Ketill. One son of
Eid * was named Thorhall, the father of Eid, the father
of Thorhall, the father of Oddny, the mother of Geirlaug, the mother of Snælaug, the mother of Markus of
Melar.

There was a man of high degree called Harald Ring ;
he came with his ship into Vestrhop or Westhope and
abode for the first winter near to the place where he had
first landed, and which is now called Ringstead. He
settled Vatnsnes (Waterness) all out to Ambattar (Bondmaid's) river to the west and eastward up to Thwart or
Cross river and over there thwartwise to Bjargaos or
Rocksmouth, and and all that side of the rocks, as far
as the sea, and he dwelt at Holar. His son was Thorbrand, the father of Asbrand, the father of Solvi the
Proud in Aegis sea-side, and Thorgeir, who dwelt at
Holar ; his daughter was Astrid, whom Armod, the son
of Hedin, had for wife ; their son was Hedin. Another
daughter of Thorgeir was Thorgerd, whom Thorgrim
married, the son of Peter from Os. There was a man
named Soti who settled Westhope and dwelt under Sotfell.

Hunda-Steinar was the name of an Earl in England.
He had for wife Alof, the daughter of Ragnar Lodbrog ;

---

* *i.e.* Eid Skeggison above.

their

[PART III, CHAPTER I.]
their children were these: Bjorn, the father of Audun
Skokul and Eric, the father of Sigurd Bjodskalli, and
Isgerd, whom Earl Thorir in Vermaland had for wife.
Audun 'Skokul' went to Iceland and settled Vididale,
and dwelt at Audunstead; with him came out Thorgil
gjallandi (yelling), his fellow, the father of Thorarin the
'godi.' Audun 'Skokul' was the father of Thora 'Mo-
shal's' ('Mewsneck') the mother of Ulfhlid, the mother
of Asta, the mother of St. Olave the King.

The son of Audun 'Skokul' was Asgeirr at Asgeir's
river; he had for wife Jorun, the daughter of Ingimund
the Old; their children were Thorvald, the father of
Dalla, the mother of Gizur the Bishop, and Audun the
father of Asgeir, the father of Audun, the father of Egil
who married Ulfeid the daughter of Eyjolf the son of
Gudmund, and their son was Eyjolf, who was slain at
the Althing and who was the father of Orm the chaplain
of Thorlak the Bishop. Another son of Audun 'Skokul'
was Eystein, the father of Thorstein, the father of Helgi,
the father of Thororm, the father of Odd, the father of
Hallbjorn, the father of Sigvat the Priest. The daughter
of Asgeir of Asgeir's river was Thorbjorg, bench setter off.

There was a man named Orm who settled Ormsdale
and dwelt there; he was the father of Odd, the father of
Thorodd, the father of Helgi, the father of Harri, the
father of Jora, the mother of Thordis, the mother of
Thordis, the mother of Tanni, the father of Skapi.

*Ingimund the Old from Norway. Prediction of the witch
wife concerning his Talisman. Its singular story. He
settles Vatnsdale and resides at Hof.*

CHAPTER II. Ketillraumr was the name of a renowned
'Hersir' in Raumsdale in Norway; he was the son of
Orm Skeljamola (Shellmeal), the son of Horsebjorn, the
son

son of Raum, the son of Giant-Bjorn from the north in
Norway. Ketill married Mjoll the daughter of An Bend-
the-bow ; their son was called Thorstein, who slew in
the wood leading to the Upplands, at the egging on of
his father, Jokul, the son of Ingimund, Earl of Gautland.
Jokul gave him his life* and afterwards Thorstein married
Thordis Jokul's sister. Their son was Ingimund the
Old, he was brought up in Hefni with Thorir, the father
of Grim and Hromund. Heid the witchwife predicted to
them all that they should settle in that land which was
then undiscovered west in the ocean, but Ingimund said
he would guard against that, but the witchwife said he
might not do so, and said the token† thereof was, that
even now would his talisman‡ have disappeared out of his
pouch, and he would there find it where he should dig
for the foundations of his high seat pillars upon that land.

Ingimund was a great Viking and harried always in
Viking raids to the west.§ His partner was named Sæm-
und, a man from the Hebrides ; they came back from
their harrying at that time ‖ when King Harald Fairhair
was fighting for the land and gave battle in Hafursfirth
to Thorir Longchin and his allies ; Ingimund wished
to go and give aid to the King, but Sæmund would not,
and there they parted company. After the battle the
King gave to Ingimund for wife Vigdis, the daughter of
Earl Thorir the Silent. She and Jorund Neck were his
bastard children.

---

* While bleeding to death from a wound inflicted by Thorstein, he still had
the power to kill him, but gave him his life and bade him marry his sister. See
Vatnsdæla Saga, Chap. III.

† The Icelandic word is 'jartegn' and signifies a token as a ring, knife,
sword, belt, or the like—properly a token which a messenger had to produce in
evidence that his message was true.

‡ The Icelandic term for talisman here is 'hlutir,' a little image or images
which people used to wear about their persons—in the present instance these
were the silver images of the god Frey.

§ The Hebrides and the British Islands generally.

‖ Date 872 A.D.

[PART III, CHAPTER II.]

Ingimund felt at home nowhere; therefore Harald the King urged him to seek his fortune in Iceland. Ingimund said that that was what he had never set his mind upon, but he sent there two Finns * on a wizard's journey in hamforum † to Iceland after his talisman, which was the image of Frey ‡ and made of silver. The Finns came back and said they had found the whereabouts of the talisman but could not lay hold on it. They however marked out to Ingimund the position of the place in a valley between two hill rises, and told Ingimund all about the trend of the land, and as to how it was shapen, where he was to settle.

After that Ingimund set out upon his voyage to Iceland and with him Jorund Neck his brother-in-law,§ and Eyvind Sorkvir and Asmund and Hvati his friends, and his thralls Fridmund, Bodvar, Thorir, Refskegg, Ulfkell. They made land in the southern part of Iceland and were all through the winter at Hvanneyri, with Grim the foster brother of Ingimund, but in spring they went north over the heaths. They came to that firth where they found two rams, and that they called Hrutafirth or Ramfirth, thence they went north over the countrysides and gave proper names to places wideabout there; he was for one winter in Vididale in Ingimundsholt; thence they saw mountains snowless towards the south east and went thitherward in the spring. There Ingimund recognised the aspect of the country which the seer had marked out for his abode.

Thordis, his daughter, was born in Thordisholt. Ingi-

---

* The art of sorcery or witchcraft was so much practised by the Finns that the names Finn and Sorcerer or Magician became identical.

† The Icelandic word here used is "hamfarir" and has a mythical sense—meaning the *faring* or travelling in the shape of an animal, fowl, deer, fish, or serpent, with magical speed over land and sea, the wizard's own body in the meantime lying lifeless and motionless.

‡ Frey is the male god—the brother of Freya—they were the children of Niord.

§ Ingimund was married to his sister, Vigdis, as stated above.

mund

[PART III, CHAPTER II.]
mund took to himself all Vatnsdale up from Helgavatn
and Urdarvatn and dwelt at Hof, and there found his
talisman, where he digged for the foundations of his high
seat posts. His sons by Vigdis were Thorstein and
Jokul and Thorir Hegoat's-thigh and Hogni. The son
of Ingimund by a bondsmaid was Smid, and his daughters
by her were Jorun and Thordis.

*Ingimund finds three white bears at Hunavatn. Sends them
to King Harald in Norway. Finds one hundred swine
in Swinedale.*

CHAPTER III. Jorund settled land out from Urdvar-
vatn to Mogilsbrook and dwelt at Grund * under Jorund-
fell, his son was Marr † at Marstead. Hvati settled land
out from Mogilsbrook to the Gills river and dwelt at
Hvatistead. Asmund settled out from Helgavatn about
the countryside of Thingeyrar and dwelt under Gnup.
Fridmund settled Forsæludale. Eyvind Sorkvir settled
Blandadale, his sons were Hermund and Hromund the
Halt. Ingimund found a she bear and two white bear
cubs on Hunavatn (when laid with ice), the place was on
this account called Hunavatn. ‡ After that he went out
and gave the bear to King Harald. Before this men had
not seen white bears in Norway.

Then King Harald gave to Ingimund a ship loaded
with a cargo of timber § and he sailed with the ships to
the northern portion of the land and was the first of men

---

*Grund in Icelandic is literally *green field* from a cognate word. Numerous
farms are so called in High Furness, *e.g.* Sandgrund, Parkgrund, &c.

†Marr is a common surname in Lakeland. Compare also Mardale near
Hawswater.

‡Hunavatn is literally 'the water of the young bears' from Hunn a young
bear which is, in the Book of the Settlement, used of other place names in Iceland as Hunafloi, Hunavatns Thing, Hunavatns Sysla. See those names on map.

§ The Icelandic phrase for cargo of timber is viðar-farmi from viðr=wood,
and farmr=fare, freight, or cargo.

[PART III, CHAPTER III.]

to double the Skagi, and he sailed up into Hunavatn to the place which is now called Stiganda-hrof by Thing-eyrat. After that was Hrafn the Norwegian with Ingi-mund, he had a good sword which he took with him into a temple, wherefore Ingimund took the sword from him, as it was forbidden to go with weapons into the hallowed edifice. Hallorm and Thororm, brothers, came out and were with Ingimund, and Hallorm married Thordis his daughter and she obtained as a dowry all the estate of Korn's-river; their son was Thorgrim the godi of Korn's-river. Thororm dwelt at Thorormstongue. Ingimund lost ten swine which were found the following harvesttide in Swinedale,* where were a hundred swine; the boar was named Beigad, he leaped into Swinewater or Swine-pool and swam about until his kloofs came off, and he died from the over exertion at Beigad's-knoll.

Hrolleif the Great and Ljot his mother settle in Hrolleifsdale. Settlement results in a series of deadly family feuds.

CHAPTER IV. Hrolleif the Mickle or Great, and Ljot his mother, come out to Iceland and landed in Burgfirth, they wandered north over the country sides but they found nowhere a chance of settled abode until they came to Skagafirth to Sæmund. Hrolleif was the son of Arn-hall, the brother of Sæmund, wherefore he sent them north to Headstrand to Thord, who assigned him land in Hrolleifsdale, and he dwelt there. Hrolleif defiled Hrodny, the daughter of Uni from Unisdale; Odd, the son of Uni, lay in wait for him and slew Ljot his cousin, and wounded him in the foot but his sword would not pierce his kirtle. Hrolleif slew Odd and two men beside,

---

* Compare Swindale, a valley and parish in Westmorland; also Swinside and Swinsty.

and

[PART III, CHAPTER IV.]

and two men escaped.   On account of that Thord * o'
Head made him an outlaw from the countryside (heraðssekan) † as wide as water-shed sent running streams to
sea in Skagafirth.‡

Then Sæmund sent Hrolleif to Ingimund the Old;
Ingimund placed him down in Odds-ridge opposite Hof.
He had the fishing in Vatnsdale river with Ingimund,
on such terms that he was to quit the river when the
men of Hof came to fish in it, but he would not quit it
for the sons of Ingimund, so they fought about the river;
this was told to Ingimund; he was then blind and he
caused a boy to lead the horse whereon he rode into the
river between them.   Hrolleif shot his spear· through
him, and therewith he and the boy went home.   Ingimund sent the lad to tell the news to Hrolleif, but he,
Ingimund, was dead in his High Seat when his sons came
home.   Hrolleif told these things to his mother.   She
said that they would come to find out which would avail
most, the fortune of the sons of Ingimund or her own
skill in magic; then she bade him betake himself away
to begin with.

It was allotted to Thorstein to follow up Hrolleif in blood-
feud, and for that he was to have what heirloom he should
choose for himself.   The sons of Ingimund did not sit
down in the High Seat of their father § ; they went north
to Geirmund, and Thorstein gave him sixty hundreds in
silver that he might get Hrolleif out of the way.   They
tracked his spoor from the north across the Necks to

---

* He was called Hofda Thord because he dwelt at Hofði = Head or Headland.

† Heraðssekan.   The legal term used here means *exiled from a district or
jurisdiction* as opposed to being exiled from the country generally.   The meaning of the word herað or district varies, but as in the present instance, it is for
the most part merely geographical, *i.e.*, a district, valley, fjord, or country, as
being bordered by the same mountains or within the same river basin.

‡ For Skagafirth see Skagafjordr in Map.

§ They could not do that until lawful revenge was taken for the slaying of him.

Vatnsdale

[PART III, CHAPTER IV.]

Vatnsdale. Thorstein sent his house-carle to the Ridge*
to spy; he repeated twelve verses (of incantations) before
anyone came to the door. He saw heaps of clothes on the
brands,† beneath which red clothes appeared. Thorstein
said that Hrolleif was there and that Ljot had sacrificed
in order that she might obtain long life for him. They
then went to Ridge and Thorstein would sit above the
door, but could not have his way on account of Jokul,
because he also wished to be there.

A man came out and looked round; then another led
forth Hrolleif after him; then Jokul burst forth from his
hiding place amongst the fuel logs and tumbled the pile
of firewood down, but cast a stick from it to his brothers.
After that he rushed upon Hrolleif and they both rolled
over the brink, but Jokul was the uppermost in the end;
then came up Thorstein and they took to their weapons.
Then Ljot came out walking back foremost and she had
her head between her legs and her clothes slung over her
back.

Jokul hewed off the head from Hrolleif and threw it in
the face of Ljot. Then she said that she had been too
late, "for otherwise would the earth have turned inside
out before my very sight but you would all have become
crazed." After that Thorstein chose Hofsland and
Jokul kept the sword and dwelt in Tongue. Thorir had
the priesthood and dwelt at Underfell ‡ and had fits of
frenzy (bersarksgang). § Hogni got the ship Stigand, he
was a seafarer; Smid abode at Smidstead. Thorstein

---

* *i.e.* Odds-ridge, see before.
† The Icelandic word used for describing this is "brandar" and refers to the
"skiðahlaði" which is mentioned afterwards, so that "brandar" here seems
to be synonymous with fuel logs.
‡ The genuine old name of this place is now proved to have been Undornfell.
§ Bersarksgang was the name of fits of frenzy to which the ber-serkr were
subject, during which they howled like wild beasts, foamed at the mouth and
gnawed the iron rim of their shields. During these fits, they were according to
the popular belief, proof against steel and fire, and made great havoc in the
ranks of the enemy, but when the fever abated they were weak and tame.

married

[PART III, CHAPTER IV.]

married Thurid Gydja or Temple Priestess, the daughter of Solmund in Asbjorn'sness, their son was Ingolf the fair and Gudbrand. The son of Bard, the son of Jokul, was Jokul, whom King Olave the Saint caused to be killed. Jokul the Highwayman foretold that for a long time there should be manslaughter by mishaps in that family.

Thorgrim dwelt at Hjallaland (Hill-land.) The sons of Ingimund and the sons of Jorund fought about the ownership of Deildarhjalli, and Hogni fell there and a freeman of Thorstein, and out of the band of Mar there fell a daughter's son of Jorund and five men beside. Jokul hewed at the thigh of Thorgrim and then they fled forth. Mar paid eighty hundreds in silver and retained Hjallaland. Thorstein and Jokul slew Thorolf Hellskin and two men beside. Thorolf Sledge dwelt at Sledgestead, up from Helgavatn, he gave chase to Hallvard, the Norwegian of Thorstein, till he plunged into the deep in a fen, to spite those brethren, and he killed Hallvard and another man. Berg the Rank, sister's son of Finnbogi the Strong of Borg came out (to Iceland from Norway.)

Thorgrim married the daughter of Skidi from Skidistead in Vatnsdale. There Jokul struck Berg with the hilt of his sword at a wedding feast,* for this Thorstein was required to go under three turfs † or sods at Hunavatns Thing and he would not. Then Finnbog challenged Thorstein to the Holmgang ‡ and Berg challenged Jokul.

---

* The Icelandic word is Brudlaup, that is the wedding journey or wedding procession.

† Three turfs or sods—in Icelandic Ganga undir jardarmen or to "gang or creep under a sod," partially detached from the earth and to let the blood mix with the mould as an ordeal.

‡ Holmganga—The Holmgang or Holmgoing was the duel or wager of battle fought on an Islet or Holm, which with the ancients was a kind of last appeal or ordeal, and wherever a þing or Parliament was held, a place was appointed for the wager or battle, as the Holm on the Aze river in the Alþing. The Holmgang differed from the duel in being accompanied by rites and governed by rules, while the latter was not. Some champions named in the Landnama or Book of Settlement were nicknamed from this as Holmgongu-Starri, Holmgongu-Krafn, Holmgongu-Mani. About A.D. 1006, the Holmgang was abolished by law in the Parliament on account of the unhappy feud between Gunnlaug Snaketongue and Skald Hrafn.

Faxe-Brand

[PART III, CHAPTER IV.]

Faxa-Brand dwelt above the Knolls, he accompanied Thorstein to the place of single combat in Vididales Island. There Jokul raised the pole of shame* to Finnbogi.

Groa and Thorey came out to Iceland from Norway. Groa dwelt at Grostead near to Hof. Thorey dwelt at Vesthope at Thorey's Gnup. There Groa made a Harvest Feast to Thorstein and the brothers. Thorstein dreamed three times that he ought not to go. Then Groa let loose; by means of witchcraft, a landslip falling down upon all the men who were present there. Thorstein vowed an offering to him who had created the sun, to the end that bearsark's fury might leave Thorir, that he might bring up Thorkel Krafla, Thorgrim's son from Korn river; by that means Thorgrim obtained the goðorð (Priesthood.†) Ingolf composed a love song on Valgerd, the daughter of Ottar. Then Ottar set afoot a lawsuit against Ingolf but that suit came to naught.

Then Thorir died but Ottar migrated thence. Gudbrand dwelt at Gudbrand's Stead. Thorir was outlawed on account of a woman. He went as a hired assassin ‡ to Ingolf, being enticed thereto by Ottar. He made a rush at Gudbrand, but Gudbrand slew him. Then they wanted to set on Ottar, but could not catch him. Ottar paid a penalty of five hundred of silver. Then Swart came

---

* This Niÿ-stong or pole of shame is described below in a note at III, 5. The custom has been kept up in Iceland to modern times. Upon the mountain roads and passes are stone pyramids on which passing travellers inscribe poetical ditties of a scurrilous nature, inscribing them to the person who may next pass. A horse head is placed there as in old times. In Lakeland such verses used to be placed on a heap of stones in the Pass of Nan Beild, and there was, I believe, something of a similiar character upon a stone near the Raise on the road between Grasmere and Thirlmere.

† The story is told in Vatnsdæla Saga how Thorir promised his godord to Thorstein, if by his vow to him who created the sun he should be healed of the fits of bearserk's fury that troubled him. He was healed of his distemper but lost his godord.

‡ The word is "Flugumadr," that is, fly man, a man who swallows the offered reward for his crime, as a fish does a fly-bait.

out

[PART III, CHAPTER IV.]

out to Mindakseyri from the Hebrides in a disabled ship; he was sent as a hired assassin against Ingolf and Gudbrand. Ingolf warded off the danger, but Swart slew Gudþrand. between the summer dairy and the winter folds* but there lay Swart also behind (fallen) on Swart's moor. Then Ottar paid in redemption three hundred in silver. Then Ingolf married Hild, the daughter of Olaf from Haukagil (Hawkgill.) Ingolf slew of the cavemen two men with one blow, in the summer shed in Micklagil (Micklegill) and three men beside. There his comrade fell and he was himself so sorely wounded that he died a short time afterwards.

Thorgil Yeller dwelt at Svinavatn (swinewater) and had come out with Audun Skokul; his sons were Digr-Orm and Thorkel, who slew Skarphedin Vefred's son at Vatnskard. Glædir was Thorgil Yeller's brother's son and sister's son of Gudmund the Mighty. Thorkell Krafla slew Thorkel from Helgavatn at a public meeting at Korn river, being 11 years old. Afterwards Thorkel Krafla went abroad and was with Sigurd, the son of Hlodver.† Thorkel, the son of Thorgils, married Hild, the daughter of Thororm from Thorormstongue, and at the bridewain Thorkell slew Glædir. Hildr, the daughter of Hermund, the son of Eyvind, kept company with him; he hid himself in Krafla-cave, under a waterfall in Vatnsdale-river.

Thordis the Seer gave this counsel, that Thorkel should throw the metal-bossed end of her belt, which was called Hegnuðr ‡ (the avenger) at the head of Gudmund the Mighty, when at the Doom of Judgment Seat, and he, Gudmund, would then forget what he should say; but

---

* ' Sel,' a dairy away from the house in outlying pastures, used in summer; ' vetrhús,' winter houses, folds or pens for grown sheep in winter.

† Earl of Orkney.

‡ Hegnuðr, *the chastiser* was the official name of the staff so used and this was a formal act.

they,

[PART III, CHAPTER IV.]

they, Gudmund and his, received two hundreds in silver. Then took Thorkel the lands of Hof=The Temple; and the Priesthood, and had it whilst he lived; he married Vigdis, the daughter of Olaf from Haukagil. In that time came out Fridrek the Bishop, with Thorvald, the son of Kodran, and abode at Gillriver with Orm Kodranson and his sons. The Bishop was at an autumn feast at Olaf's, and there the Bishop consecrated the fire *; there also were two Bearserks and they were both named Hauk; they walked through the fire and were both burned, and the place was afterwards named Haukagil; there was Thorkel baptised and all the Vatnsdalers. He caused a church to be reared at Hof † and there were all the men of his district interred.

Eyvindr settles Svindale. Ævarr comes to Blanda river mouth. Settles Langdale all across the Hause and shares his lands with his ship's crew. Vefreyd settles Moberg. Gaut settles Gauts-dale and Hauk settles near Hauk's pits. Holti at Holtisland. Fostolf and Thorstolf settle Engihlid in Langdale. Fatal feud between them and Ulfhedin.

CHAPTER V. There was a man named Eyvindr Audkula; he settled all Svindale (Swinedale) and dwelt at Audkulastead. There was a man named Thorbjorn Kolka; he settled Kolka-moors and abode there while he lived. Eyvinder Sorkvir settled Blandadale, as has been written before; his son was Hromund the Halt, who slew Hogni, the son of Ingimund, then when Mar and Ingimund fought about Deildarhjalli, for this he was

---

* Ok vigði biskup þar elda. The Bishop consecrated the fire so that the Berserks could not walk through it unharmed, which was the ordinary method by which they displayed their power of witchcraft.

† This is an example of the place where was an heathen temple becoming the site of a Christian place of worship.

exiled

exiled from the Northern Quarter. His sons were Hastein and Thorbjorn, who fought with Steilu-Helgi in Hruta-firth. Another son of Eyvind was Hermund, the father of Hild, whom Avaldi the son of Ingald had for wife; their children were Kolfinna, whom Gris the son of Seming had to wife, and Brand who slew Galti the son of Ottar at the Hunavatn's Thing on account of a libellous * rhyme by Hallfled.

There was a man named Ævarr, the son of Ketil Helluflagi=(slate river or slate splitter) and Thurid the daughter of King Harald Goldbeard from Sogn. Ævarr had with his wife a son named Vefreyd. The sons of Ævarr bastard-born were these: Karli and Thorbjorn Strug and Thord the Mickle. Ævarr went to Iceland, leaving off Viking raids, together with his sons, all but Vefreyd. With him went out to Iceland Gunnsteinn his kinsman, and Audolf and Gautr; Vefreyd remained behind sea-roving.

Ævarr brought his ship to Blanda mouth; by that time all the lands to the west of Blanda were occupied. Ævarr went up along Blanda to seek for himself a landtake, and when he came to that place which is called Moberg's-brinks, he stuck up there a long pole and said that there he took a dwelling site for his son Vefreyd. After that he settled all Langdale up from thence and likewise north across the Hause †; there he shared lands with his ship's crew.

Ævarr abode in Ævar's Skard. Vefreyd came out afterwards to the mouth of the Gaunga Skard's-river and

---

* The term for libel or contumely as here used is " Nid," as a law term this kind of libel made a man subject to outlawry. Another, and graver kind of libel, was the carving of a person's likeness (tre-nid) in an obscene position upon an upright post or pole (nidstong). When the post was put up a horse's head was also put up and a man's head was carved upon the end of the pole with dire runes and imprecations.

† Icelandic " Hals," a mountain neck or pass, and is equivalent to Hause found with the same meaning in Lakeland.

walked

[PART III, CHAPTER V.]

walked from the north to his father, and his father knew him not ; they wrestled so fiercely that all the benches in the house were forced out of their places before Vefreyd told who he was. He set up house at Moberg as it had been planned, and Thorbjorn Strug at Strugstead, and Gunstein at Gunsteinstead, and Karli at Karlistead, and Thord at Micklestead, Audolf at Audolfstead. Gaut settled Gautsdale, * he was one-handed (einhender). Eyvind Sorkvir and his friends put an end to themselves for they were unwilling to live after Ingimund the Old.

Hauk † dwelt at the place which now is called Hauks-grafir=Hauksgraves (meaning Hauks pits). Vefreyd married Gunnhild, the daughter of Eirek from Goddales, the sister of Holmgang-Starri. Their sons were Ulf-hedinn, whom Thjostolf slew at Grindalæk (Grind-brook) and Skarphedinn, whom Digr-Ormr slew in Vatnskard, and Hunraud the father of Mar, the father of Haflidi. The daughter of Hunraudar was named Halldora, the mother of Vigdis, the mother of Ulfhedinn, the father of Rafn, the father of Hallbera, the mother of Valdis, the mother of Snorri, the father of Hallbera, whom Markus of Melar the son of Thord had for wife. There was a man named Holti, who settled Langdale out from Moberg, and dwelt at Holti'sstead, he was the father of Israud, the father of Isleif, the father of Thorvald, the father of Thorarin the sage. The daughter of Thorvald was Thordis, whom Halldor, the son of Snorri the godi took to wife. Their daughter was Thorkatla whom Gudlaug Thorfinnson in Straumfjord ‡ had for wife, thence are the Sturlungs § descended and the men of Oddi.

---

* Compare Goats or Gaitswater in High Furness, also Gaitscale and Gaits Hause near to it.
† Compare Hawkshead, Hawkesdale.
‡ Streamfirth.
§ The Sturlungs were the most noted family in Iceland.

Another

[PART III, CHAPTER V.]

Another daughter was Gudrun who was the wife of Kjartan the son of Asgeir from Vatnsfirth, their children were Thorvald and Ingirid, whom Gudlaug the priest married; Foslolf and Thjoslolf settled in Eingihlid in Langdale. They took in a certain outlaw, named Thorgrim, the same whom Hunraud and Thoralf Leikgodi slew on the Keel-mountain.

After that Fostolf and Thjostolf slew Ulfhedin, the brother of Hunraud, at Grindbrook, they abode then at Holt; but Finn of Breida-bolstead in Vestrhope, the kinsman of Fotslof, and son of Jorund gave them quarter and Thorkell got them a berth far abroad. Ulfhedinn concealed his wounds and begged that no revenge should be sought, saying he was minded to think that it was fated to no one to wreak it. Afterwards Fostolf and Thjostolf slew east in Norway, Skum the freedman of Hunraud—very rich* in possessions and sent all his wealth out to Hunraud and then they were wholly at peace again. There was a man named Holmgang-Mani, who settled Skagaströnd to the west of the Foss† river, and to the east to Mani's-Hummock and dwelt in Mani's-wick, his daughter was the wife of Thorbrand in Dales, the father of Mani, the father of Kalf the Scald.

Eilif Eagle settles land from Manis-Hummock to Gunnguskeld river and Lax-river-dale. Sæmund from the Hebrides brings his ship to the mouth of Gaunga-skards river. Settles land from Sæmunds slope to Vatn's-Skard. Skefil contemporary with Sæmund settles land beyond the Sand river. Settlements of his descendants. Ulfljot settles Langholt. Alfgeir settles Algeirs fields up to Machfells river. Settlement by Hrosskell in Svart-river-dale.

---

* The Icelandic word is " fe " meaning moveable possessions. In Scotland it is used in this sense :—" My riches are my penny fe."—Burns.
† Foss is the Icelandic equivalent of Lakeland Force, a waterfall.

CHAPTER

[PART III, CHAPTER VI.]

CHAPTER VI. There was a man named Eilif Orn*=
eagle, the son of Atli, the son of Skidi the Old, the son of
Bard in Al. The son of Eilif *the eagle* was Kodran at
Gill river and Thjodolf the godi at Hof=Temple on
Skagastrand, and Eystein, the father of Thorvald Tinrod
and Thorstein 'heidrnenning' and Orn in Fljot. Eilif
settled land up from Mani's-Hummock to Gaungaskard-
river and Lax-river-dale and abode there. Eilif had for
wife Thorlaug the daughter of Sæmund from Hlid; their
sons were Solmund the father of Gudmund the father of
Slaughter-Bardi and his brothers. Another was Atli the
Strong, who had for wife Herdis the daughter of Thord
from Hofdi; their children were Thorlaug whom Gudmund the mighty had for wife, and Thorarinn, who had
for wife Halla, the daughter of Jonund Neck, their son
was Styrbjorn, who had for wife Yngvild the daughter
of Steinraud, the son of Hedin of Hedinshofdi, their
daughter was Arndis whom Hamall the son of Thormod
the son of Thorkel Moon, had for wife. Sæmund from
the Hebrides was the companion of Ingimund the Old and
as has been written he brought his ship to the mouth of
the Gaungu Skard† river. Sæmund settled all Sæmund's
slope to Vatns Skard,† above Sæmund's brook, and dwelt
at Sæmunds-stead; his son was Geirmund who abode
there afterwards. The daughter of Sæmund was Regin-

---

* Orn and Ari, both meaning eagle, are often found as men's names, and
compounded as place names. Ari, the compiler of the Book of the Settlement,
is the most eminent example of its use as a man's name.

† This word Skard occurs often in the Book of the Settlement and is worthy of
special note as entering into the origin of many place names. Skard, as a common noun, means (1) a *notch* or *chink* in the edge of a thing, (2) a *mountain
pass*, as in the phrase 'vestr yfir skordin'=west over the mountain passes;
with this meaning it is used of the place names in the text, and also as the origin
of many names in Iceland, *e.g.*, Skard, Skord, Skardverjar=the men from
Skard, Skardaleid=the way through Skard or the mountain pass (compare
Scarf Gap, a pass in Cumberland). Skardsheidr, Skardsstrond, Vatnsdal's
Skard, Ljosavatns Skard, Kerlingar Skard, Haukadale Skard, Geita Skard.

[PART III, CHAPTER VI.]

leif whom Thorodd hjalmr* had for wife; their daughter was Hallbera, the mother of Gudmund the mighty, the father of Eyjolf, the father of Thoreyj, the mother of Sæmund the learned. Another son of Sæmund was named Arnhalld, the father of Rjupa, whom Thorgeir, the son of Thord from Hofdi had for wife, their son was Halldor from Hof.

There was a man named Skefill who came to the mouth of Gaungaskard river in the same week as Sæmund, and whilst Sæmund marked out for himself his landtake by fire, Skefill occupied all the land beyond the Sand † river, which he took from Sæmund's landtake without his leave (ólofi ‡) and Sæmund allowed it to be so settled. There was a man named Ulfljot, he settled all Longholt below Sæmund's brook. Thorkell Vingnir was the son of Skidi the old, he settled all the land about Vatn's Skard, and Swart river dale, his son was Arnmod the squinter, the father of Galti, the father of Thorgeir, the father of Styrmir, the father of Hall, the father of Kolfinna.

There was a man named Alfgeir who settled land about Alfgeir's fields and up to Mælifells river and abode in Alfgeirs fields. There was a man named Thorvid, who settled the land from Mælifells river to Gill's river.

Hrosskell was the name of a man who settled the whole of Swart-river-dale and all the lands of Yrarfell by

---

* Hjalmr=the Helm or Helmet from the sense of covering; it is also applied to the clouds which were called hulid's hjalmr=a hiding helm or cap of darkness. The Helm is the cloud that descends upon Cross fell, when the Helm winds prevail. The Helm winds take their name from this Helm or cloud covering.

† Sand has the same meaning as common noun, and in place names in Icelandic and in English.

‡ Ólofi is from ó or u=*not*, and lofa (1) To praise, (2) To permit, and hence means as in this passage *without permission*. The process is something like what is called *squatting* in the American Settlements. There are place names in Cumberland and also in Yorkshire which seem to indicate that the original settler has taken land without leave as Unthank.

the

[PART III, CHAPTER VI.]
the advice of Eirek, he took land as far down as Gilhagi
and abode at Irafell; he had a thrall who was named
Rodrek whom he sent up along Mælifell's-dale to seek
for settlements southwards about the mountain tracts.
He came to the gill which lays to the south of Mælifell,
and which now is called Rodrek's Gill, then he set down
his new barked staff which they called Land* Konnud=
land-scanner and thence withall he returned home.

*Eirek, a Norwegian, settles Goddale down to North River.
Contends with Vekell the Shapechanger.*

CHAPTER VII. There was a man of renown named
Eirek; he went from Norway to Iceland, he was the son
of Hroald the son of Geirmund the son of Eirek Ordig-
skeggja or Shockbeard. Eirek settled land from Gill's
river round all Goddale and adown to Northriver, he
dwelt at Hof in Goddales. Eirek had for wife Thurid
the daughter of Thord Skeggi, the sister of Helga whom
Ketilbjorn the Old at Mossfell had to wife. The children
of Eirek and his wife were Thorkell and Hroald, Thorgeir
and Holmgang-Starri, and Gunnhild. Thorgeir the son
of Eirek had for wife Yngveld the daughter of Thorgeir;
their daughter was Rannveig, whom Bjarni the son of
Broddhelgi had for wife. Gunnhild the daughter of Eirek
was the wife of Vefreyd, the son of Ævar.
    There was a man named Vekell, the Shapechanger,†
who settled land down from Gill's river to Mælifell's
river, and dwelt at Mælifell, he heard about the journey
of Rodrek, and a short time afterwards he went south

---

* Land Kenning=to survey land with a view to taking possession of it. By
setting down his staff Rodrek formally took possession of the land. See a
a remarkable parallel in Joshua XVIII, 8-9.
    † The word here used for Shapechanger is ham-ramr which means a man who
is able to change his shape, especially by being subject to fits that impart to him
supernatural strength.

into

[PART III, CHAPTER VII.]

into the mountain tracts in search of settlements and
came to those howes which now are called Vekell's
Howes; he shot forth an arrow between the Howes and
then turned back again.   But when Eirek in Goddales
learned this he sent his thrall who was named Raungud
south into the mountain ranges, and he went still in
search of lands that might be settled; he came south to
the head waters of the river Blanda and thence he went
up along the river which flows to the west of Vinverja-
dale, and made his way westward till he came upon the
lava between Reykjavellir and the Keel (mountain), and
there he came upon the track of a man which he judged
lay from the south; there he raised that beacon which
is now called Raungud's Beacon*; then he went back,
and Eirek gave him his freedom in return for his journey,
and from that time began journeys across the mountains
that divide the Southlanders' quarter from the Northlanders'.

There was a man named Kraku (or Crow) Hreidar and
Ofeig Danglebeard his father son of Ox-Thorir; father
and son arrayed their ship for Iceland; but when they
came within sight of land then Hereidar went up to the
mast and said that he would not cast overboard the High
Seat Pillars, and said he thought it was an idle thing to
frame one's counsel on such a custom; but that he would
rather make a vow to Thor to the end that he would
guide him to the land settlements he sought, and that
there he would fight for lands if already taken.   So he
came into Skagafirth and sailed his ship up on to Burg-

---

* Varda from Varda, to warn, is applied to a pile of stones or wood used to
warn wayfarers; in Iceland Varda is the popular name of the Stone Cairns
erected on mountains and high places to warn the wayfarer of the course of the
way, or defining, in the present instance, the meeting of landtakes, shires and
quarters.   Notices of stones thus used as land divisions are often found in the
earlier historical Books of the Old Testament; that one is most remarkable for
its resemblance to the present passage which occurs in Genesis XXXI, 45 and
following verses.

sand

[PART III, CHAPTER VII.]

sand for a wreck. Havard hegri (or heron) came to him and bade him come and be with him, and there he was at Hegraness through the winter. In spring Havard asked him what he had made up his mind to do, and he said that he was minded to fight with Sæmund for land; but Havard hindered his doing this, saying that that had never come to a good end, and bade him go rather to meet Eirek in Goddale and take advice from him : "for that he is the wisest man in this country-side." This Hreidar did. But when he met Eirek he bade him give up the thought of such unpeace, saying how unbecoming it was that men should be at odds while yet there were so few folk in the land. He said that he would rather give him all that tongue of land down from Scale-moor, for thither, he said, that Thor had guided him, and thitherward had the prow (of his ship) looked, when he ran upon Burg-sand ; that landtake, he said, was plenteous for himself and his sons. With this choice Hreidar fell in and dwelt at Stonestead ; he chose to die into * Mælifell. His son was Ofeig Thinbeard the father of Bjorn, the father Tongue-stein.

Eirek and Önund the wise contend for land east of Mark Gill. Taking possession of the land by the fire arrow. Thorbrand's hospitality. Horse racing and fighting.

CHAPTER VIII. There was a man named Önund the Wise who settled land up from Mark-Gill, the eastern valley-side, all to the east thereof (*i.e.* of Mark-gill) ; but when Eirek was minded to bestir himself to take possession of the whole valley, all along the western side of the gill, then Onund cast hallowed lots† to the end that he

---

* *Die into*, for explanation see note on Holy Hill, page 52 and 53.

† 'Blótspánn' (probably the same as ' hlautviðr,' in 'Voluspá,' and ' hlutr' in many instances) a chip which accompanied by some religious rite, was dropped ('fella') from some height to the floor, to show which of two alternatives the 'face' declared. In its religious aspect the custom still lives in Iceland in choosing names for new-born infants, when the chip is let drop down from the main beam of the chancel of the church.

might

[PART III, CHAPTER VIII.]

might know at what time Eirek would go and take possession of the dale, and Önund was the quicker and shot across the river with a tinder or fire-arrow and hallowed for himself the land on the western side of the river and built his house *between the rivers.**

There was a man named Kari who settled land between the North-river and Mark-Gill and dwelt at Flattongue. † He was called Tongue-Kari; from him are the Silver-steadings descended. There was a man named Thor-brand Orrek who settled land up from Bolstead ‡ river all Silversteadslope and all North-river-dale on the northern side, and dwelt at Thorbrandstead, and let there be made so great a fire hall eldhus §(=hall or reception room), that all men who passed on that side of the river, might take through it their horses with their loads and there should meat be welcome to all men. Orreksheath up from Hakastead took its name from him, he was the most noble of men and of a most high degree.

There was a man named Hjalmolf who settled land about (Blonduhlid) Blandaslope, ‖ his son was Thorgrim Kuggi, the father of Odd in Axlarhaga, the father of Sela-Kalf, from thence are sprung the Axlhegings. Thorir Doveneb was a freedman of Ox-Thorir; he brought his ship to the mouth of the Göngu-Skard-river, then was all the countryside settled towards the west, so he went north-wards over the Jokul river at Landbrot and settled land between Glodafeykis-river and Deep river (Djupár) and

---

* Milli á = "between or among the rivers." The Latin phrase for this is "in interamnio," and the Greek equivalent is found in the Scripture name Mesopo-tamia which is the name of the territory between the Tigris and the Euphrates.

† Upon an estate which I know well, in Cumberland, two level fields situated together are called Tongue Flat.

‡ Bol means a *dwelling* and finds an equivalent, I think, in such names as Bolton, Bootle, Boot, Bothel.

§ Called eldhus or fire house because the fire was kept up there.

‖ Blonduhlid = *the slope up from the river Blanda.*

dwelt

[PART III, CHAPTER VIII.]

dwelt at Flymoor (Flugumyri). At that time a ship came to the mouth of Kolbein's River freighted with live stock but they lost a certain young mare in Brimness woods; but Thorir Doveneb bought the reversion and found her afterwards; she was the fleetest of all horses and was called Fly.

There was a man named Orn, he wandered from corner to corner through the land, and was a wizard; he waylaid Thorir in Vinverja-dale, as he was making his journey south over the Keel, and laid a wager with Thorir as to which of their horses might be the fleetest, for he had a right good horse himself. Each of them staked a hundred in silver. Afterwards they rode south across the Keel, until they came to that racing course* which was afterwards called Doveneb's Course. So great was the difference in the speed of horses that Thorir having completed his course returned back again and met Orn half-way on the course. Orn took the loss of his wager so ill that he would not live, and he went off up under that mountain which is now called Arnarfell, and there he made an end of himself, and Fluga (Fly) stood left there, for she was very weary. But when Thorir was returning from the Thing he found there by Fly, a stallion; grey with a black mane†; from him she had conceived, and from her and the stallion was sprung Eidfaxi, which was taken abroad, and gave death to seven men on the shore of the lake of Mjors in one day, and itself came to an end here. Fly was lost in a bog at Flymoor.

Kollsvein the Strong was the name of a man who settled land between Thvera‡ (=Thwart river) and Gorge-river and dwelt at Kollveinstead over against Thwart river, he kept up sacrifices at Hofstead.

---

* Skeid = 1st a race, 2nd a race course.
† The Icelandic word is " föxottan."
‡ Thver is used of a stream which is tributary or affluent to another stream.

The

⌈PART III, CHAPTER IX.⌉
The Royal connexions in Sweden and Russia of Gorm. His settlements in Iceland. Ondott's settlements.

CHAPTER IX.   There was a man named Gunnolf who settled land between the Thwart river (Thvera) and Glodafeyki's river, and dwelt at Hvamm.

There was a renowned lord in Sweden called Gorm, he had for wife Thora, the daughter of King Eirek at Upsala; their son was named Thorgils, he had to wife Elin, the daughter of King Burislaf of Novgorod in the east (*i.e.* from Russia), and of Ingigerd the sister of Dagstygg the King of the giants.   Their sons were Hergrim and Herfinn, who had to wife Halla, the daughter of Hedin, and of Arndis, the daughter of Hedin. The daughter of Herfinn and Halla was named Groa, she was the wife of Hroar, and their son was Slettu-Bjorn, who settled land first between the Grjot river and the Deild-river, before Hjalti and Kolbein came out; he dwelt at Slettubjornstead.   His children were Örnolf, who had for wife Thorljot, the daughter of Hjalti, the son of Skalp, and Arnbjorn, who had for wife Thorlaug the daughter of Thord of Hofdi, and Arnodd, who had to wife Thorny, the daughter of Sigmund, the son of Thorkel, whom Glum slew.   A daughter of Slettu-Bjorn was named Arnfrid, whom Spak-Bodvar, the son of Ondott had to wife.   Ondott came out to the mouth of Kolbein's river and bought from Slettu-Bjorn land down from Halsgrof on the eastern side and out to the mouth of Kolbein's river, and on the west side down from that brook which is met with out away from Nautabui (=cattle booths), and up unto Gorge-river and he abode at Vidvik. Sigmund of Vestfold had to wife Ingibjorg the daughter of Raudsruggu=the rocking cradle, in Naumadale, the sister of Thorstein Svarfad; their son was Kolbein who went to Iceland and settled land between Grjot river and Deildriver, Kolbeinsdale and Hjaltdale.

Remarkable

[PART III, CHAPTER X.]

Remarkable Arvals. A Drapa. Verses on the appearance of the sons of Hjalti at Thorskafjard Thing. The discovery of Vinland the Good, i.e. America. Thord and his nineteen children.

CHAPTER X. Hjalti the son of Thord Skalp came to Iceland and settled Hjaltdale by the advice of Kolbein, and dwelt at Hof. His sons were Thorvald and Thord, both men of great renown. The Arvals* of their father were the most notable held in Iceland ; there were there twelve hundred invited guests, † and all the men of high degree were seen off with gifts. At those Arvals Odd the Broadfirther brought forth that drapa (laudatory ode) which he had composed concerning Hjalti. Before this Glum the son of Geiri had summoned Odd to the Codfirth Thing ; then the sons of Hjalti went from the north by ship to Steingrimsfirth, and went from the north over the Heath by that way which is now called Hjalt-dalers' hollow ; when they came to the Thing they were so excellently apparrelled that men thought that the Aesir or Gods were come. To this effect the following stanzas were recited :—

> Hark ye, men deft of slaughter !
> No stem o' the steel[1] misdoubted
> That e'en the gods were going
> There were the sons of Hjalti,
> The hardy-hearted, strode forth
> Into the Thing assembled
> In Codfirth, all bedecked with
> The holt-fish[2] gleaming spangles.

---

* The word in the Icelandic is 'erfi' or Arvals, and in name and in other surroundings these Icelandic Arvals seem to furnish a remarable parallel to the Arval feasts that prevailed in early times in Cumberland, Westmorland, and North Lancashire.

† The Icelandic word is boðs menn or "bidden men" from bjóða *to invite.* The north English dialect word for inviting to a funeral is "bid," and the district to be invited often conterminous with a Parish or Township is called "a bidding." The word is found in Old English and the invitatory Prayer in the Liturgy is called "the bidding prayer."

(1) Stem o' the steel = warrior, man.
(2) Holt-fish = serpent, whose lair is gold.

From

⌊PART III, CHAPTER X.⌋

From the sons of Hjalti is descended a great and noble family. There was a famous man named Thord, he was the son of Bjorn byrðusmjör=*Keg-butter* the son of Hroald Rig, the son of Bjorn Ironside, the son of Ragnar *lodbrok*=hairy breeches. Thord went to Iceland, and settled Hofdistrand in Skagasfirth between Unadales river and Hrolleifdales river and dwelt at Hofdi. Thord married Thorgerd the daughter of Thorir hima and Fridgerd, the daughter of Kjarval a King of Ireland. They had nineteen children. Bjorn was a son of theirs, he married Thurid the daughter of Ref from Bard and their children were Arnorr Kerlingarnef=*old woman's nose*, and Thordis the mother of Orm, the father of Thordis, the mother of Botolf, the father of Thordis, the mother of Helga, the mother of Gudny, the mother of the Sturlusons.

Thorgeir was the name of another son of Thord he married Rjupa, the daughter of Arnhald, the son of Sæmund ; their son was Halldor at Hof. Snorri was a third son, he married Thorhild rjupa,* the daughter of Thord the Yeller. Their son was Thord *horsehead*, the father of Karlsefni who discovered Vinland † the good, the father of Snorri the father of Steinun, the mother of Thorstein Wrongdoer, the father of Gudrun the mother of Halla, the mother of Flosi, the father of Valgerd, the

---

* Rjupa=ptarmigan.

† Vinland or Wineland is the name given to the chief settlement of the early Norsemen in North America, represented by part of Massachusetts and Rhode Island. The first Norseman who saw it was Bjarne Herjulfson, who was driven there by a storm in 986, when he was voyaging from Iceland to Greenland. He did not land however. Leif, son of Eric the Red, visited the land about the year 1000, and a German in his company having found grapes growing wild as in his native land, called the land Vinland or Wineland. The most famous, however, of the Norse explorers, was Karlsefni, as mentioned above. In 1007 he sailed from Greenland to Vinland with a crew of 160 men. He remained there for three years and then returned. After this no further attempts were made by them at colonisation. Rafn (*Antiquitates Americanæ*) and Finn Magnusen show that Columbus got his first hints of a new world from these early Icelandic expeditions. Finn Magnusen establishes the fact that Columbus did visit Iceland in 1477, fifteen years before he undertook his expedition across the Atlantic.

mother

mother of Knight Erlend the Strong. Thorvald Holbarki
(=without a roof to his mouth) was the fourth son, he
came one autumn to Thorvardstead to Smidkel and
tarried there awhile; thence he went up to the cave of
Surt and recited there a drapa which he had made
on the giant in the cave. Afterwards he married the
daughter of Smidkel, and their daughter was Jorun the
mother of Thorbrand in Skarfness. Bard was the fifth
son of Thord, he married Thorarna, the daughter of
Thorodd the Helmef, their son was Dadi the Skald.
Söxolf was the sixth son of Thord, the seventh Thorgrim,
the eighth Hroar, the ninth Knorr, the tenth Thormod
Skull, the eleventh Stein. The daughter of Thord was
Thorlaug, who married Arnbjorn, the son of Sléttu-bjorn,
their daughter was Gudlaug, whom Thorleik the son of
Hoskuld had to wife, their son was Bolli. Herdis was
another daughter of Thord, and her Atli the Strong had
for wife; Thorgrima Skeidarkinn was the third, the
fourth Arnbjorg, the fifth Arnleif, the sixth Asgerd, the
seventh Thurid, the eighth Fridgerd, in Hvamm.

The son of Arnor, the son of Bjorn, the son of Thord,
was Eldjarn, the father of Hall, the father of Ragnhild,
the mother of Rafn, the father of Hallbera, the mother of
Valdis, the mother of Snorri, the father of Hallbera,
whom Markus the son of Thord at Melar had for wife.
Hrolleif the Mickle settled Hrolleifsdale, as has been
written before; Thord drove him from the north as an
outlaw, on account of the slaughter of Odd, the son of
Uni, thence he went into Vatnsdale.

*Fridleif the Swede, Floki, and other settlers. Bard from the
Hebrides, and Bruni the White settle Narrowdales.
Rotation iu the ownership of land.*

CHAPTER XI. Fridleif was the name of a man, a
Gautlander

[PART III, CHAPTER XI.]

Gautlander * by his father's side, his mother was named Bryngerd and was a Fleming by nation. Fridleif settled all Slettahlid and Fridleifsdale between Fridleifsdale's river and Staff river, and dwelt at Holt, his son was Thjodar, the father of Ari and Bryngerd, the mother of Tungu Stein. Floki, the son of Vilgerd, the daughter of Horda-Kari, went to Iceland and settled Flokadale, between the Flokadal's river and Reek-Knoll; he dwelt at Mor. Floki had for wife Gro, the sister of Thord from Hofdi, their son was Oddleif Staff, who dwelt at Staff-Knoll and had a quarrel with the sons of Hjalti; the daughter of Floki was Thjodgerd, the mother of Kodran, the father of Thjodgerd, the mother of Kodran, the father of Kar in Vatnsdale. There was a man, a Swede by kindred, named Thord Knapp (=Knob) the son of Bjorn at Haug †; there was another man named Auger-Helgi; they went in the same ship to Iceland and came to Haganess.

Thord settled land up from Stifla to the Tongue river and dwelt at Knappstead; he married Æsa the daughter of Ljotolf godi; their son was Hafr, who had for wife Thurid, the daughter of Thorkel from Goddale; their son was Thorarin, the father of Ofeig. Auger-Helgi settled land to the east up from Haganess to Flokadale's river below Bard, and up to Tongue river and dwelt at Grindill; he had to wife Gro the Keen-eyed; their children were Thorhrolf and Arnor, who fought with Fridleif at Staffs Knoll, and Thorgerd, whom Geirmund the son of Sæmund had for wife, and Ulfhlid, whom Arnor the son of Skefil in Gaunguskard had in marriage; their son Thorgeir Swaggerer, who slew Sacrifice Mar at Moberg. Thorunn Blue-cheek was yet another daughter of Auger-Helgi.

---

* From Gautland in South Sweden.
† Haug is " the How," so commonly found in northern place names.

[PART III, CHAPTER XI.]

Bard, from the Hebrides, settled land up from Stifla to Narrowdale river; his son was Hall the Narrowdaler, the father of Thurid, whom Arnorr Carline-neb had for wife. Bruni the White was the name of a renowed man, the son of Harek, an Earl of the Upplandings (in Norway); he went to Iceland at his own desire and settled land between Narrowdale river and Ulf'sdales; he dwelt at Brunastead; he married Arnora the daughter of Thorgeirr Madcap, the son of Ljotolf the godi; their sons were Ketill, and Ulfhedin, and Thord, whence are the Bardmen descended.

Ulf the Viking, and Olaf Beck * or Stream went in the same ship to Iceland. Ulf settled Ulfsdales and abode there. Olaf Beck was the son of Karl from Birchisle in Halogaland, he slew Thorri the Black, and was outlawed on account of that. Olaf settled all the dales to the west and a part of Olaf's Firth to the meeting (till mots†) with the lands of Thormod, and dwelt at Kviabekk, Foldbeck; his sons were Steinod, the father of Bjorn, and Grimolf, and Arnodd, the father of Vilborg, the mother of Karl the Red.

There was a man named Thormod the Strong, he slew Gyrd, the grandfather by the mother's side of Skjalg in Jadar, and was for that exiled and went to Iceland; he brought his ship to Siglufirth and sailed up to Thormodseyri, whence he named the bay Siglu (=mast)-firth; he settled all Siglufirth between Ulfsdales and Hvanndales, and dwelt at Sigluness; he quarrelled with Olaf Beck about the Hvanndales and killed sixteen men before they

---

* Bekkr *stream* is in place-names found frequently in the North of England. The dialect term for a small stream is almost invariably " beck," hence we have it applied as place-name to Caldbeck, Troutbeck, Kirkcambeck, also Beckermet=the meeting of the becks.

† Til mots=to the meeting. This mot, a meeting, is noteworthy, for we have it in such names as Moot Hall=meeting hall. Beckermet as above, and the mountain Muta near Bassenthwaite.

came

[PART III, CHAPTER XI.]

came to the agreement that they should have it on alternate * summers or summer about.

Thormod was the son of Harald the Viking, and he
had for wife Arngerd, the sister of Skidi from Skididale ;
their sons were Arngeirr the Keen, and Narfi the father
of Thrand, the father of Copse-isle † Narfii and Alrek,
who fought at Slettuhlid with Knor, the son of Thord.
Gunolf the Old, the son of Thorbjorn Thjoti=the rusher,
from Sogn ; he slew Vegeir, the father of Vebjorn, the
Sygna-kappa ‡=the Sogna champion, and went after-
words to Iceland ; he settled Olafsfjord on the eastern
side up to Reek river, and out to Vomula, and dwelt at
Gunnolf's river ; he had for wife Gro, the daughter of
Thorvard from Urdir, their sons were Steinolf, Thorir,
and Thorgrim.

Bjorn exiled from a burning in, in Sweden. Goes to Ire-
   land in Vestrviking. Eyvind his son settles in Ireland.
   Helgi the Lean, son of Eyvind, brought up in the Heb-
   rides. His adventures and final settlement in Iceland.

CHAPTER XII.   There was a man of great renown in
Gautland § named Bjorn, he was the son of Hrolf from
Am, he had for wife Hlif, the daughter of Hrolf, the son
of Ingjald, the son of Frodi the King; their son was
named Eyvind.   Bjorn got into strife with Sigfast, a

---

* The Icelandic phrase is " skyldi sitt sumar hvarr hafa "=each should have it
for his own summer. In some parts of Lakeland the system of such alternate
ownership was practised until very lately.
   † Hriseyjar-Narfi=Narfa of the Copsewood Island.
   ‡ Sygna-kappr or Sogni-kappr appears to mean that in the Province of Sogni
he was a sort of A.I. or " Cock of the walk." To kap in the Icelandic means to
beat or conquer. To cap, also, in the Cumberland dialect means to beat in
athletic or other contests. Anderson says of Kit Kraffit :—
         " He wan sebben belts afoor he was twenty,
            An in Scaleby needa teuk off the fit-bo ;
            Yet he kent o the Beyble, Algebera, Josephus,
            And *capt* the skeulmaister, exciseman an'o."
   § Gautland=Part of South Sweden.

relation

[PART III, CHAPTER XII.]

relation of Solver King of the Gauts (Sweden) concerning land, and Bjorn burned him in his house with thirty men. After that Bjorn went to Norway with eleven men, himself the twelfth, and Grim the hersir, the son of Kolbjorn Sneypis *=snaper or checker, took him in and he was with him for one winter. Then Grim wished to kill Bjorn for his money, so Bjorn went to Ondott Crow, who dwelt in Hvinisfirth in Agdir and he took him in.

Bjorn was in summer tide on Viking raids in the west vestrviking,† and in winter with Ondott, until Hlof, his wife, died in Gautland. Then came Eyvind, his son, from the eastward and took over the warships of his father; then Bjorn took to wife Helga, the sister of Ondott Crow, and their son was Thrand. Eyvinder went then on Viking raids in the west, and had a fleet fitted out for the coasts of Ireland. He married Rafarta, the daughter of Kjarval,‡ the king of the Irish, and settled down there; therefore he was called Eyvind the Eastman. He and Rafarta had a son who was called Helgi, whom they handed over for fostering into the Hebrides, and when they came there two winters afterwards, he was so starved that they did not know him; they brought him away with them and called him Helgi§ the Lean. He was brought up in Ireland, and when he was grown up he became a man of great honour; then he married Thorun the Horned, the daughter of Ketil Flatnose, and they had many children; their sons were named Hrolf and Ingjald. Helgi the Lean went to Iceland with his wife and children; there was with him also Hamund Hellskinn, his son-in-law, who had for wife Ingun, the daughter of Helgi.

---

* Snápe in the Cumberland dialect means to check or restrain.
† Vestrviking, *i.e.*, harrying in the west of British Islands.
‡ Kjarval was the King of Ossory.
§ He became one of the most distinguished of the Early Settlers, and the epithet of " The Lean," which he retained to the end of his life, must have constantly reminded him of his semi-starvation in the Hebrides.

Helgi

[PART III, CHAPTER XII.]

Helgi was very shifty in his faith*; he believed in Christ, but made vows to Thor for sea-faring and hardy deeds. Then when Helgi sighted Iceland, he went to inquire of Thor where he should make land, the answer directed him northward round the land; then Hrolf, his son, asked whether Helgi must hold into Dumbshaf (=the foggy sea†) if Thor should direct him thither, because the crew thought that now it was high time to leave the sea, inasmuch as the summer was in a great measure spent. Helgi took land outside Hrisey but inside of Svarfadardale; he was the first winter in Hamundstead. They had a very hard winter.

In the spring he went up to the top of Sunfell‡; there he saw how the land looked much blacker up the firth,§ which they called Island Firth, on account of the islands that lay there outside. After that Helgi bare to his ship all that he had there, while Hamund abode there behind. Helgi landed there at Boars' crag (Galtahamar), where he put ashore two swine, and the boar was named Solvi; they found them three winters afterwards in Solvadale, and then there were seventy swine. Helgi kenn'd, *i.e.* (surveyed with a view to settling) the whole district that summer, and settled all Island Firth between Sigluness and Rowanness, and made a great fire at every river mouth and thus hallowed to himself the whole district. He abode that winter at Bild's river, and in the spring he moved his household to Christness, and dwelt there during the remainder of his life. In the removing of his

---

* Helgi was very shifty in his belief. In Icelandic this is :—Helgi var blandinn mjök í trú. This mixed state of faith seems to have been common to the early settlers; we are told, however, in the concluding chapter of the Book of the Settlement that even this uncertain state of Chrisrian belief became extinguished in the course of generations, so that the land was entirely Heathen for nearly one hundred years on Icelandic form 120 winters.

† Dumbshaf, the misty or foggy sea, is here put for the Polar Sea.

‡ Solarfjall.

§ *i.e.* much more free from snow.

household

[PART III, CHAPTER XII.]

household Thorun was delivered of a child in Thorun's-isle in Island Firth river. There she brought forth Thorbjorg Holme-sun. Helgi believed in Christ and therefore gave his name to his dwelling. After that men took to settling in the landtake of Helgi, by his advice.

Settlement of Thorstein Svarfad. Origin of the Saga of the men of Svarfadar-dale. Hamund Hellskinn shares his lands with Orn.

CHAPTER XIII. There was a man named Thorstein Svarfad, the son of Raud Cradle in Naumudal; he married Hild, the daughter of Thrain, the black giant. Thorstein went to Iceland and settled Svarfad's-dale, by the counsel of Helgi. His children were Karl the Red, who dwelt at Karl's river, and Gudrun, whom Hafthor, the Viking, had for wife; their children were Klaufi and Groa, whom Griss Merryheart had for wife.

There was a man named Atli Illing, he slew Hafthor, and put Karl in irons; then Klaufi came unawares and slew Atli, and released Karl from out of irons. Klaufi had for wife Yngvild Redcheek, the daughter of Asgeir Redcloak, the sister of Olaf Knuckle-breaker, and of Thorleif; to spite them he ripped open a bag filled with club-moss * which they had gathered in his land; then sang Thorleif this verse :—

A hairless bag
Of mine cut Boggvir,
And Aleif's strap
And cloak, in likewise.
So shall Boggvir,
For bale † e'en ready,
Upon my life,
Be cut asunder.

---

* In Icelandic, jafnabelg=a bag filled with jafni, which is a herb used by dyers and called botanically lycopodium clavatum, or club-moss.

† The Icelandic word here used for misfortunes is böl. Dialect " bale," as in bale-fire, also baleful.

Therefrom

[PART III, CHAPTER XIII.]
Therefrom sprung the Saga of the men of Svarfad's-dale. There was a man named Karl who settled all Strönd (=the Strand*) out from Upsar to Migandi.

Hamund Hellskinn, the son of Hjor the King, shared lands with Orn his kinsman, when he came from the west, him, to wit, who had settled Ornfirth, and he dwelt at Orn's-ness; his daughter was Idunn, whom Asgeir Red-cloak had for wife. The son of Orn was Narfi, from whom Narfa-skerries take their name. He had for wife Ulfeid, the daughter of Ingjald from Gnupufell; their sons were Asbrand, the father of Slate-Narfi, and Eyjolf, father of Thorkel in Hagi, and Helgi, the father of Grim in Kalfskinn.

There was a man named Galmi, who settled Galma-strand, between Thorvald's-dale river and Reistar river; his son was Thorvald, the father of Orm, the father of Bairn-Thorodd, the father of Thorunn, the mother of Dyrfinna, the mother of Thorstein Smith, the son of Skeggi. Hamund gave land to Thorvald between Reistar river and Horg river, but before that he had had his abode in Thorvald's-dale.

There was a man named Geirleif, he settled Horg river-dale up to Mirk † river; he was the son of Hrapp and dwelt at Hagi the ancient, ‡ his son was Bjorn the rich, from whom the Audbrink-men are descended.

Settlement of Thord the Tearer and his relations in Horg-river-dale. Verses on the conflict between Steinrand and Blacksmith and Geirhild the witch-wife. Settlement of Audolf and Eyvind in Horgrivers-dale.

CHAPTER XIV. There was a man named Thord the

---

*The Strand as used here corresponds in meaning and application to the Strands in Netherwasdale, at the foot of Wastwater.
† Myrk=dark, Scottish mirk.
‡ Forna old corresponds with fairnis in bible of Ulphilas.

Tearer

[PART III, CHAPTER XIV.]

Tearer, he settled Horg* river-dale on one side from
Mirk river down to Drangi; his son was Ornolf, who
had for wife Yngvild, Sister-of-all, their sons were Thord
and Thorvard in Kristness, and Steingrim at Kropp.
Thord the Tearer gave Skolm, his kinsman, a share in
his landtake; his son was Thorolf the Strong, who
dwelt at Mirk river. Thorir Gianthunter was the name
of a man who was brought up in Ömd in Halogaland,
and fell out with Earl Hakon, the son of Grjotgard, and
went for that reason to Iceland. He settled all Oxen-
dale, and dwelt at Vatns river; his son was Steinraud (or
Redstone) the Strong, who restored many men to whom
fairies had done harm. There was a woman named
Geirhild, a woman skilled in witchcraft and a doer of
evil. Men who had the power of second sight saw how
that Steinraud came upon her unawares and she changed
herself into the semblance of a neat's skin full of water.
Steinraud † was a blacksmith and had a large iron goad
in his hand, of their meeting this was sung :—

> He who makes hammers clatter,
> Lets rod, of rods the biggest,
> E'er at his utmost, yell on
> The fluid-bag of Gunnhild.
> High, iron-staff inflicteth
> A pain exceeding heavy
> On the side o' th' hag of Hjalteyr,
> The troll's ribs are all swollen.

The daughter of Steinraud was Thorljot who married
Thorvard in Christness.

There was a man named Audolf, he went from Jadar

---

* Horga or Horg river doubtless takes its name from a Hörg, which was a
heathen place of worship.
 † This Steinraud or Redstone as applied to a blacksmith, seems to be taken
from his trade, the hematite being called red stone from its colour. In Furness
the iron miners are called red workers.

to

⌊PART III, CHAPTER XIV.⌋

to Iceland and settled Horg river-dale down from Thvart river to Bægis river and dwelt at the southernmost Bægis river.* He had for wife Thorhild, the daughter of Helgi the Lean, their daughter was Yngvild, who was the wedded wife of Thorodd Holm, the father of Arnljot, the father of Halldor, the father of Einar, the father of Jorun, the mother of Hall, the father of Gizur, the father of Thorvald, the father of Earl Gizur. Eystein, the son of Raudulf, the son of Ox-Thorir, settled land down from Bægis river to Kraeklingahlid, and dwelt at Lón, his son was Gunnstein, who had for wife Hlif, the daughter of Hedin from Mjola ; their children were Halldora, whom Fighting-Glum had for wife, and Thorgrim and Grim (Grim Shingle-leg.) Eyvind Cock was the name of a man of much renown, he came out late in the time of the land-takes, he owned a ship with Thorgrim, the son of Hlif, he was a kinsman of the sons of Ondott, they gave him land and he dwelt at Cockton and was called Town-cock, that place is now called Marbæli, he had for wife Thorny, the daughter of Storolf, the son of Ox-Thorir, his son was Snorri Hlidmannagodi or *the godi of the lea-men.*

Quick voyage of Thrand much sailing from the Orkneys. Grim slays Ondott. Grim burned in his house by the sons of Ondott. Terrible conflict resulting therefrom.

CHAPTER XV. Ondott Crow, who was mentioned before, became a mighty man when Bjorn his brother-in-law died. Grim the Hersir claimed for the King all his inheritance, inasmuch as he was a foreigner and his sons were west beyond sea. Ondott held to the wealth on behalf of Thrand his sister's son, and when Thrand heard of the death of his father, he sailed from the Hebrides by

---

* Implying that there were two Bægis rivers, one to the south of the other.

such

[PART III, CHAPTER XV.]

such a swift sailing that he was on that account named
Thrand *much-sailing*. When he had taken possession of
his inheritance he went to Iceland and took a settlement on the South land as will be related later on, and
because he did not receive the inheritance on behalf of
the King therefore Grim slew Ondott, and then in the
same night Signy, the wife of Ondott, carried on board
their ship all their chattels and went with their sons
Asgrim and Asmund, to Sighvat, her father, and then
sent her sons to Hedin, her foster father, in Sokndale;
not feeling at home there, however, they wanted to go
back to their mother; they came at Yule-tide to Ingjald
the Trusty in Hvin, and he took them in at the entreaty
of Gyda his wife.

In the summer after, Grim the Chieftain prepared an
entertainment for Audun, the Earl of King Harald, and
in the night when the ale was being brewed at the house
of Grim, the sons of Ondott burned him in his home and
took then a boat * belonging to Ingjald their foster
father and rowed away. Audun came to the entertainment as had been bespoken, and missed there a friend
instead; and early in the morning came the sons of
Ondott there to the sleeping-bower, *i.e.*, bedroom where
Audun lay, and hurled a beam at the door. Asmund
kept watch over the two house carles of the Earl and
Asgrim placed his spear point before the breast of the
Earl and bade him deliver up the weregild for his father;
he then handed over to him three gold rings and a kirtle
of costly stuff, from thence Asgrim gave to the Earl a
nickname and called him Audun Goat (*i.e.* coward.)

Afterwards they went to Sorreldale (Surnadalr) to the
house of Eirek Ale-fain, who took them in; then dwelt

---

* Icelandic Bátr, a boat of two or four oars.

there

[PART III, CHAPTER XV.]

there Hallstein Horse, another landed man,* and they held their Yule-drink together. Eirek first entertained Hallstein well and faithfully, then Hallstein afterwards entertained Eirek, but in an unfriendly manner and struck him with a deer's horn †; from thence Eirek went home but Hallstein sat behind with his house carles; then Asgrim went in and dealt to Hallstein a great wound, but the house carles gave out they had killed Asgrim, but he got out into the wood and a woman took him into a house underground and healed him so that he was quite whole of his hurt.‡

That summer Asmund went to Iceland and found that Asgrim his brother was dead. Helgi the Lean gave to Asmund, Krækling-slope, and he dwelt at Gler river, the southernmost, and when Asgrim was whole of his wounds Eirek gave him a long ship and he harried to the west by sea, but Hallstein died of his wounds. When Asgrim returned from the wars Eirek gave him Geirhild, his daughter, in marriage, and Asgrim went to Iceland. He dwelt at Gler river the northermost. Harald the King sent Thorgeir from Hvin to slay Asgrim; he was for one winter on the Keel in Hvinmen's-dale and brought nought about concerning the blood revenge. The son of Asgrim was Ellidagrim, the father of Asgrim, the father of Sigfus, the father of Thorgerd, the mother of Grim, the father of Sverting, the father of Vigdis, the mother of Sturla of Hvamm.

---

* Lendr madr " is a chieftain who holds lands from the King.
† The deer's horn was generally used, as on the present occasion, for a drinking cup.
‡ In an old Landnama Text (that of the Mela bok) which differs in some places much from the Copenhagen edition (1843) there is a curious addition to this story. It is there said that when Asgrim was in the wood overcome by the cold that the servants of Hallstein overtook him and wounded him fearfully with their spears. He afterwards came to an old woman (Kerling) who having killed a calf, which she had, placed the entrails upon him in such a way that when the servants of Hallstein came there after, they thought that these were his own entrails and that he was wounded to death. When they returned home however, the old woman tended and cured him in a cave.

[PART III, CHAPTER XVI.]

Settlement of Hamund " hellskin," Audun, Thorgeir, sons-in-law, and Ingjald, son of Helgi the Lean.

CHAPTER XVI.—Helgi the Lean gave Hamund his son-in-law, land between Merkgill and Skjalgdale's river, and he dwelt at Asp-knoll the southernmost, his son was Thorir, who abode there afterwards; he had for wife Thordis, the daughter of Kadal, their sons were Thorarin, who dwelt at Asp-knoll the northermost, and Thorvald Crook at Grund, but Thorgrim of Madder-fell was not her son, Vigdis was their daughter.

Helgi gave Thora his daughter, together with land up from Skjalgdales river to Neck or Haws, to Gunnar, the son of Ulfljot, who brought out laws to Iceland. He dwelt at Deepdale, their children were Thorstein, Ketill, and Steinmod, and their daughter Yngvild and Thorlaug.

Helgi gave Helga, his daughter, to Audun Rotten, the son of Thorolf Butter, the son of Thorstein Scurf, the son of Grim Kamban, together with land up from Neck or Haws to Villingdale; he dwelt in Saurby. Their children were Einar, the father of Eyjolf, the son of Valgerd, and Vigdis, the mother of Halli the White, the father of Orm, the father of Gellir, the father of Orm, the father of Halli, the father of Thorgeir, the father of Thorvard and Asi, the father of Gudmund the Bishop.

Einar, the son of Audun, had for wife Valgerd, the daughter of Runolf, their son was Eyjolf, who had for wife Hallbera, the daughter of Thorolf Helm, and they resided at Jorunstead for a long time, and afterwards at Madder-meads. Hallfrid was the daughter of Einar, the son of Eyjolf; she was the mother of Halldor, the father of Snorri, the father of Gudrun, the mother of Hrein the Abbot, the father of Valdis, the mother of Snorri, the father of Hallbera, whom Markus the son of Thord had for wife.

Vigfus

[PART III, CHAPTER XVI.]

Vigfus, the son of Fighting-Glum, slew Bard, the son of Halli the White, and on him was written the Poem of Bard wherein this is the refrain :—

> Bard cuts with the " skid "[1] of harbours,
> . The land of billows pathway.[2]

But Brúsi the brother of Bard and Orm composed these verses when Glum ran away from the Thing :—

> Oh, Gondul of the border![3]
> We have an even share in
> The honours of this fighting
> With steering trunks o' the stem-stud :[4]
> Yet Hlokk[5] that years for splendour,
> Methinks the trunks o' the fire
> O' the ship's garth[6] hied yet faster,
> Down brink than I e'er recked of.

Hamund " hellskin " married Helga, the daughter of Helgi, after Ingun her sister died, and their daughter was Yngvild, who was called Sister-of-all, whom Ornolf had for wife. Helgi gave to Hrolf, his son, all the lands to the east of Island-firth river, from Orn's-knoll upward, and he dwelt at Gnupufell, and raised there a great temple ; he married Thorarna, the daughter of Thrand Spindleshanks, their children were Haflidi the bountiful, and Valthjof, Vidar, Grani, and Bödvar, Ingjald, and

---

(1) " Skid." A well-known word as used by coach drivers for an iron slip for wheels to rest in on going down hill; is the same word as Icelandic skið, Norwegian " Ski," the ancient name being öndurr, in English commonly rendered snow shoe—" Skid of harbours=ship.

(2) The land of billows pathway=the tract over which the wave finds its way =surface of the sea, hence, sea, ocean.

(3) Gondul, a Valkyrja ; G. of the border=woman.

(4) Stem-stud=ships; steering trunks=commanders : the whole kenning= sea rovers, warriors, men.

(5) Hlokk, a valkyrja ; H. that yearns for splendour=woman fond of orna- ments, or of white shining flaxen garments.

(6) Ship's garth=shield ; the fire thereof=flashing sword, the trunk thereof= warrior, man.

Eyvind

[PART III, CHAPTER XVI.]

Eyvind, and a daughter Gudlaug, whom Thorkell the Black had for wife. Valthjof was the father of Helgi, the father of Thorir, the father of Arnor, the father of Thurid, the mother of Thordis, the mother of Vigdis, the mother of Sturla in Hvamm.

Helgi the Lean gave to Ingjald, his son, land out from Orn's-knoll to Thwart river the outer, he dwelt at Thwart river the inner and raised there a great temple; he had for wife Salgerd, the daughter of Steinolf, their son was Eyjolf, the father of Fighting-Glum, and Steinolf, the father of Thorarin the Evil, and of Arnor the Good of Red River (Rauðæingr.) Fighting-Glum was the father of Mar, the father of Thorkatla, the mother of Thord, the father of Sturla.

Helgi gave Hlif, his daughter, to Thorgeir, the son of Thord the Beam, together with land out from Thwart river to Ward-gorge (Varð-gjá), they resided at Fishbrook, their children were Thord and Helga.

There was a man of much renown in Mæri (in Norway) named Skagi, thé son of Skopti, he had a dispute with Eystein Glumra (=the clatterer) and went out thence to Iceland. He settled by the advice of Helgi, Islandfirth-strand, the easternmost out from Ward-gorge to Hnjoska-dale's river and dwelt at Sigluvik, his son was Thorbjorn, the father of Hedin the bounteous, who caused Svalbard to be built sixteen years before the Christian religion was introduced into Iceland; he had for wife Ragneid, the daughter of Eyjolf, the son of Valgerd.

Gaut clears his forecastle of Vikings by a blow of his tiller, hence called Tiller-Gaut. Verses on his settlement. Thorir worships the grove. Verses in welcome of Hallstein.

CHAPTER XVII. There was a man named Thorir Snip

[PART III, CHAPTER XVII.]

Snip, son of Ketill Seal (brimil)*; he arrayed himself for a journey to Iceland: a shipmate of his was named Gaut, but while they lay ready for sea some Vikings came upon them and were minded to plunder them, but Gaut struck the man upon the forecastle with the tiller of his helm (hjálmunvölr) and thereat the Vikings made off. After that he was called Hjalmun-Gautr, *i.e.* Tiller-Gaut.

Thorir and his companions came to Iceland and brought their ship in at the mouth of the Skjalfandafljot.† Thorir settled Cold-chine between Shadow-rocks and Lightwater-pass; he did not remain there but migrated thence; then he sang this :—

> Driver of keels ! here lieth
> Cold-chine throughout all time ;
> But hence, O Tiller-Gaut, we
> All put off, well beholden.

Thorir afterwards settled all Hnjoskadale to Odeila, and dwelt at Lund ‡=the Grove. He worshipped the grove. § His son was Orm Wallet-back, the father of Hlenni the Old, and Thorkell the Black in Hleidrargard, he had for wife Gudlaug, the daughter of Hrolf, their sons were Aungull the Black, and Hrafn, the father of Thord at Stock-lade (Stokkahladir) and Gudrid, whom Thorgeir, the godi at Lightwater, had for wife.

---

* Brimill=phoca fetida masc; a large kind of seal.
† The Icelandic word "fljot" which enters into the composition of this place-name and also into many other place-names in the Book of the Settlement, means "river" in its more modern application, and we seem to have it in a like usage in English river names, as the Fleet river in London—hence Fleet Street; North Fleet and South Fleet in Kent. Fljot is the name of a County in the North of Iceland.
‡ Lund was applied as the name of a sacred grove, is used in place-names, and also surnames in the North of England.
§ Hann blotaði lundinn=he worshipped the grove. See Exodus xxxiv, 13,— "But ye shall destroy their altars, break their images, and cast down their groves." Judges, vi, 25,—"Throw down the altar of Baal that thy father hath and cut down the grove that is by it."

Thengili

[PART III, CHAPTER XVII.]

Thengil *much-sailing* went from Halogaland to Iceland, he settled land with the advice of Helgi out from Hnjosk river to Furwick; he dwelt at Head; his sons were Vemund, the father of Asolf of Head, and Hallstein, who sang this verse * when he returned home from sea and heard of the death of his father :—

> Now droops the Head
> For Thengill dead—
> Fell slopes laugh greeting
> At Hallstein's meeting.

There was a man named Thormod, who settled Firwick and Whale-litter, and all the Strands out to Thorgeirsfirth, his son was Snart, from whom the Snartlings are descended. There was a man named Thorgeir, who settled Thorgeirsfirth and Whalewaterfirth.

There was a man named Lodin Angle, he was brought up in Angle-isle in Halogaland, he set out for Iceland on account of the tyranny of Earl Hakon, son of Grjotgard, and died at sea, and Eyvind, his son, settled Flateydale up to Gunn-stones, which he worshipped. There lies Odeila between his land and the landtake of Thorir Snip. Asbjörn Dettias (Falling Beam) was the son of Eyvind, the father of Finnbogi the Strong, the father of Narfi, the father of Yngvild, the mother of Jodis, the mother of Halla, the mother of Thorgils, the father of Geirny, the mother of Valgerd, the mother of Helga, whom Snorri, the son of Markus of Melar had for wife.

---

* This verse is used metaphorically of the country, of which the hills are said to laugh in welcoming a guest among them and to droop at his departure from them. " Why hop ye so ye high hills " is a phrase used in the Psalms.

[PART III, CHAPTER XVIII.]

Settlements of Bard of the Peak. Settlements of Kamp-Grim from the Orkneys and his descendants. Settlements of Heidan and Hoskuld, sons of the Giant.

CHAPTER XVIII.　Bard, the son of Heyjang-Bjorn, brought his ship to the mouth of Skjalfandafljot and settled all Bard-dale up from Calf Burgh river and Isle-dale river, and dwelt at Lund-brink * for a time; then he observed from the winds that the land breezes were more genial than the sea breezes, and therefore he concluded that there must be better lands to the south of the heath. He sent his sons south about the middle of the month Goi,† there he found goibeytla, *i.e. equisetum vernum hyemele i.e.* horsetail, and other vegetation, and in the next spring after, Bard made a sledge for every creature that could walk, and let each drag its own fodder and some chattels; he went by Hope-pass (Vonarskard) which afterwards was called Bardargata ‡ *i.e.* the road of Bard; he afterwards settled Fljotshverfi and dwelt at Peaks (Gnupar) and was thence called Peaks-Bard § (Gnúpa-Barðr). He had many children; his son was Sigmund, the father of Thorstein, who married Æsa, the daughter of Hrolf Red-beard, their daughter was Thorun, whom Thorkel Loaf (Leifr) had for wife, and their son was Thorgeir, the godi of Lightwater. Another son of Bard was Thorstein, the father of Thorir, who was at Fitjar with Hakon the King, and cut a rift in the hide of an ox and used it for a shield, therefore he was nicknamed Leather Neck,‖ he

---

* Lundarbrekka, "the slope of the wood."
† The month Goi had thirty days, from the middle of February to the middle of March.
‡ Gate for way is often found in Cumberland, Westmorland, and the Lake District, *e.g.* Rickergate, Caldewgate, Botchergate, in Carlisle; Highgate, Stricklandgate, in Kendal; Outgate, Clappersgate, Soutergate, &c.
§ Compare "Peveril of the Peak" in Scott.
‖ I have heard a man nicknamed Ledder Neck in Cumberland.

married

[PART III, CHAPTER XVIII.]

married Fjorleif, the daughter of Eyvind, their sons were Havard in Fell Mull, Herjolf at Midgewater, Ketill at Housewick, Vemund Kogr, who had for wife Halldora, the daughter of Thorkel the Black, and Askel and Hals, he dwelt at Helgistead.

Kampr-Grimr went from the Hebrides to Iceland, he was tossed about upon the sea for the whole summer and wrecked his ship at the mouth of the Skjalfanda-fleet; he settled Cold-chine a second time and afterwards sold to sundry people portions thereof; his daughter was Arnbjorg, whom Asolf of Hofdi had in marriage.

There was a man named Thorfin Moon, the son of Askel Turfy, he settled land below the Isle-dale river to the Londsmot and some also about Lightwater Pass, and dwelt at Ox-river. Thorir, the son of Grim Grayfell-muzzle (grafeldarmuli) from Rogaland, settled about Lightwater Pass, his son was Thorkell Loaf the High (leifr enn háfi) the father of Thorgeir godi. Thorgeir first had to wife Gudrid, the daughter of Thorkell the Swart, their sons were Thorkell Flake and Hoskuld, Tjorfi, Kolgrim, Thorstein, and Thorvard, and a daughter, Sigrid. After that he married Alfgerd, the daughter of Arngeir the Eastman or Norwegian.; Thorgeir also had for wife Thorkatla, the daughter of Dales-Koll; his sons with these wives were the following: Thorgrim, Thorgils, Ottar, these were bastard born: Thorgrim and Finn the Dreamwise, his mother was named Lecny, of foreign kindred.

Hedin and Hoskuld, sons of Thorstein the Giant, went to Iceland and settled above Tongue-heath (Tunguheidi). Hedin dwelt at Hedin's Hofdi and married Gudrun; their daughter was Arnrid, whom Ketill, the son of Fjorleif, had to wife; their daughter was Gudrun, whom Hrolf had for wife. Hoskuld settled all the land to the south of the Lax river and dwelt in Skard-wick; from him

him Hoskuld's water takes its name, because he was drowned there. In their landtake is Housewick where Gardar had his abode for one winter·* The son of Hoskuld was Hroald, who had for wife Ægileif, the daughter of Hrolf, the son of Helgi.

Settlements of Vestman, Ulf, Eyvind, Grenjad. Shipwreck and settlement of Bodolf. Foretelling the weather by means of ship's beaks. Grettis verses concerning Thorir.

CHAPTER XIX.   Vestman and Ulf being foster-brothers, went in one ship to Iceland, they settled all Reek-dale to the west of Lax river up to Vestman's water. Vestman had for wife Gudlaug. Ulf abode under Scratch-fell †; his son was Geirolf, who had for wife Vigdis, the daughter of Konal, the widow of Thorgrim; their son was Hall. There was a man named Thorstein Head, he was a Hersir from Hordaland, his sons were Eyvind and Ketil the Hordlander ; Eyvind took the fancy to go to Iceland after the death of his father, and Ketil asked him to take land for them both in case he should make up his mind to go afterwards. Eyvind brought his ship into Housewick and settled Reek-dale up from Vestman's water, he dwelt at Helgastead and there was laid in howe. Nattfari, who had gone out with Gardar, had before this possessed himself of Reek-dale, and had put his marks upon the trees, but Eyvind drove him off and only allowed him Nattfari's-wick.

Ketil went out at the word sending of Eyvind; he dwelt at Einarstead ; his sons were Konal and Thorstein, the father of Einar, who resided there afterwards.

---

* Cf. Pt. I, ch. 1.

† Skratti is in Iceland the name of a monster or hobgoblin, and Skrattaskér is in Iceland the name of a rock where wizards were appointed to die. Skratta is the name of a demon or hobgoblin in the North of England.

The

[PART III, CHAPTER XIX.]

The son of Eyvind was Askel, the godi, who had for wife the daughter of Grenjad; their sons were Thorstein and Fight-Skuta; the daughter of Eyvind was Fjorleif. Konal had for wife Oddny, the daughter of Einar, and sister of Eyjolf, the son of Valgerd; their children were Einar, who had six sons, and a daughter Thorey, who was the wife of Steinolf the son of Mar, and another daughter they had named Eydis, who was the wife of Thorstein, the godi from Asbjorn's-wick. Thord, the son of Konal, was the father of Sokki at Broadmire, who was the father of Konal. A daughter of Konal was Vigdis, who was the wife of Thorgrim, the son of Thorbjorn Skagi, and their son was Thorleif, the step-son of Geirolf.

There was a man named Grenjad, the son of Hrapp, the brother of Geirleif; he settled Hushed-dale (Theigjandadale) and Lavaheath (Hraunaheidi) or Thorgerd's fell and Laxriver-dale the lower; he dwelt at Grejad's-stead; he married Thorgerd, the daughter of Helgi Horse; their son was Thorgil's Vormuli, the father of Onund, the father of Hallbera, the mother of Haldora, the mother of Thorgerd, the   of Hall, the Abbot, and of Hallbera whom Hrein, the son of Styrmir, had for wife.

There was a man named Bodolf, the son of Grim, the son of Grimolf from Agdir; Bodolf was the brother of Bodmod; he had for wife Thorun, the daughter of Thorolf Deep-in-love; their son was Skeggi. They all went to Iceland and wrecked their ship at Fjornes, and were at Audolfstead the first winter; he settled all Fjornes between the Tongue-river and Os. Botolf had for wife afterwards Thorbjorg Holme-sun, the daughter of Helgi the Lean; their daughter was Thorgerd, who Asmund, the son of Ondott had for wife; their son was Thorleif, the father of Thurid, whom Valla-Ljot had for wife.

Skeggi

[PART III, CHAPTER XIX.]

Skeggi, the son of Bodolf, settled Kelduhverfi up to Kelduness, and dwelt at Micklegarth ; he had for wife Helga, the daughter of Thorgeir of Fishbrook ; their son was Thorir the Seafarer ; he caused a ship to be built in Sogn ; Bishop Sigurd consecrated it ; from this ship were the ships' beaks * used for weather spaeing (or weather foretelling) before the door at Micklegarth.

Grettir has composed concerning Thoris the following :

> In no wise shall I ride out
> Against those stems [1] shield-heeding !
> Alone shall I depart hence,
> This thane [2] is in for trouble.
> I will not have a meeting
> With Vidrir's tempest-makers [3] ;
> I shall abide my chances,
> Though brave ye may not deem me.
>
> I keep away where Thorir's,
> Great crowds are coming onwards ;
> To me 'tis nowise handy
> To join in with their thronging.
> I shun the famed men's meeting,
> I take me to the woodland,
> And save my life ; I needs must
> Heed well the sword [4] of Heimdal.

The son of Thoris was named An, the father of Orn, the father of Ingibjorg, the mother of Skum, the father of Thorkel the Abbot.

---

* The Icelandic word is "brandar," used always in plural of ships' beaks or figureheads used as ornaments over the chief door of dwellings. They are mentioned also in Grettis Saga (116) where it can be seen that the "brandar" were two one on each side of the door.

(1) Shield-heeding stems=warriors or men.

(2) This man, *i.e.* " I," Grettir himself.

(3) Makers of Vidrir's tempest. Vidrir=Odin, his tempest=a battle, makers thereof=warriors or men.

(4) Sword of Heimdal=the head, *i.e.* the speaker's own head. The head is called the sword of Heimdal because it is said that he was smitten through with the head of a man. See Snorris Edda.

Mani

[PART III, CHAPTER XX.]

Mani from Halogaland settles between Fljots and Raudaskridu (Red Screes). Einar, Vestman, and Vemund from the Orkneys consecrate to themselves by place-names, Axfrith, Eagle's hummock and Cross ridge. Ketill Thistle settles Thistle Firth.

CHAPTER XX. There was a man named Mani, he was brought up at Omd in Halogaland, he went to Iceland and wrecked his ship upon Tjorsness and dwelt at Mani's river for several winters. Afterwards Bodolf drove him from thence, and then he settled down below Kalfburg river between Fljot and Red Screes (Raudaskrida) and dwelt at Mani's-fell; his son was Ketill, who had for wife Valdis, the daughter of Thorbrand, who bought Red Screes lands from Mani; his daughter was Dalla, the sister of Thorgeir, the son of Galti, her Thorvald, the son of Hjalti, had for wife.

There was a man named Ljot the Unwashed, who settled Helduhverfi up away from Keldunes, his son was Gris, the father of Galti in As, he was a wise man and much given to manslaughters. Onund settled Kelduhverfi from Keldunness and dwelt in As, he was the son of Blæing, the son of Soti; Onund was the brother of Balki in Ramfirth. The daughter of Onund was Thorbjorg, whom Hallgils, the son of Thorbrand from Red Screes had for wife.

Thorstein, the son of Sigmund, the son Gnup Peaks'-Bard, dwelt first at (Myvatn) Midgewater, his son was Thorgrim, the father of Arnor in Reykjahlid, who married Thorkatla, the daughter of Bodvar, the son of Hrolf from Peakfell; a son of theirs was called Bodvar. Thorkell the High came when young to Iceland, and dwelt first at Greenwater, which branches out from Midgewater. His son was named Sigmund, and had for wife Vigdis, the daughter of Thorir from Aspknott; him Glum slew in the

[PART III, CHAPTER XX.]

the field. The daughter of Thorkel was Arndis, whom Vigfus the brother of Fight-Glum had for wife. Thorkel had a son in his old age, who was called Day, he was the father of Thorarin, who had for wife Yngvild, the daughter of Hall o' Side, then a widow after Eyjolf the Halt. There was a Norwegian named Geiri, who first of men dwelt at the south of Midgewater in Geirstead, his sons were Glum and Thorkel. Father and sons fought with Thorberg Cutcheek, and slew Thorstein his son, and for those manslaughters they were outlawed from the countrysides in the north. Geiri remained for one winter at Geristead upon Hunawater, and afterwards they went to Breidaford and dwelt at Geridale in Kroksfirth. Glum married Ingun, the daughter of Thorolf, the son of Veleif, their children were Thord, who married Gudrun, the daughter of Osvif, and Thorgerd, whom Thorarin, the son of Ingjald had to wife, their son was Helga-Steinar.

Earl Turf-Einar (of Orkney) had a daughter in his youth, she was called Thordis. Earl Rognvald brought her up and gave her in marriage to Thorgeir Klaufi, their son was Einar, he went to Orkney to see his kinsmen; they would not own him for a kinsman; then Einar bought a ship in partnership with two brothers, Vestman and Vemund, and they went to Iceland and sailed round the land by the north and west abour Stetta into the firth; they set an Ax in Reistargnup, and called it (Oxarfjord) Axfirth; they placed up an Eagle on the west of it and called the place (Arnarthufu) Eagle's-hummock, and in the third place they set up a Cross and they named the spot Crossridge; thus they hallowed to themselves all Axfirth.*

---

* Sva helguðu þeir sér allan Oxarfjord=so they hallowed to themselves all Axfirth. This is an evidence that the Norsemen regarded giving place-names to their settlements as a solemn religious ceremony, by which they consecrated or hallowed the land to their own use. See Oxarfjord on Map.

The

[PART III, CHAPTER XX.]

The children of Einar were these: Eyjolf, whom Galti the son of Grisar slew, and Ljot, the mother of Hroi the Sharp, who avenged Eyjolf and slew Galti. The sons of Gliru-Halli, Brand and Berg, were the sons of a daughter of Ljot, they fell in Bodvarsdale. Reist, the son of Bearisle-Ketil and of Hild, the sister of Ketil Thistle, was father of Arnstein the godi. Reist settled land between Reistgnup and Redgnup, and dwelt at Miryhaven.

There was a man named Arngeir, who settled all Sletta between Havor's-lagoon and Sveinung-wick; his children were Thorgils and Odd and Thurid, whom Steinolf in Steer's river-dale had for wife. Arngeir and Thorgils went from home in a snowstorm to search for sheep, and came not home again. Odd went to seek them and found them both dead; a white bear had killed them and lay sucking the blood from one of the corpses when Odd came upon him. Odd slew the bear and conveyed him home, and men said that he ate the whole of it and maintained he had wrought blood revenge for his father when he killed the bear, and for his brother when he ate it.

Odd was afterwards evil and troublesome to deal with, and was seized with such a fit of frenzy that he went from home, from Lavahaven, one evening and came in the morning after to Steer's river-dale, to the aid of his sister, whom the men of Steer's river-dale were on the point of stoning to death for sorcery and witchcraft.

Sveinung settled Sveinung's-wick, and Kolli settled Kolli's-wick, and each abode afterwards at the place named after him. Ketil Thistle settled Thistle-firth between Hound's-ness and Sheepness, his son was Sigmund, the father of Einar of Bath-brink (Laugarbrekka.)

Now have been written down the landtakes in the Northlanders' Quarter; and these are there the most

renowned

renowned settlers: Audun Skokul, Ingimund, Ævar, Sæmund, Eirek in Goddales, Hofda (o'Head) Thord, Helgi the Lean, Eyvind the son of Thorstein Hofdi (Head), and there were 1440 husbandmen (bondi) in that quarter when their census was taken.* *Bondi*=Husbandmen who owned the land which they tilled.

FOURTH PART.

These men have taken land in the Quarter of the Eastern Firths, which must now be reckoned up—taking the direction from the North to the boundaries of the Quarter from Longness to Sunhome-sand, and men have said that this Quarter was the first to be fully settled.

Gunnolfsvik and Gunnolfsfell settled by Gunnolf Kroppa and others. Eyvind the Weaponed gives the name to Weapon-firth=Vapnafjord.

CHAPTER I. There was a man named Gunnolf Kroppa, son of the hersir† Thorir Hawkneb. He settled Gunnolfswick and Gunnolfsfell, and Longness all outside Helkundheath, and dwelt at Fairwick; his son was Skuli the Hardy (herkja), the father of Geirlaug. There was a man named Finni, who settled Finnafirth and Woodfirth; his son

---

* This refers to the census taken by the second Bishop of Skalholt, Gizur (1080—1118) about 1097, of all householders whose duty it was to pay the so-called "þing fararkaup" or tax for paying those who met yearly at the Althing their travelling expenses; when it was found that in the Eastfirthers' Quarter there were 700=840, in the Southlanders' Quarter 1000=1200, in the Westfirthers' Quarter 900=1080, and in the Northlanders' Quarter 1200=1440, in the land altogether therefore 4560 such householders. Hungrvaka ch. vi, Biskupasögur i, 69.

† Hersir=a chief or lord, the political name of the Norse chief of the earliest age before the time of Harold Fairhair and the settlement of Iceland; respecting the office and the authority of the old hersar, *the records* are scanty, as they chiefly belonged to pre-historical times. They were probably not liegemen but resembled the godar (see godi) of the old Icelandic Commonwealth, being a kind of patriarchal and hereditary chiefs; in this matter this Book of Settlement is our chief source of information. See Part I, Chap. X of this work.

[PART IV, CHAPTER I.]

was Thorarin, the father of Sigurd, the father of Gliru-Halli. Hrodgeir the White, son of Hrapp, settled Sandwick to the north of Digranes, all to Woodfirth, and dwelt at Skeggi-stead; his daughter was Ingibjorg, whom Thorstein the White had for wife; she was the mother of Thorgils, the father of Helgi, the father of Bjarni, the father of Yngvild, the mother of Amundi, the father of Gudrun, the mother of Thordis, the mother of Helga, the mother of Thord the Priest, the father of Markus of Melar. A brother of Hrodgeir was Alrek, who came out with him; he was the father of Ljotolf the godi in Svarfad's-dale.

Eyvind the Weaponed, and Ref the Red, sons of Thorstein Thickleg, arrayed themselves for Iceland from Strind in Thrandheim, because they were at variance with King Harald, and each had his own ship. Ref was driven back by stress of weather, and the King put him to death, but Eyvind came to Weaponfirth and settled the whole dale from Westdale's river, and dwelt at Crosswick the innermost; his son was Thorbjorn.

The son of Ref the Red was named Steinbjorn Court (Kort); he betook himself to Iceland and came to Weaponfirth. Eyvind, his foster brother, gave him all the land between Weaponfirth river and the Westdale river; he lived at Hof. His sons were these: Thormod Stikublig, who resided at Sundale; another was Ref at Ref's-stead; a third was Egil at Egilstead—the father of Thorarin and Thrast and Hallbjorn and Hallfrid, whom Thorkell Geitisson had for wife. Hroald Bjola was foster brother of Eyvind the Weaponed. He took land to the west of Westdale river, half the dale, and all Sel river-dale out to Digranes. He resided at Torfi's-stead; his son was Israud, father of Gunnhild, whom Oddi, the son of Asolf in Hofdi, had for wife. Gunnhild was the mother of Grim, the father of Halldora, the mother of Markus, the father

father of Valgerd, the mother of Bodvar, the father of
Thord the Priest, the father of Markus of Melar.

There was a man named Olver the White, son of
Osvald, son of Oxen-Thorir; he was a landed man and
resided at Almdales; he fell into strife with Earl Hakon,
son of Grjotgard, and he went to Yrjar and died there;
but Thorstein the White, his son, went to Iceland and
his ship came to Weaponfirth after the time of the land
settlement was gone by; he bought land from Eyvind
Weaponed and dwelt for some winters at Toptavoll or
Toft field outside Sirek's-stad, before he possessed himself
of Hofsland in this manner, that he claimed the payment
of his loan from Steinbjorn Kort, who had nothing
wherewith to pay except the land. Thorstein lived there
seventy winters after, and was a wise and good man.
He had for wife Ingibjorg, the daughter of Hrodgeir the
White; their children were these: Thorgils and Thord,
Onund, Thorbjorg, and Thora. Thorgils had for wife
Asvor, daughter of Thorir, the son of Porridge-Atli.
Their son was Brodd-Helgi; he married first Halla, the
daughter of Lyting, the son of Arnbjorn; their son was
Fighting-Bjarni. He had for wife Rannveig, the daughter
of Eirek from Goddales; their son was Skeggbroddi, and
their daughter Yngvild, whom Thorstein, son of Hall,
had for wife. Skeggbroddi married Gudrun, the daughter
of Thorarin Sæling, with his wife Halldora the daughter
of Einar; their children were Thorir and Bjarni House-
long. Thorir took to wife Steinun, the daughter of
Thorgrim the Tall. Their daughter was Gudrun, whom
Flosi, son of Kolbein, had for wife. Their son was
Bjarni, the father of Bjarni, who had for wife Halla, the
daughter of Jorund; their children were these: Flosi the
Priest and Torfi the Priest, Einar Bride, and Gudrun,
whom Thord Sturluson had for wife, and further Godrun,
whom Einar Bergthorson had for wife, and Helga, the
mother

[PART IV, CHAPTER I.]
mother of Sigrid, the daughter of Sigvat. Flosi the
Priest had for wife Ragnhild, the daughter of Bork at
Baugstead; their children were Bjarni and Einar, Halla,
the mother of Knight Kristoforus, and Thordis, mother
of Lady Ingigerd, the mother of Lady Gudrun and of
Hallbera. Valgerd was the name of a daughter of Flosi,
she was the mother of Knight Erlend the Strong, the
father of Hauk* and Valgerd.

*Weaponfirth settled by Thorstein Turf, Lyting and Thorfid.
Hakon settles Jokulsdale west of Jokul's river. Tongue
lands between Lagarfljots and Jokuls river settled by
Thord and his descendants. Arneid finds buried treasure.*

CHAPTER II. Two brothers, Thorstein Turf and
Lyting, went to Iceland. Lyting settled all the eastern
shore of Weaponfirth, Bodvarsdale, and Fairdale, and
lived in Crosswick; from him the Weaponfirthers are
descended. His son was Geitar, the father of Thorkel,
the father of Ragneid, the mother of Halla, the mother
of Botolf, the father of Thordis, the mother of Helga, the
mother of Thord the Priest, the father of Markus of
Melar.

There was a man named Thorfid, who first resided at
Skeggistead, by the counsel of Thord Haulm; his son
was Thorstein the Fair, who slew Einar, the son of
Thorir, the son of Porridge-Atli; Thorfid's sons and
Einar's two brothers were also Thorkel and Hedin, who
slew Thorgils, the father of Brodd-Helgi. Thorstein
Turf took all the Hlid east away from Osfells west to
Hvann river and dwelt at Forcefield; his son was Thor-
vald, the father of Thorgeir, the father of Hallgeir, the
father of Hrapp at Forcefield.

---

* Last Editor of the Book of Settlement.

There

[PART IV, CHAPTER II.]

There was a man named Hakon, who settled all Jokul's-dale to the west of Jokul's-river and above Teig-river, and dwelt at Hakonstead; his daughter was Thorbjorg, whom the sons of Brynjolf the Old, Gunnbjorn and Hallgrim had for wife. Teig lay unclaimed between Thorstein Turf and Hakon. That plot they dedicated to a Temple and it is now called Temple-Teig. Skjoldolf, the son of Vemund and brother of Berdla-Kari, settled Jokulsdale to the east of Jokul's-river up from Knefilsdale river and dwelt at Skjoldolfstead; his children were these: Thorstein, who married Fastny, the daughter of Brynjolf, and Sigrid, the mother of Bersi, the son of Ozur.

There was a man named Thord, the son of Thorolf Haulm and brother of Helgi Brownhead; he settled all Tongue lands between Lagarfljot and Jokul's-river, beyond Rang river; his son was Thorolf Haulm, who had for wife Gudrid, the daughter of Brynjolf; their son was Thord Thvari,* the father of Thorodd, the father of Brand, the father of Steinun, the mother of Rannveig, the mother of Sæhild, whom Gizur had for wife. Ozur Stagakoll settled between Orm's river and Rang river; he had for wife Gudny, the daughter of Brynjolf; their son was Asmund, the father of Mord.

Ketil and Porridge-Atli, sons of Thorir Thidrandi, went from Veradal to Iceland and settled in Fljotsdale before Brynjolf came out, both Lagarfljot's-strands. Ketil settled on the west of the Fljot between Hang-force river and Orms river. Ketil went abroad and abode with Vethorm, the son of Vemund the Old, there he bought from Vethorm Arneid, the daughter of Earl Asbjorn Skerryblaze, whom Holmfast, the son of Vethorm had taken captive, when he and Grim, the sister son of

---

* Thvari corresponds with the old Cumberland word "Thyvel," used for stirring porridge.

Vethorm

[PART IV, CHAPTER II.]

Vethorm, slew Earl Asbjorn. Ketil bought Arneid, the daughter of Asbjorn, for twice the price at which Vethorm estimated her at first, and when the bargain was made, then Ketil married Arneid lawfully. After that she found much buried treasure (grafsilfr) under the root of a tree and Ketil offered her to flit her to her kinsfolk, but she preferred then to be with him. They went out to Iceland and abode at Arneidstead; their son was Thidrandi, the father of Ketil in Njardvik. Joreid, the daughter of Thidrandi, was mother of Thorstein, the father of Gudrid, the mother of Rannveig, the mother of Salgerd, the mother of Gudrun, the mother af Abbot Hrein, the father of Valdis, the mother of Snorri, the father of Hallbera, who was the wife of Markus Thordson at Melar.

Porridge-Atli settles eastern shore of Lagarfljot to Gils river (Gilsá). Thorgeir and others settle there. Hrafnkel's dream. Settles Hrafnkelsdal.

CHAPTER III. Porridge-Atli settled the eastern shore of Lagarfljot, all between Gils river and. Vallaness, to the west of Oxbrook; his sons were Thorbjorn and Thorir, who married Asvor, the daughter of Brynjolf. There was a noble man named Thorgeir Vestarsson, he had three sons, one was Brynjolf the Old, another Ævar the Old, the third Herjolf. They all went to Iceland, each in his own ship. Brynjolf brought his ship to Eskifirth and settled land on the upland side of the mountains, all Fljotsdale up dale from Hengiforce river to the west of the Fljot, and up dale from Gils river on the east side of the valley, all Screesdale, and also on the Fields out to Eyvind river, and he took a large portion from the landtake of Uni Gardar's son and settled on that land his kinsmen and relations-in-law; he had already then ten children, but later on he married Helga, the widow of Herjolf his
brother

[PART IV, CHAPTER III.]

brother, and they had three children; their son was Ozur, the father of Bersi, the father of Holmstein, the father of Orækja, the father of Holmstein, the father of Helga, the mother of Holmstein, the father of Hallgerd, the mother of Thorbjorg, whom Lopt, son of the Bishop,* had for wife.

Ævar the Old, the brother of Brynjolf, came out to Reydarfirth and up across the mountain; Brynjolf gave him all Skreesdale beyond Gils river; he dwelt at Arnaldstead; he had two sons and three daughters. There was a man named Asraud, who married Asvor, the daughter of Herjolf, brother's daughter and step daughter of Brynjolf; there went with her from home, *i.e.* there was to her for a dowry all the lands between Gils river and Eyvind's river; they dwelt at Ketilstead. Their son was Thorvald Hollowmouth, the father of Thorberg, the father of Hafljot, the father of Thorhadd Scale. Thorun was the daughter of Hollowmouth, and her Thorbjorn, son of Porridge-Atli, had for wife. Another daughter of Hollowmouth was Astrid, the mother of Asbjorn Shaggy-head, the father of Thorarin in Seydfirth, who was the father of Asbjorn, the father of Kolskegg the Wise and of Ingileif, mother of Hall, the father of Finn the Speaker-at-law.

There was a man named Hrafnkel, the son of Hrafn; he came late in the time of the Settlement; he was the first winter in Broaddale, and in the spring he went up across the mountain, and baited in Screesdale and slept, and then he dreamed that a man came to him and bade him stand up and go forth as swiftly as possible, and when he awoke he went forth, then the whole mountain rushed down and there were buried under it a hog and a bull that he had with him. Afterwards Hrafnkel

---

* Son of Páll Jónsson, Bishop of Skalholt.

settled

[PART IV, CHAPTER III.]
settled Hrafnkelsdale and dwelt at Steinraud's-stead; his
sons were Asbjorn, the father of Helgi, and Thorir, the
father of Hrafnkel the godi, the father of Sveinbjorn, the
father of Thorstein, the father of Botolf, the father of
Thordis, the mother of Helga, the mother of Thord the
Priest, the father of Markus of Melar.

Uni (son of Gardar first discoverer) and his companions slain
  by Leidolf in a deadly feud. Drawing and carving by
  Tjorvi. His satirical verses result in the death of Hroar
  and his sister's sons. Vetrlidi settles Borgfirth (Borgar-
  fjord.)

CHAPTER IV. Uni, the son of Gardar, who first discovered Iceland, went to Iceland by the advice of King
Harald Fairhair, for the purpose of conquering the land;
and when that should be accomplished, the King had
promised him to make him his Earl.* Uni settled near
the place which is now called Uni's Inlet and set up
house there; he took land to himself to the south of
Lagarfljot, all the country-side to Uni's-brook. But
when the people of the land got aware of his design they
began to show ill-feeling towards him, and would not sell
him cattle or provisions, so that he might not hold out
there. Uni went to Swanfirth the southernmost, but was
not able to effect a settlement there; then he went from
the east with twelve men, and came in winter to Leidolf
Champion in Skogahverfi, who took them in.

Uni made love to Thorun, daughter of Leidolf, and she
was with child in the spring; then Uni tried to run off
with his men, but Leidolf rode after him and overtook
him at Flangastead, and there they fought, because Uni
would not go back with Leidolf; there fell some men on

---

* Herein we have in evidence, as elsewhere also in the Landnama, that Harald
after having by his unbearable tyranny driven the Norse chieftains to seek homes
elsewhere, yet follows them up and endeavours to enslave them in the land of
their refuge.

Uni's

[PART IV, CHAPTER IV.]

Uni's side, and he went back unwilling, because Leidolf
wished him to take his daughter to wife and to settle
down and take inheritance after him. Some time after
Uni ran away when Leidolf was not at home. He traced
him and found him at Calfpits (Kalfagrafir) and was so
angry that he slew Uni and all his companions. The son
of Uni and Thorun was Hroar Tongue-godi; he took all
the inheritance of Leidolf; he was a man of the highest
mettle; he had for wife a daughter of Hamund, who was
sister of Gunnar from Lithend; their son was Hamund
the Halt, who was a most warlike man. Tjorvi the
Mocker, and Gunnar, were the sister sons of Hroar.
Tjorvi asked for the hand of Astrid Manwit-breaker,
daughter of Modolf, but her brothers, Ketil and Hrolf,
refused her to him, and gave her in marriage to Thorir,
the son of Ketil. Then Tjorvi drew their likeness upon
the wall of the chamber and every evening when he and
Hroar went to the chamber he would spit upon the likeness of Thorir and kiss the likeness of Astrid, until Hroar
scraped them off the wall. After that he carved them
upon his knife handle and composed this verse :—

> The young wealth-Thrud [1] and Thorir
> I painted erst together
> There on the wall—the deed was
> A set off 'gainst an insult [2]
> Now the sea-acorn's-Hlin [3] I
> Have carved on my haft of alder;
> Right many a talk I've had with
> The bright Syn of the hawk-stall. [4]

---

(1) Wealth-Thrud: Thrud, the daughter of Thor, a goddess; the goddess of
wealth, a woman whose personal ornaments are of precious metal.

(2) The insult ('gletta') was that Astrid was refused him in marriage. The
prep. 'við'=against, justifies the translation.

(3) Sea-acorn or acorn of the sea=a stone, boulder, or pebble, thence precious
stone, jewel, the Hlin or goddess—Hlin was one of the goddesses of Asgarth—
of jewels=woman.

(4) Hawk-stall, the stall whereon the hunting falcon perches, hand, the Syn=
goddess of the hand, that is, the fine or delicate or jewel-bedecked hand=
woman. Syn is counted in Snorri's Edda among the female deities of Asgarth;
she was the doorkeeper in Valhall.

Hereof

[PART IV, CHAPTER IV.]
Hereof arose the slaughter of Hroar * and his sister's sons.

There was a man named Thorkel the Full-Sage, who settled all Njardwick and dwelt there; his daughter was Thjodhild, whom Ævar the Old had for wife, and their daughter was Yngvild, mother of Ketil in Njardwick, the son of Thidrandi. There was a man named Vetrlidi, a son of Arnbjorn, the son of Olaf Longneck; Vetrlidi was the brother of Lyting and Thorstein Turf, and Thorbjorn in Eagle-holt. Olaf Longneck was the son of Bjorn Trout-side. Vetrlidi settled Borgfirth and dwelt there. There was a man named Thorir Line who settled Broadwick and dwelt there; his sons were Sveinung and Gunnstein. Now has Kolskegg † dictated the story henceforth of the Settlements.

Lodmund the Old and Bjolf come from Norway to Iceland. Lodmund guided by his High Seat Pillars settles between Hegoat-river and Jokul's-river on Solheima-sand—names his dwelling Solheim=Sunhome. Lomund and Thrasi agree that Jokul's-river shall divide the East and South Quarters.

CHAPTER V. Thorstein Gadfly (Kleggi ‡) first settled Housewick and dwelt there; his son was An, from whom the Housewickings are descended. There was a man named Lodmund the Old, and another named Bjolf, his foster brother; they went to Iceland from Vors out of Thulaness. Lodmund was exceedingly strong and a great wizard; he cast his High Seat Pillars overboard while out at sea and vowed that he would settle there

---

* Hroar married the sister of Gunnar of Lithend—the hero of the Njala.
† This refers to Kolskegg Asbiornson the Learned, who according to this passage, described or dictated the story of the Eastfirths Settlement.
‡ Nickname, meaning horsefly or gadfly. Compare Cumberland "cleg."

[PART IV, CHAPTER V.]
where they came to land. These foster brothers made the Eastfirths and Lodmund settled Lodmundsfirth, and dwelt there that winter; then he heard of his High Seat Posts in the Southern land. After that he bore on board ship all his goods; and when the sail was hoisted he lay down and bade no man be so daring as to name him, but when he had lain a short while, there befell a mighty din and men saw how a great landslip fell upon the homestead at which Lodmund had lived. After that he sat up and uttered these words: "It is my spell that the ship sailing out from here shall never come whole from the sea." He then held south round the Horn and west along the land and beyond Hjorleifshofdi and landed a little further to the west. He settled there where his High Seat Pillars had come ashore and that was between Hegoat's river and Foulbrook, that is now named Jokul's river on Solheima-sand; he dwelt at Lodmundhvamm and called his home there Sunhome (Solheimar).

Then when Lodmund was old, Thrasi dwelt at Skogar; he was skilled in the art of magic; it happened once upon a time that Thrasi saw one morning a great rushing forth of waters and with his magic power he turned the waters to the east of Solheimar. Then a thrall of Lodmund's saw this and said that the sea was rushing upon them from the north of the land. Lodmund was then blind; he bade the servant bring him in a bilge water tub what he called the sea, and when he brought it Lodmund said, "that does not seem to me to be sea water"; then he bade the thrall guide him to the water, "and stick thou my staffs-pike," he said, "into the water": and Lodmund held the staff clasped with his two hands, biting the ring in it at the same time; then the waters began to flow to the west-ward beyond Skogar again; and in this manner each would lead the waters away from himself, until they met at certain gorges, where they made peace on the terms
that

[PART IV, CHAPTER V.]
that the river should run there where the way was
shortest to the sea; it is now called Jokul's river and
parts the Quarters of the land.*

*Bjolf settles Seydisfjord. Egil the Red settles Northfirth
(Nordfjord). Freystein the Fair settles Sandvik and
Cavefirth (Hellisfjord). Thorir the High settles Krossavik (Crosswick) Reydarfjord (Troutfirth). Vemund
settles Faskrudsfjord. Thorhadd the Old settles Stodvarfjord.*

CHAPTER VI. Bjolf, a foster brother of Lodmund,
settled all Seydisfjord, and dwelt there all his life. He
gave Helga, his daughter, to An the Strong, and she
received as a dowry all the western strand of Seydisfjord
to Westdale river. The son of Bjolf was named Isolf;
he dwelt there afterwards, and the Seydfirthers have their
origin from him.

There was a man named Eyvind who came out with
Brynjolf, and afterwards moved his household to Narrowfirth and dwelt there; his son was Hrafn, who sold
Narrowfirthland to Thorkel Klaka, who dwelt there
afterwards; from him are descended the family of Klaka.

There was a man named Egil the Red, who settled
North firth and dwelt there out at Ness; his son was
Olaf, from whom the family called Nessmen are descended.

There was a man named Freystein the Fair; he settled
Sandwick dwelling at Bardsness and made his own also
Woodfirth and Cavefirth; from him are the Sandwick
men and the Woodfirthers and the Cavefirthers descended.
Thorir the High and Krum, both went from Vors to Ice-
land, and there they settled; Thorir settled Crosswick

---

* That is the Eastfirths Quarter and the Southlanders Quarter. According to
the explanation here given, the division is made at the watershed or waterparting.
See Map.

between

[PART IV, CHAPTER VI.]

between Gerpir and Troutfirth, thence are the Crosswick men descended. Krum settled Hafraness to Thernaness, and all the outlying parts, both Skruday and the other outer islands off the shore and three landtakes on the other side opposite to Thernaness, thence are the Krymlings descended. Ævar was first in Troutfirth, before he went up across the mountain, but Brynjolf was left in Eskifirth, before he went up to settle Fljotsdale, as was written before.

There was a man named Vemund, who settled all Faskrudsfirth, and dwelt there all his life; his son was Olmod, from whom the Olmodlings are descended. Thorhadd the Old was Temple Priest at Thrandheim in Mæri.* He desired to go to Iceland, and before going he took down the Temple and brought with him the Temple Mould and the High Seat Pillars, and when he came to Stodvarfjord he hallowed the whole firth after the fashion that obtained at Mæri, † and would not let them destroy any cattle there except such as were for domestic use. He dwelt there all his life and from him the Stodfirthers are descended.

Hjalti settles Broaddale; Herjolf settles Hvalness Screes; Thjodrek settles Berufjord and Bulandness. The ring in each chief Temple. Form of the oath upon the ring.

CHAPTER VII. There was a man named Hjalti, who settled Kleifland and all Broaddale upward; his son was Kolgrim, and many men are descended from him. There was a man named Herjolf, who settled land all out to Hvalsness Screes; his son was Vapni, from whom the

---

* A county in Norway; it also gives its name to Mæri, a famed Temple in Drontheim.
† Literally "he made a holy Mæri of the whole firth."

Vapnlings

[PART IV, CHAPTER VII.]

Vapnlings are descended. Herjolf, brother of Brynjolf, settled Heydaleland down below Finnadale's river and out to Orm's river; his son was Ozur, from whom the Broaddalers are descended. There was a man named Skjoldolf, who settled Street all out from Gnup, and inward on the opposite side to Os * and Skjoldolfness by Fagradale river in Broaddale; his son was Haleyg, who dwelt there afterwards, and from him the family of Haleygar are descended.

There was a man named Thjodrek, he first settled all Broaddale, but he had to bolt from thence before Brynjolf south into Berufjord, and settled all the northern strand of Berufirth and to the south out round Bulandness and up the other side unto Red Screes, and dwelt three winters in that place which is now called Scale; then Bjorn the High bought lands from him, and from him are the Berufirthers descended.

There was a man named Bjorn " Singed-horn," who settled the northernmost Swanfirth in from Red Screes and Svidinhornadal or Singedhornsdale. Thorstein Trumpet-bone was the name of a kinsman of Bodvar the White and he went with him to Iceland and settled land out from Miry-Creek to Whaleness Screes; his son was Koll the Gray, the father of Thorstein, the father of Thorgrim in Burghaven, the father of Steinun, whom Gizur the Bishop married. Bodvar the White was son of Thorleif Middling, a son of Bodvar Snowthunder, the son of Thorleif Whaleskuft, the son of An, the son of King Orn the Horny, the son of Thorir the King, the son of Swine-Bodvar, the son of Kaun the King, the son of King Solgi, the son of Hrolf from Berg; he (Bodvar the White) and Brandonund his kinsman, went from Vors to Iceland and came to Swanfirth the southernmost. Bod-

---

* That is, "the river's mouth."

var settled the land in from Miry-Creek and all the dales that lie there and out on the opposite side to Muli and dwelt at Hof; he built there a large Temple.

The son of Bodvar was Thorstein, who had for wife Thordis, the daughter of Ozur Keiliselg, the son of Hrollaug; their son was Side Hall; he married Joreid, the daughter of Thidrandi, and from thence are descended a great kindred. Thorstein was a son of theirs, he was the father of Amundi, the father of Gudrun, the mother of Thordis, the mother of Helga, the mother of Gudny, the mother of the sons of Sturla. Brandonund settled to the north of Mula-Kambsdale and Melrakkanes, and up to Hamar's river, and many men are descended from him.

Thord Skeggi, son of Hrapp, son of Bjorn buna, married Vilborg, daughter of Osvald, and of Ulfrun, the daughter of Eadmund. Thord went to Iceland and settled in Lon, to the north of Jokul's river, between it and Lon's Heath, and dwelt at Bær *or By* for ten winters longer. There he heard news of his High Seat Pillars being found * in Leiruvag or Miry-Creek, south of the Heath, † so he betook himself westward thither and abode at Skeggistead as was written before. He then sold his lands in the Lon to Ulfljot, ‡ who brought laws out hither from Norway to Iceland. The daughter of Thord was Helga, whom Ketilbjorn at Mosfell had for wife.

[*It was the beginning of the preamble of the heathen laws that men should not take ships to sea with carved figure heads upon their stems, but if they did, they should take them off before they came in sight of land and not sail to land with gaping heads or yawning snouts lest the guardian feys of the land should be scared thereat.*]

---

* A.D. 927.
† That is south of the Heath of Mossfell, Miry Creek being in the neighbourhood of Reykjavik.
‡ For institution of Althing, see page 16. In another MS. of the Landnama it is stated that Ulfljot brought out law from Norway to Iceland in 927, when he was 60 years old; and that three years after this he instituted the Althing.

A ring

[PART IV, CHAPTER VII.]

A ring weighing two ounces or more should lie on the stall in every chief Temple, and this ring should every chief or godi have upon his arm at all public law-motes (logthing) at which he should • be at the head of affairs, having first reddened it in the blood of a neat which he himself had sacrificed there. Every man who was there to transact any business, as by law provided by the Court, should first take an oath upon that ring and name for the purpose two or more witnesses and repeat the following words:—" I call to witness in evidence, he was to say, that I take oath upon the ring, a lawful one (lögeid) so help me Frey and Niord and the Almighty God, to this end that I shall in this case prosecute or defend or bear witness or give award or pronounce doom according to what I know to be most right and most true and most lawful, and that I will deal lawfully with all such matters in law as I have to deal with while I am at this Thing." Then was the land divided into Quarters, and it was decided that there should be three Things in each Quarter and three Temples in each Thing Commune i.e. Thing District or Community, and that men should be selected according to wisdom and righteousness to have ward of the Temple, and they were to nominate Courts of Judges at the Things and to regulate the proceedings of lawsuits, and therefore were they called godar or Priests ; and every man should pay toll to the Temple as now they pay tithes to the Church.]*

Thorstein Leg goes from the Hebrides to Iceland—settles all lands from north of the Horn to Jokul's-river—returns to the Hebrides. Rögnvald Earl of Mæri and his three sons, of whom Hrollaug is sent to Iceland and Einar volunteers for the Orkneys.

CHAPTER VIII. Thorstein Leg,† son of Bjorn Blue-tooth, went from the Hebrides to Iceland, and settled all

---

* Originally a shire having a meeting or Parliament of its own.

† Throughout the Book of the Settlement is found evidence, as in this instance, of the settlement of the Norsemen in the Hebrides, and of their passing to and from Iceland. The Place Names of the Hebrides bear abundant testimony to this. There we find that almost every local name is Norse. The names of the farms end as in Norway in *seter* and *ster*, and the hills are called how, hog, and holl. The names of the smaller burghs have the Norwegian suffix *vœ* as Westvœ, Aithsvœ, Laxvœ, and Hammavœ. We find also Burrafiord, Saxaford, Lerwick, and Sandwick.

lands

[PART IV, CHAPTER VIII.]   .

lands from the north of the Horn to Jokul's-river in Lon,
and dwelt at Bodvarsholt three winters, and then sold
his lands again and went back to the Hebrides.

Rögnvald, Earl of Mæri, son of Eystein Glumra, the·
son of Ivar, an Earl of the Upplendings, the son of
Halfdan the Old, had for wife Ragnhild, the daughter of
Hrolf the Beaked ; their son was Ivar, who fell in the
Hebrides, fighting with King Harald Fairhair. Another
son was Gaungu-Hrolf* who conquered Normandy; from
him are descended the Earls of Rouen and the Kings of
England ; the third was Earl Thorir the Silent, who had
for wife Alof Year-betterment, the daughter of King
Harald Fairhair, and their daughter was Bergljot, the
mother of Earl Hakon the Mighty.

Earl Rögnvald had three base-born sons : one called
Hrollaug, another Einar, a third Hallad, who tumbled
from his station of Earl in the Orkneys, and when Earl
Rögnvald heard thereof, he called together his sons and
asked who of them was then minded to go to the islands,
and Thorir bade the Earl do as he pleased concerning his
journey ; the Earl said he had spoken well, but said he
should abide there (at Mæri) and have that dominion
there after his day. Then Hrolf stepped forward and
volunteered to go (to Orkney) ; Rögnvald said it suited
him well, inasmuch as he was both strong and valiant,
but he was minded to think that his temper was too wild
for him to settle down now already in the rule of lands.
Then Hrollaug stepped forward and asked if it was his
will that he should go ; but Rögnvald said he would not be
likely to become an Earl ; thy ways lead out to Iceland ;
in that land thou wilt be deemed a noble man and become
prosperous in thy kindred, but here destiny hath nought

---

* Gaungu-Hrolf = Rolf the Ganger, see chapter on Harald Fairhair in the
Introduction to this volume.

[PART IV, CHAPTER VIII.]
in store for thee. Then Einar stepped forward and said: let me go to Orkney, and I will promise thee what thou wilt deem the best, that thereafter I shall never come within the sight of thine eyes. The Earl answers: I am well content that thou go away, however scanty hope I have about thee, for all thy mother's kin is thrall-born. Thereupon Einar fared west and subdued to him the islands as is told in his saga. But Hrollaug betook himself to King Harald and stayed with him for a while, because, after this, father and son could not agree together.

Voyage and Settlement of Hrollaug—keeps up allegiance with Harald Fairhair—accepts from him sword, alehorn, and gold ring. Settlement of Hrollaug's sons.

CHAPTER IX. Hrollaug went to Iceland by the advice of King Harald, and had with him his wife and sons. He came up in the east at Horn and there cast overboard his High Seat Pillars, which were borne to land in Hornfirth, but he himself was driven away beyond the land to the westward and fell in with a rough tossing about with scarcity of water. They landed in Miry-Creek in the Nesses; there he was the first winter. Then he had news of his High Seat Pillars, and from thence he went to the east; he was for another winter under Ingolf's-fell. Thence he went eastward to Hornfirth and took land eastward of Horn in westward to Folds'-river, and resided first under Skard-brink in Hornfirth, but afterwards he abode at Breidabols-stead in Fellshverfi. By then he had parted with those lands which were north from Borgarhofn, but he retained until the day of his death the lands which were south from Hreggsgerdismuli. Hrollaug was a great lord and kept up friendship with King Harald, but never went abroad. King Harald sent to Hrollaug a sword, an alehorn and a gold ring which weighed five ounces. Afterwards

[PART IV, CHAPTER IX.]

Afterwards Kol, son of Side Hall, owned that sword, and Kolskegg Deep-in-lore had seen the horn. Hrollaug was father of Ozur Keilis-elk, who married Gro, the daughter of Thord Evilmind; their daughter was Thordis, the mother of Hall o' Side. Another son of Hrollaug was Hroald, father of Ottar Hvalro, the father of Gudlaug, the mother of Thorgerd, the mother of Jarngerd, the mother of Valgerd, the mother of Bodvar, the father of Gudny, the mother of the Sturlungs. Onund was the third son of Hrollaug. Hall o' Side had for wife Joreid, the daughter of Thidrandi; their son was Thorstein, the father of Magnus, the father of Einar, the father of Magnus the Bishop. Another son of Hall was Egil, father of Thorgerd, the mother of Bishop John the Holy. Thorvard, the son of Hall, was the father of Thordis, the mother of Jorun, the mother of Hall the Priest, the father of Gizur, the father of Bishop Magnus, and of Thorvald, the father of Earl Gizur. Yngvild, the daughter of Hall, was mother of Thorey, the mother of Sæmund the Priest Deep-in-lore. Thorstein, the son of Hall, was father of Gudrid, the mother of Joreid, the mother of Ari the Priest Deep-in-lore. Thorgerd, the daughter of Hall, was the mother of Yngvild, the mother of Ljot, the father of Jarngerd, the mother of Valgerd, the mother of Bodvar, the father of Gudny, the mother of the sons of Sturla.

Ketil, Audun the Red and Thorstein the Squinter buy land of Hrollaug. Vors-Ulf settles Papyli and Breidabolstead. Thord Evilmind wrecks his ship upon Broadriversand. Settles between Jokul's-river and Folds-river. Sons of Asbjorn settle round Ingolf's-stead. Peak-bird settles Fljotshverfi and the Peaks.

CHAPTER X. There was a man named Ketil, to whom Hrollaug sold Hornfirthstrand, east of Horn,

west

[PART IV, CHAPTER X.]

west to Hamrar; he dwelt at Middlefell; from him are the Hornfirthers descended. Audun the Red bought land of Hrollaug westward from Hamrar and out on the other side to Vidbord; he dwelt at Hofsfell or Templefell, and raised there a great Temple; from him are the Hofs-fellings descended. Thorstein the Squinter bought land of Hrollaug, all from Vidbord south over the Meres and to Heinaberg-river; his son was Vestmar, from whom the Meremen are descended. Ulf from Vors bought land of Hrollaug south from Honeberg-river to Hreggsgerdis-muli, and dwelt at Scalefell first of all men; from him are the Vorsmen descended. Afterwards Ulf moved his abode to Papyli and dwelt at Breidabolstead and there is his burial mound and also the burial mound of Thor-geir. Thorgeir was the son of Vors-Ulf and dwelt at Hof in Papyli.

Thord Evilmind, son of Eyvind Oak-crook, wrecked his ship at Broadriversand. Hrollaug gave him land between Jokul's-river and Folds-river and he dwelt under the fell at Broad-river; his sons were Örn the Strong, who quarrelled with Thordis, the Earl's daughter, the sister of Hrollaug, and Eyvind the Smith; his daughters were Groa, whom Ozur had for wife, and Thordis, the mother of Thorbjorg, the mother of Thordis, the mother of Thord Evilmind, who slew Fighting-Skuli.

There was a man named Asbjorn, son of Heyjang-Bjorn, a hersir from Sogn, he was the son of Helgi, the son of Helgi, the son of Bjorn Buna. Asbjorn went to Iceland and died at sea, but Thorgerd his wife, and their sons came out and settled all the countryside of Ingolf's-head between Folds-river and Jokul's-river, and she dwelt at Sandfell; and Gudlaug, the son of her and Asbjorn, after her; from him the Sandfellings are descended. Another of their sons was Thorgils, from whom the Hnappfellings are descended; the third was Ozur, the father

[PART IV, CHAPTER X.]

father of Thord Freys-godi, from whom many men are descended.

Helgi was another son of Heyjang-Bjorn, he went to Iceland and dwelt at Redbrook; his son was Hildir, from whom the Redbrookmen are descended. Bard, who has been mentioned before, was a third son of Heyjang-Bjorn, he first settled Barddale in the north, and then he went south over Hope Pass by the Bardgate (Bardargata) and settled all Fljotshverfi, and dwelt at Peaks; then he was called Peak's-Bard. His sons were Thorstein and Sigmund, third Egil, fourth Gisli, fifth Nefstein, sixth Thorbjorn Krum, seventh Hjor, eighth Thorgrim, ninth Bjorn, the father of Geiri at Lundar, the father of Thorkel the Leech, the father of Geiri, the father of Thorkel the Canon regular, a friend of Bishop Thorlak the Saint, who founded the monastery at Thickby.

Eyvind Carp settles near Allmens'-Fleet. Ketil the Foolish from the Hebrides settles between Geirland's-river and Firth-river—lives at Kirkby, former abode of the Papar. Vilbald from Ireland comes ashore at Kudafljot's-mouth and dwells at Buland.

CHAPTER XI. Eyvind Carp settled land between Allmens'-Fleet and Geirland's-river, and dwelt at Fors to the west of Modolfsgnup; his sons were these: Modolf, the father of Hrolf and Ketil and Astrid Manwit-breaker, another was Onund, father of Thraslaug, the mother of Tyrfing and of Halldor, the father of Tyrfing, the father of Teit. Before Allmens'-Fleet burst out (of the glacier) the stream there was called Rafter's-brook.

There was a man named Ketil the Foolish, son of Jorun Manwit-breaker, the daughter of Ketil Flatnose; he went from Sodor to Iceland. He was a Christian and settled land between Geirland's-river and Firth-river,

above

[PART IV, CHAPTER XI.]

above Newcome. Ketil dwelt at Kirkby (Kirkjubæ)—
there the Papar had formerly had their abode, and no
heathen men might settle there. Ketil was father of
Asbjorn, the father of Thorstein, the father of Surt, the
father of Sigvat the Speaker-at-law, the father of Kolbein.
The daughter of Asbjorn was named Hild, the mother of
Thorir, the father of Hild, whom Skarphedin had for
wife. Thorbjorg was the name of the daughter of Ketil
the Foolish ; her Vali, the son of Lodmund the Old, had
for wife.

There was a man named Bodmod, who settled between
Driving and Firth-river and up to Bodmod's-horn ; he
dwelt at Bodmod's-Tongue. His son was Oleif, from
whom Oleif's-Burg received its name : he lived at Holt.
His son was Vestar, the father of Helgi, the father of
Gro, whom Glasdir had for wife. Eystein the Big went
from Sunnmæri to Iceland; he settled to the east of
Geirland's-river, over against the claim of Ketil the
Foolish, and dwelt in Geirland ; his son was Thorstein
of Ditch-Peak. Eystein, son of Hrani, the son of Hildir
Parak, went from Norway to Iceland: he bought lands
of Eystein the Big, which he had settled there and which
he said were called Middle-lands; he dwelt at Skard;
his children were Hildir and Thorljot, whom Thorstein
at Ditch Peak had for wife. Hildir wished to flit his
dwelling to Kirkby after Ketil, thinking that a heathen
might dwell there, but when he came near the fence of
the homefield, he died very suddenly and he lies there in
Hildir's-Howe.

There was a man named Vilbald, brother of Askel
Knokkan ; he went from Ireland to Iceland and he had
that ship which he called ' Kudi,' and he came to Kuda-
fljots-mouth ; he settled Tongueland between Shaft-river
and Holm's-river, and dwelt at Buland; his children were
Bjolan, father of Thorstein and Olver Mouth and Bjollok,
whom Aslak ' orgodi ' had for wife.   There

[PART IV, CHAPTER XI.]

There was a man named Leidolf Champion; he settled land to the east of Shaft-river unto Driving and dwelt at River to the east of Shaft-river out from Skal, and he had another homestead at Leidolf-stead under Leidolf's-fell, and there were at that time many dwellings. Leidolf was father of Thorun, the mother of Hroar Tongue-godi. Hroar married Arngunn, the daughter of Hamund, a sister of Gunnar from Hlidarendi; their children were Hamund the Halt, and Ormhild. The son of Hroar and a bondwoman was named Vebrand; Hroar seized Thorun Brow, the daughter of Thorgils from Hvamm in Midgedale; their son was named Thorfinn. Hroar dwelt first at Ridges, afterwards he took Loon-Peak's-land (Lomagnupsland) from Eystein, son of Thorstein Titling and of Aud, the daughter of Eyvind, a sister of Modolf and Brandi.

Thraslaug was the daughter of Thorstein Titling, and her Thord Freysgodi had for wife. Onund Walletback, a kinsman of the children of Thorstein, challenged Hroar to the Holmgang at Skaplafell Thing and fell at the feet of Hroar. Thorstein Upplending took Thorun Brow and had her with him abroad. Hroar also went abroad and in that journey he slew Thrast the Bearserk at the Holmgang, because he wished to marry Sigrid, his wife, against her will, but Thorstein and Hroar made peace between them.* The sons of Modolf were at the slaughter of Hroar, also Thorir their brother-in-law, Brandi from Peaks, and Steinolf his neighbour. Hamund took vengeance for the slaughter of Hroar and his company.

---

* That is in respect of Thorstein's robbery of Thorun Brow, the concubine of Hroar.

Hrafn

[PART IV, CHAPTER XII.]

Hrafn Haven-Key foretells a volcanic eruption. Death song of Vermund the Blacksmith. Mould-Gnup the Black-smith, his brother, settles Kudafleet and Swqn's-haunts. Bjorn, his son, dreams of the rock-dweller ; his great prosperity resulting therefrom.

CHAPTER XII. There was a man named Isolf. He came out late in the Landnamtide and challenged Vilbald to the Holmgang for his lands. Vilbald would not fight but went away from Buland. He then became possessed of land between Kudafljot and Shaft-river. His son was Hrani of Hranastead, and his daughter was Bjorg, whom Onund, the son of Eyvind the Carp, had for wife. Thraslaug was their daughter, whom Thorarin, son of Olvir at Head, had for wife.

Hrafn Haven-Key was a great Viking, he came to Ice-land and settled land between Holm's-river and Isle's-river and dwelt at Din-Shaws (Dynskogar). He foretold a volcanic eruption, and moved his dwelling to Low-isle (Lágey): his son was Aslak 'orgodi' and from him the Lowislanders are descended. There was a man named Hrolf the Hewing, he dwelt at Nordmæri, at a place named Mould-Town (Molda-tún); his sons were Vermund and Mould-Gnup; they were men great at manslaughters and smiths in iron. Vemund sang the following, once when he was in his smithy :—

> Alone I bore
> From those eleven [1]
> The weird of bane [2]:
> Blow thou faster.

Gnup went to Iceland on account of his own and his brother's manslaughters and settled land between Kuda-

---

(1) "I bore it from the eleven"=it rests on me, it is the *burden of fate* I carry away from the encounter. I slew them all.
(2) *Letale fatum.*

fleet

[PART IV, CHAPTER XII.]

fleet and Isles-river, and all Swans Haunts (Alftaver);
there was a great standing-water then and swan catches
thereon. Molda Gnup sold from his landtake to many
men, and it became thickly peopled, until the earth-fire
i.e. lava flowed adown there; when they fled westward to
Head-Brink (Hófda-brekka), and made there tent-dwellings
in the place which now is called Tent-field (Tjaldavöllr).
But Vermund, the son of Sigmund Kleykir, would not
allow them abidance there, so they went to Horse-garth
(Hrossgard) and made a house there and sat there over
the winter and quarrels and manslaughters befell there
among them. But in the following spring Molda-Gnup
and his companions went west to Grind-wick and took
up their abode there. They had a scanty store of live-
stock. By then the sons of Mould (Molda) Gnup, Bjorn
and Gnup, Thorstein Hrungnir and Thord Leg-wielder,
were of ripe age.

Bjorn dreamed one night that a rock-dweller came to
him and made him an offer of partnership and he thought
he accepted it; whereupon a he-goat (hafr) came to his
goats, and his flocks then bred so quickly that he was
speedily rolling in riches; thence he was called Hegoat-
(Hafr) Bjorn (or Bjorn of the he-goat). Men who had
the power of second sight saw that all the guardian spirits
of the land followed Hegoat-Bjorn to the Thing, and
that they accompanied Thorstein and Thord in hunting
and fishing.

Hegoat-Bjorn had for wife Jorun, the step-daughter of
Gnup his brother; their son was Sverting, who had for
wife Hungerd, the daughter of Thorodd, the son of
Tungu-Odd and of Jofrid the daughter of Gunnar. Their
daughter was Thorbjorg, the mother of Sveinbjorn, the
father of Botolf, the father of Thordis, the mother of
Helga, the mother of Gudny, the mother of the sons of
Sturla. Gnup, son of Molda-Gnup, had for wife Arnbjorg,
the

[PART IV, CHAPTER XII.]
the daughter of Rathorm; a daughter of Molda-Gnup
was called Idun, whom Tjorvar of Swans-ness had for
wife; a son of theirs was Thormod, as has been written
before.

Eystein wrecks his vessel and settles Fairdale. Olver, son of
Eystein, settles land east of Grim's-river. Sigmund
Kleykir settles land from Grim's-river to Carlines-river.
Names of most distinguished settlers in Eastfirth's Quarter.

CHAPTER XIII. There was a man named Eystein,
son of Thorstein-Drangakarl (that is fond of climbing
sea-rocks, 'drangar'); he went to Iceland from Halogaland * and wrecked his ship and was hurt himself among
the spars. He settled Fairdale, but a Carline (old woman)
was washed ashore from his ship into Carlines † Firth
(Kerlingarfjord) where now there is Headriver-sand (Höf-
dársandr). Olver, son of Eystein, settled land to the
east of Grim's-river; no man had dared to settle there on
account of the guardian spirits of the land since Hjorleif
was slain. ‡ Olver dwelt at Head; his son was Thorarin
at Head, a brother by one and the same mother of
Halldor, the son of Ornolf, whom Mord Oraekja slew
under Hamrar and brother by one and the same mother
of Arnor, whom Flosi and Kolbein, the sons of Thord
Freysgodi, slew at Skaptafells Thing.

Sigmund Kleykir was the son of Onund Bill, he took
land between Grim's-river and Carlines-river, which fell
there to the west of Head; from Sigmund are three
Bishops descended, Thorlak, and Pal, and Brand.

---

* " Halogaland " means literally " the land of the northern lights," and is the
country in Norway which begins to the north of Naumdale.
† Carline, Icelandic Kerling, still means old woman or witch in the west of
Scotland.
‡ For an account of the murder of Hjorleif, see Book of Settlement, Part I,
Chapter 6.

There

[PART IV, CHAPTER XIII.]

There was a man named Bjorn, rich and a great dandy, he went to Iceland from Valdres and settled land between Carlines-river and Hegoat-river, and dwelt at Reynir (*i.e.* the Rowan Trees). He had ill dealings with Lodmund the Old. From Reyni-Bjorn the Holy Bishop Thorlak is descended. Lodmund the Old settled land between Hegoat's-river and Foul-brook, as was writ afore; what was then named Foul-brook is now called Jokul's-river on Sunhome-sand, which divides the land quarters. Lodmund the Old, at Solheim, had six sons or more; one of his sons was named Vali, the father of Sigmund, who married Oddlaug, the daughter of Eyvind from Orkney. Another son of Lodmund was named Sumarlidi, the father of Thorstein Hollowmouth in Mark, the father of Thora, the mother of Stein, the father of Thora, the mother of Surt the White, the step-son of Skapti, he was the son of Sumarlid. Skapti the Lawspeaker married Thora later than Sumarlidi, as is told in the landtake of the race of the Olfusings. The third son of Lodmund was named Vermund, the father of Thorkatla, whom Thorstein Vifil had for wife; their daughter was Arnkatla, the mother of Hroi and Thordis, whom Stein Brandsson had for wife; their daughter was Thora. The fourth was named Ari, the fifth was named Hroald, the sixth son of Lodmund was named Oleif, a bastard, he had to wife Thraslaug, the daughter of Eyvind from Orkney; she was sister to Oddlaug; from all these many men are descended.

Now has been written of the landtakes of the Eastfirth Quarter, according to what able and learned men have said; in that quarter there have been many men of greatness and many matters for great sagas have befallen there. These have been the greatest settlers, namely: Thorstein the White, Brynjolf the Old, Porridge-Atli, and Ketil, the sons of Thidrandi-Hrafnkel the godi, Bodvar the White, Hrollaug, son of Earl Rögnvald,

Ozur

[PART IV, CHAPTER XIII.]
Ozur, son of Asbjorn, son of Asbjorn, the son of Heyjang-Bjorn, from whom the Freysgydlings are descended; Ketil the Foolish and Leidolf Champion.

FIFTH PART.

Here begins the Landnam in the Southern Firths, which had the highest reputation of all Iceland, both on account of the richness of the land and on account of those Chieftains who settled there, both learned and unlearned.

The East Firths were settled first in Iceland; between Hornfjardar and Reykjanes they were latest in being fully settled, as there the storm and the surf impeded men's progress in settlement, on account of the harbourless and storm-swept coast.

Some that came out first settled close to the mountain and marked out for themselves the best land, as their cattle selected the pasturage between the coast and the mountain. Those who came out later on, deemed that the former settlers had appropriated too extensive lands to themselves; but King Harald made them agree to this, that no man should appropriate more land to himself than he and his ship's crew could carry fire across in one day.

They should make fires when the sun was rising in the east (and also smokes should be raised to give them an idea of each others bearings) but the fires that they made in the east were to burn until nightfall, meantime they should walk (carrying fire) until the sun reached the west, and there they were to make other fires (which with the fires they had made in the morning were to form the bounds of the landtake).*

Thrasi settles between Kaldaklof-river and Jokul's-river. Hrafn the Foolish settles between Kaldaklof-river and Lambfell-river.

CHAPTER I. There was a man named Thrasi, the son of Thorolf Hornbreaker, he went from Hordaland to Ice-

---

* This portion has been put in Italics as it appears in Italics in the original Icelandic.—Translator.

land

land and took land between Kaldaklof-river and Jokul's-river; he abode at Skogar the easternmost; he was a man of exceeding great strength, and had quarrels with Lodmund the Old as is written before. The son of Thrasi was Geirmund, the father of Thorbjorn, the father of Brand of Skogar.

Hrafn the Foolish was the name of a man, the son of Valgard, the son of Vermund Wordplane, the son of Thorolf 'Vaganef,' the son of Hrærek Ringslinger, the son of Harald Hildtooth—the King of the Danes. He went out of Thrandheim to Iceland and took land between Kaldaklof-river and Lambfell-river; he abode at Raudfell the easternmost and was the noblest of Lords. His children were these; Jorund the godi, and Helgi Bluelog and Freygerd.

Asgeir "Kneif" settles land between Lambfell-river and Seljaland-river. Thorgeir settles land between Lambfell-river and Ira-river. Asgerd upon the murder of Ofeig, her husband, by Harald Fairhair, sets out for Iceland with her children; settles between Seljaland-mull and Mark-fleet. Ancestors of Burnt Nial.

CHAPTER II. There was a man named Asgeir "Kneif," the son of Olaf the White, the son of Skæring, the son of Thorolf, his mother was Thorhild, the daughter of Thorstein Howebreaker; Asgeir went to Iceland and took land between Lambfell-river and Seljaland-river, and dwelt at the place now called Audnar (Wastes); his sons were Jorund and Thorkel, the father of Ogmund, the father of Bishop Jon the Holy. The daughter of Asgeir was Helga, the mother of Thorun, the mother of Thorlak, the father of Thorhall, the father of Bishop Thorlak the Holy.

Thorgeir of Hordaland, the son of Bard Wheghorn, set

out

[PART V, CHAPTER II.]

out from Viggjar in Thrandheim for Iceland, he bought land from Asgeir Kneif between Lambfell-river and Ira-river and abode at Holt. A few winters later he wedded Asgerd, the daughter of Ask the Speechless, and their sons were Thorgrim the Mickle, and Holt-Thorir, father of Thorleif Crow and Skor-Geir.

Ofeig was the name of a renowned man in Raumsdale-folk, he had for wife Asgerd, the daughter of Ask the Speechless. Ofeig came to be at enmity with King Harald Fairhair, and on that account arranged himself for a journey to Iceland, and when he was all ready King Harald sent men upon him who took his life, but Asgerd set off with their children./ She took up land between Seljaland-mull and Mark-fleet and the whole of Longness all up to Jalda-stone, and abode in the northern skirt of Kataness. The children of Ofeig and Asgerd were these : Thorgeir " gollner " and Thorstein Bottlebeard, Thorbjorn the Quiet and Alof Ellidi-shield, whom Thorberg Cornmull had for wife; their children were Eystein and Hafthora, whom Eid, the son of Skeggi, had for wife. Another daughter of Ofeig was Thorgerd, whom Finn, the son of Otkel, had for wife.

Thorolf, the brother of Asgerd, took land by her counsel to the west of the Fleet, between two rivers both called Dealing-river, and he abode at Thorolf's-fell ; there he brought up Thorgeir " gollner," who afterwards abode there; his son was Nial, who was burnt in his house. Asbjorn, the son of Reyrketil, and Steinfinn took land above Cross-river to the east of the Fleet. Steinfinn abode at Steinfinn's-stead, and from him no offspring is come. Asbjorn hallowed his land unto Thor and called it Thorsmark ; his son was Ketil the Wealthy, who had for wife Thurid, the daughter of Gollnir ; their children were called Helgi and Asgerd.

Ketil

[PART V, CHAPTER III.]

Ketil Salmon avenges the murder of Thorolf by burning in their house Harek and Hrærek, two of Thorolf's deadliest enemies; afterwards goes to Iceland and settles land between Rang-river and Hroars-brook. His son, Sighvat the Red, settles above the Dealing or 'dividing' river. Three cornered plot of land hallowed by fire and set apart for a Temple.

CHAPTER III. Ketil Salmon was the name of a much renowned man in Naumdale-folk, a son of Thorkel the Earl of Naumdale, and Hrafnhild the daughter of Ketil Salmon out of Hrafnista. Ketil was then abiding in Naumdale, when King Harald Fairhair sent Hallward Hardfare and Sigtrygg Swiftfarer to Thorolf, the son of Kveldulf, who was a kinsman of Ketil. Then Ketil drew together a band and was minded to give aid to Thorolf; but King Harald went by inland ways over Eldueid and got ships in Naumdale-folk and thus went north to Sandness in Alost and took the life of Thorolf Kveldulf's son, and then went from the north by an outer course and came upon many men who were minded to go and aid Thorolf and his people. At the same time the King dispersed them. But a short time afterwards Ketil Salmon went north unto Torgar and burnt within their house Harek and Hrærek, sons of Hildirid, who had slandered Thorolf with a slander unto death, but after this Ketil betook himself to a journey to Iceland, together with Ingun his wife, and their sons.

He brought his ship unto Rang-river mouth and was the first winter at Hrafn-tofts. Ketil took unto him all the lands between Thiors-river (*Steers*-river) and Markfleet, and within there by the counsel of Ketil, many noble men afterwards took lands. Ketil made especially his own the land between Rang-river and Hroars-brook, all down below Frontwater and abode at Hof. So when

Ketil

[PART V, CHAPTER III.]

Ketil had brought most of his goods to Hof, his wife gave birth to Hrafn, who was the first Speaker-at-Law in Iceland, hence the place is called Hrafn-tofts. Salmon kept to himself all lands east of Rang-river the easternmost, together with Vatnsfell all unto the brook that flows east of Broad-lair-stead, as well as the lands above Cross or *Thwart*‑river (Thvera) all but Dafthak's-holt and the moor which he gave to a man called Dafthak; Salmon was a man of exceeding great strength. Another son of Salmon was called Helgi, he had for wife Valdis Jolgeir's daughter, and their daughter was Helga, whom Oddbjorn Ash-smith had for wife; after him Addbjorn's tomb bears its name. The children of Oddbjorn and Helga were these: Hroald, Kolbein, Holfinna, and Asvor. A third son of Salmon was Horolf, whose children were these: Orm the Strong, Otkel, and Hrafnhild, whom Gunnar, the son of Baug, had for wife; their son was Hamund, the father of Gunnar of Lithe-end. A fourth son of Salmon was called Vestar, who had for wife her who was called Moeid; their daughter was Asmy, who was the wife of Ofeig Snake; their children were these: Asmund Beardless, Asbjorn, Aldis, the mother of Brand of Vellir, and Asvor, the mother of Helgi the Swart; another daughter was called Asa. A fifth son of Salmon was called Herjolf, who was the father of Sumarlidi, the father of Vetrlidi the Scald, both of whom lived at Sumarlidis-by, a place that now is called Under-Brinks (Undir-Brekkum). Thangbrand the Priest and Gudleif Arason of Reek-Holar slew Vetrlidi for lampooning them. Sæbjorn the godi was a son of Hrafn, the son of Hœng (Salmon), he had for wife Unn, the daughter of Sigmund; a son of theirs was called Arngeir.

Sighvat the Red was the name of a noble man in Halogaland, who had for wife Rannveig, the daughter of Eyvind Lambi and of Sigrid, whom Thorolf, the son of

Kveldulf

[PART V, CHAPTER III.]

Kveldulf, had had for wife before. Rannveig was the sister of Finn the Squinter. Sighvat went to Iceland by his own desire, and took land by the counsel of Salmon in his landtake, to the west of Markfleet, the Mark of Einhyrning, to wit above Dealing-river, and he abode at Lairstead (Bolstad) ; his son was Sigmund, the father of Mord Gig,* and of Sigfus in Hlid, and of Lambi at Lambi's-stead, and of Rannveig, whom Hamund Gunnar's son had for wife, and of Thorgerd, whom Onund Bill in Floi had for wife. Another son of Sighvat was Barek, the father of Thord, the father of Stein. Jorund the godi, the son of Raven the Foolish, settled to the west of the Fleet at a place now called Sverting's-stead, where he reared a great temple. A three-cornered plot of land lay unappropriated to the east of the Fleet, between Cross-river and Jalda-stone. This plot of land Jorund went round by fire and set it aside for the temple. Jorund had for wife Thurid, the daughter of Thorbjorn from Gaular ; their son was Valgard the godi, the father of Mord, and Ulf the "orgodi," from whom are descended the men of Oddi and the Sturlungs, and from Jorund are come many great men in Iceland.

Thorkel Bandaged-leg took land by the counsel of Salmon, round about Three Corner (Thríhyrning) and abode beneath that mountain, he was a man of exceeding great strength. The children of Thorkel were these : Bork the Bluetooth-beard, the father of Starkad beneath Three Corner, and Thorny, whom Orm the Strong had for wife, and Dagrun the mother of Bersi.

---

* Gig=Fiddle : and in the Saga of Burnt Nial, of which he is one of the most distinguished characters, he is called Fiddle Mord. See Dasent's "Burnt Niall."

Baug

[PART V, CHAPTER IV.]

Baug settles Fleet-Lithe. Fatal fight at Sandholar-ferry between the followers of Sigmund and followers of Stein the Snell. Sons of Stein outlawed from Lithe. Many and fatal blood suits result therefrom between Stein, Onund, and their families.

CHAPTER IV. There was a man named Baug, who was the foster-brother of Salmon, he went to Iceland and was the first winter at Baug-stead, and the next with Salmon ; he settled the whole of Fleet-Lithe (Fljotshlid) by the counsel of Salmon, down from Broad-lairstead to the boundary of Salmon and abode at Lith-end. His sons were Gunnar at Gunnarsholt and Eyvind at Eyvind Mull, a third son was Eyvind the Snell, and a daughter he had called Hild, whom Orn in Væla-garth had for wife. Stein the Snell and Sigmund the son of Sighvat the Red, were journeying together from the west from Eyrar * and came to Sandholar-ferry all at one and the same time, that is to say, Sigmund and the travelling company of Stein, and each party wished to cross the river first ; Sigmund and his party butted off the house-carles of Stein, and drove them away from the ferry-boat, and therewith Stein came up and dealt Sigmund forth-with a death blow. For this manslaughter all the sons of Baug were made outlaws from the Lithe,† and Gunnar went away to Gunnar's-holt, and Eyvind went east to the fells, Isle Fells (Eyjafjöll) to Eyvind's-holar, but Snell-Stein to Snell-Stein's-head. The daughter of Sigmund was grieved that her father's murderer should go out thither, and she egged on Onund, her husband, to avenge Sigmund. So Onund went with thirty men unto Snell's-head and set fire to the abode there, and Snell-

---

* Now Eyrar-bakki.
† Lithe – Hlid = *The Slope.*

[PART V, CHAPTER IV.]

Stein went out and gave himself up, and they took him to the Head and slaughtered him there, and the blood suit for that slaughter was taken up by Gunnar, who at that time had for wife Hrafnhild, the daughter of Storolf, and sister to Orm the Strong. Their son was Hamund, and they were both men of exceeding great mettle as to strength and prowess.

Onund was found guilty of the murder of Snell-Stein, and abode at home with a large company of men for two winters. Orn of Væla-garth kept spies upon Onund. The third winter, past yule-tide, Gunnar went with thirty men upon Onund at the suggestion of Orn; Onund happened to be going from some sports with his horses accompanied by eleven men, and both parties met in Battledale (Orrostudal) where Onund and three men fell, while there fell one of Gunnar's band. Gunnar had on a blue cape and rode up along the Holts unto Steer's-river, and a short way from the river he fell off his horse dead from his wounds. When the sons of Onund, Sigmund Kleykir, and Eilif the Wealthy grew up they besought their kinsman, Mord the Gig, to take up the blood suit; but Mord said it was no easy matter seeing that the man was a guilty outlaw; but they answered that of Orn, who was their nearest neighbour they had the greatest dislike, so Mord advised that they should set afoot against Orn a suit whereby to saddle him with the guilt of outlawry, and get him driven out of the countryside. So the sons of Onund undertook a suit against Orn for unlawful grazing and the verdict of guilt against him came to this that he should fall, unatoned, at the hands of the sons of Onund, anywhere but within Vælagarth and within an arrowshot's range outside his own land. The sons of Onund were continually laying ambush for him, but he took good heed to himself. But in this manner they got an opportunity of Orn, that he was driving cattle out of

his

[PART V, CHAPTER IV.]

his land and thus they slew him, and those concerned were disposed to think that he had fallen an unhallowed man.*

Thorleif Spark, the brother of Orn, made a bargain with Thormod, the son of Thiostar, that he should hallow Orn; Thormod had then just come out to Eyrar from abroad and he shot an arrow from a hand bow so far that the fall of Orn was within such bounds as the range of his bowshot hallowed. Then Hamund Gunnar's son and Thorleif took up the blood suit after Orn but Mord backed up the brothers, the sons of Onund; they had no fine to pay but had to quit the countryside of Floi. Then Mord wooed, on behalf of Eilif, Thorkatla, the daughter of Ketilbjorn, and as dowry from home there went with her the lands of Head, and there Eilif took up his abode; but on behalf of Sigmund, Mord wooed Arngunn, the daughter of Thorstein Drang-carle, and he betook himself east into those countrysides; then also Mord wedded Rannveig, his sister, to Hamund, the son of Gunnar, who thereon betook himself back to the Lithe (Fleet-lithe, Fljóts-hlíd) and their son was Gunnar of Lithe-end.

Hildir and Hallgeir and their sister Ljot were all descended from a stock in the Western Islands,† they came to Iceland and took up land between the Fleet and the Rang-river, the whole of the countryside of Eyjar up to Thvera. Hildir abode at Hildisey; he was the father of Moeid; Hallgeir dwelt in Hallgeirsey, and his daughter was Mabil, whom Helgi, the son of Salmon, had for wife, but Ljot had her dwelling at Ljotstead.

---

* Oheilagr.
† That is from Scotland or Ireland.

Remarkable

[PART V, CHAPTER V.]

Remarkable combat of Dufthak and Storolf in Oldugrof.
Orm the Enthralled first to settle Westman-Isles. Eilif
from Sogn settles land up to Troutwater and Viking-
brook. Bjorn from Sogn lives at Svinhagi and settles
land along Rang-river. Kol, son of Ottar Ball, settles
land east of Troutwater and Stot-brook with Troll-wood.
Fatal fight of Egil, his son, with Gunnar; other fatal
fights with Gunnar. Hrolf Redbeard settles land of
Holm between Fish-river and Rang-river; resides at
Force (the Falls); he worships the Force; his remark-
able power of distinguishing his sheep; fortells his own
death and destructlon of his flocks.

CHAPTER V.   Dufthak cf Dufthaksholt was a freedman
of those brothers, he was a man of exceeding great
strength, as was also Storolf the son of Salmon, who
then abode at Hvol. Between them there befell a dispute
about grazing rights. A second-sighted man saw one
evening nigh to nightfall, that a great bear went out from
Hvol and a bull likewise out from Dufthaksholt, and they
met on Storolf's-wold and set in anger on each other, and
the bear got the best of it. In the morning it was seen
that a dell was left where they had encountered each
other, and the soil looked as if it had been turned inside
out and there the place is now called Alda-grove; both
of them were hurt.*

Orm the Enthralled, the son of Bard, the son of Barek,
the brother of Hallgrim Ṣinged-balk, was the first to
people the Westman-Isles, where heretofore there had
only been a fishing station, and which few or none had
made a winter abode of. The daughter of Orm was
Haldora, whom Eilif, the son of Wall-Brand, had for wife.

Two brothers, Eilif and Bjorn, went away from Sogn

---

* Dufthak and Storolf were hurt—who by their magical power of shape-
changing had contended in the assumed forms of a bull and a bear.

[PART V, CHAPTER V.]

to Iceland. Eilif settled Oddi-the-little up to Trout-water and Viking-brook; he had for wife Helga, the daughter of Onund Bill; their son was Eilif the Young, who had for wife Oddny, the daughter of Odd the Slender; their daughter was Thurid, whom Thorgeir of Oddi had for wife; their daughter again was Helga.

Bjorn abode at Svinehagi, and took land up along Rang-river; his children were these: Thorstein, the father of Grim Holt-scull and Hallveig, the mother of Thorun, who was the mother of Gudrun, the mother of Sæmund, the father of Bishop Brand.

There was a man named Kol, the son of Ottar Ball, who took up land to the east of Troutwater and Stot-brook west of Rang-river, together with Troll-wood, and abode at Sandgill; his son was Egil, who lay in ambush for Gunnar, the son of Hamund, at Knave-hills, and fell there himself, together with two Norwegians who were with him, and his house-carle Ari, while of Gunnar's company there fell Hjort, his brother. The sons of Gunnar were Hrani and Hamund. Gunnar had also a fight with Otkel from Kirkby near the home-field enclo-sure at Hof, where fell both Otkel and Skamkel. Geir the godi and Gizur the White, Asgrim the son of Ellida-grim and Starkad from Three-corner, who was the son of Bork Bluetooth-beard, the son of Thorkel Bandaged-leg, who had for wife Thurid, the daughter of Egil of Sandgill. All these went by the road called Leet-race and came by night with thirty men to Lithe-end, where Gunnar had to face them with only one man of ripe age; two men fell out of the company of Geir; but sixteen were wounded ere ever Gunnar was laid low.

There was a man called Hrolf Redbeard, he took all the land of Holm, between Fish-river and Rang-river, and abode at Force; his children were these: Thorstein Redneb, who abode there afterwards, and Thora, the mother

[PART V, CHAPTER V.]

mother of Thorkel Moon, and Æsa, the mother of Thorun, the mother of Thorgeir of Lightwater, and Helga, the mother of Odd from Mjosyndi. The daughter of Odd was Asborg, who was the wife of Thorstein godi, the father of Bjarni the Sage, the father of Skeggi, the father of Markus Speaker-at-Law. Thorstein Redneb was a great man at blood-offerings, he worshipped the force, and all leavings of blood-offerings he commanded to be thrown into the force; he was also a man of keen sight into things to come. Thorstein caused to be counted out of a fold two thousand and four hundred sheep of his, whereupon all the remainder in the fold rushed out (uncounted); although his sheep were so many yet in autumn he could tell which of them looked likely to die (in the winter) and them he slaughtered. But the last autumn he lived, he spoke at the sheepfold: "Cut ye now down whichever sheep ye like, for now, either I am a death-doomed man or else all my sheep are doomed, or all of us together." But that winter on the same night that he died all his sheep were driven into the force (by tempest).*

---

* The power of knowing and distinguishing sheep is very extraordinary amongst mountain shepherds at present, and the Translator knows a case in his own district in which a farmer passing a field more than twenty miles from his home, recognised and picked out from the sheep amongst which they were feeding, a number of sheep that had been stolen from him. He identified them in a Court of Justice, and they were eventually satisfactorily proved to have belonged to his farm, though since he had lost them they had been sheared and every mark had been removed that seemed likely to lead to their identity. The face of the sheep is that to which the shepherd chiefly looks for recognition, and to the practised shepherd the face of a sheep seems to be as easily distinguishable from that of others as that of one man from another. Of course the shepherds of Iceland had at a very early period to adopt some more definite means of the recognition of their sheep than by the face and general appearance as implied here in the case of Thorstein, and it appears from the Grágás or collection of the Laws of the Icelandic Commonwealth, that a general system of ear-marking (lög-mark) was adopted from very early times on Icelandic farms and that each farm had an hereditary mark of its own. These marks were called hamar (hammer) and were often cut on the top of the sheep's ears and belonged originally to the heathen age denoting the Holy Mark of the Hammer of Thor. The marking known in Lakeland as key-bitting seems most closely allied to it in form. Close cropping or cutting off the whole of the sheep's ears was forbidden under penalty of the lesser outlawry, unless the matter had first been proclaimed at the Lögretta or Public Court of Law.

Harald

[PART V, CHAPTER VI.]

Harald Fairhair causes Asgrim to be killed by Thororm.
Thorstein Asgrim's son burns Thororm in, and then with
Thorgeir, his brother, sails for Iceland. By advice of
Flosi he settles the Rang-river plains above Viking-brook.
Buried treasure at Tent-stead.

CHAPTER VI. Ulf the Gilder was the name of a
mighty hersir in Thelamark and he lived at Fiflavellir
(Dandelion-field); his son was Asgrim, who there abode
afterwards. King Harald Fairhair sent Thororm of
Thruma, his kinsman, to claim taxes from Asgrim, but
he yielded none; so the King sent Thororm a second time
for his head, and then he slew Asgrim. At that time
Thorstein, the son of Asgrim, was out on Viking journeys
and Thorgeir, another son of his, was but ten winters old.
Some time afterwards Thorstein came back from the
wars and laid his ship against Thruma, and burnt * Thororm in his house, together with all his household; the
stock he cut down and stole all the chattels; whereupon
he went to Iceland, together with Thorgeir his brother
and a mother-sister of theirs called Thorun, who settled
all the Thorun Haws (necks).

Thorgeir bought the land of Oddi, from Hrafn, the son
of Salmon, both the strands and Warmdale, and all the
land between Rang-river † and Hroar's-brook; he abode
first at Oddi, and then wedded Thordis, the daughter of
Eilif.

By the advice of Flosi, who had already made all
Rang-river plains his own, Thorstein took up land above

---

* These "burnings in" though recognised in blood feuds, were the most
barbarous cruelties practised by the northmen. The doors and windows of the
house were fastened from the outside, hay was placed against the house round
about, and set on fire, and the inmates when trying to escape were butchered or
driven back into the flames. The earliest mention of a "burning in" is in
Heimskringla at Upsula; see Chapter 40; see also Egil's Saga 22 for "burning
in" of Thorolf by Harald Fairhair.

† Rang-ring, literally the wrong or "crooked" water probably takes its
name from the angle or bend near Oddi.

Viking-brook

[PART V, CHAPTER VI.]

Viking-brook unto the boundary of Bjorn of Svinhagi, and he abode in Skard the easternmost; in his day there came a ship into Rang-river-mouth, on board which there was much sickness, and men would lend them no help. So Thorstein went to them and brought them to the place which is now called Tent-stead, and put up a tent over them and tended them himself while they were still alive, but they all died at last; but the longest lived of them buried a great treasure which has never been yet found. From these things Thorstein was called Tent-steading; his sons were called Gunnar and Skeggi.

Flosi goes from Norway to Iceland on account of manslaughter of King Harald's bailiffs. His settlements by the Rang-river. Ketil the One-handed, Ketil Char, Orm the Wealthy, and other settlers by the Rang-river.

CHAPTER VII. There was a man called Flosi, a son of Thorbjorn from Gaular, who slew three bailiffs of King Harald Fairhair, and then went to Iceland. He took to himself land east of Rang-river, the whole of the eastern Rang-river plains. His daughter was Asny, the mother of Thurid, whom Brand o' the Fields had for wife. A son of Brand o' the Fields was Flosi, the father of Kolbein, the father of Gudrun, whom Sæmund Deep-in-Lore had for wife. Flosi was wedded to Gudrun, the daughter of Thorir, the son of Skeggbroddi, and their sons were these: Kolbein, who has been named afore, and Bjarni, the father of Bjarni, the father of Flosi, the father of Valgerd, the mother of Lord Erlend, the father of Hauk. For this reason Loft the Old went to do blood-offering at Gaular, that Flosi was an outlaw in Norway. Flosi the Norwegian had for wife Thordis the Mickle, the daughter of Thorun the Wealthy, the daughter of Ketil the One-handed, and their daughter was Asny, whom Thorgeir had for wife.   Ketil

[PART V, CHAPTER VII.]

Ketil the One-handed was the name of a man who was the son of Audun Thunnkar; he took to him the whole of the western Rang-river plains above Brook-bottoms, and on the eastern side of Steer's-river, and abode at A (A=river); he had for wife Aleif, the daughter of Thorgils. Their son was Audun, the father of Brynjolf, the father of Bergthor, the father of Thorlak, the father of Thorhall, the father of Bishop Thorlak the Holy.

Ketil Char, the son of a brother of Ketil the One-handed, took land on the western side of Steer's-river and abode at Vellir the westernmost; his son was Helgi Roe, who had for wife Helga, the daughter of Rolf Redbeard, and their son was Odd the Slender, the father of Asborg, whom Thorstein godi had for wife, and of Oddny, whom Eilif the Young wedded.

Orm the Wealthy, the son of Ulf the Keen, took land along Rang-river, by the counsel of Ketil the One-handed, and abode at Housegarth, where also dwelt after him his son Askel; but his son was the first to rear an abode at Vellir and from him are come down the family of Vellir.

Thorstein Lunan was the name of a man of Norway who was a great sea-farer; about him it had been prophesied that he would die in a country which, at that time, was not yet peopled. Thorstein went in his old age to Iceland, together with his son Thorgils; they settled the upper parts of Steer's-river-holts, and abode at Lunan's-holt, and there Thorstein was buried in a howe. A daughter of Thorgils was Asleif, whom Ketil the One-handed had for wife, and their sons were these: Audun, aforenamed, and Eilif, the father of Thorgeir, the father of Skeggi, the father of Hjalti in Steer's-river-dale; he was the father of Jorun, the mother of Gudrun, the mother of Einar, the father of Bishop Magnus.

Gunnstein Bearserks'-Bane, the son of Bolverk Blinding-snout, slew two Bearserks, one of whom had slain

Earl

[PART V, CHAPTER VII.]

Earl Grjotgard at Solvi on the inner side of Agdaness. Afterwards Gunstein was shot by a Finnish arrow on board his ship, north in Hefnir. A son of Gunnstein was Thorgeir, who had for wife Thorun the Wealthy, the daughter of Ketil One-handed, and their daughter was Thordis the Mickle.

Settlements of Rathorm and Jolgeir from the west, and Askel Hnokan, Thorkel Furcoat, Lopt the son of Orm, Thorvid the son of Ulfar, and Thorarin, son of Thorkel.

CHAPTER VIII.　Rathorm and Jolgeir, two brothers, came from west away over sea to Iceland, and took land between Steer's-river and Rang-river; Rathorm became owner of land to the east of Redbrook, and abode in Vætleifsholt; his daughter was Arnbjorg, whom Sverting, the son of Hrolleif, wedded, and their children were Grim the Speaker-at-law and Jorun. Afterwards Arnbjorg was the wife of Gnup, the son of Molda Gnup, and their children were Hallstein of Hialli (Hill) and Rannveig, the mother of Skapti the Speaker-at-law, and Geirny, the mother of Scald-Raven. Jolgeir became owner of land to the west of Redbrook unto Stonebrook, and abode at Jolgeir's-stead.

Askel Hnokan, the son of Dufthak, the son of Dufnial, who was the son of Kjarval, King of the Irish, took up land between Stonebrook and Steer's-river, and abode in Askel's-head; his son was Asmund, the father of Asgaut, the father of Skeggi, the father of Thorvald, the father of Thorlaug, the mother of Thorgerd, the mother of Bishop Jon the Holy.

Thorkel Furcoat, the foster-brother of Rathorm, got ownership of all lands between Rang-river and Steer's-river, and abode at Haf; he had for wife Thorunn from Orkney, and their daughter was Thordis, the mother of

Skeggi

[PART V, CHAPTER VIII.]

Skeggi, the father of Thorvald of As; from thence Hjalti, his brother-in-law, got riding horses to the Althing for himself and eleven followers when he came out with Christianity; but no one else dared avail Hjalti in this manner on account of the overbearing ways of Runolf, the son of Ulf, who had made Hjalti guilty of blasphemy.

Now are set down in writing the men who have taken up lands within the landtake of Ketil Salmon.

Lopt, the son of Orm, the son of Frodi, came from Gaular to Iceland while still in his youth, and took land west of Steer's-river, between it and Rothay (Rauða) and up as far as Skuf's-brook, also Broadmere the easternmost up as far as Sulaholt, and he abode in Gaulverjaby together with his mother Oddny, who was the daughter of Thorbjorn of Gaular.

Lopt went abroad every third summer on behalf of himself and his mother's brother, Flosi, in order to do sacrifice at the temple, of which Thorbjorn, his mother's father, had been the guardian. From Lopt many great folk are descended, such as Thorlak the Holy, Paul, and Brand.

Thorvid, son of Ulfar, and brother of Hild, went away from Vors to Iceland, but Lopt, his kinsman, gave him land on Broadmere, and he abode at Vorsby. His children Hrafn and Hallveig, whom Ozur the White had for wife, and their son was Thorgrim Cheekbeard.

There was a man named Thorarin, son of Thorkel from Alvidra, who was the son of Hallbjorn, the Hordlander's Champion; he brought his ship into Steer's-river-mouth and had a Steer's head at the stem thereof, and from that the river got its name. Thorarin took land above Skufsbrook unto Rothay, along Steer's-river; his daughter was Heimlaug, whom Loft took it into his head to wed when sixty years of age.

Ancestry

⌊PART V, CHAPTER IX.⌋

Ancestry of Harald Fairhair. Hastein driven by him from
Sogn betakes himself to Iceland; throws his Seat Stocks
overboard for an omen; they come ashore at Stockseyri;
settles between Rotnay (Red-river) and Olvis-river up to
Full-brook. Settlements of Hallstein, Thorir, son of
hersir Asi, Hrodgeir the Sage, and Onund Bil.

CHAPTER IX.   Harald Goldbeard was the name of a
King in Sogn *; he was married to Solvor, the daughter of
Earl Hundolf, and sister to Earl Atli the Slender; their
daughters were these: Thora, the wife of Halfdan the
Black, King of the Uplanders, and Thurid, the wife of
Ketil Slate-river.   Harald the Young was the son of Halfdan and Thora; to him Harald Goldbeard gave his name
and his realm.   King Harald died the first of them, and
next to him Thora, but Harald the Young last; and
then the realm came to King Halfdan, and to the rule
thereof he appointed Earl Atli the Slender.

Later King Halfdan † wedded Ragnhild, the daughter
of Sigurd Hart, and their son was Harald Fairhair.
When King Harald stepped into the reign in Norway and
allied himself with Earl Hakon, the son of Grjotgarth, he
handed over to Hakon, his father-in-law, the folk of Sogn,
while he himself (Harald) went east into the Wick.   But
Earl Atli would not give up the rule till he should have
seen King Harald on the matter.   Over this the Earls
strove with great mettle, and each drew an armed host
together, and they met at Stafnessvag in Fjalir and
fought.   There Earl Hakon fell, and Atli was wounded

---

* Sogn = district represented by Sogne fiord and its coasts in modern map of
Norway.   .
† The reign of Halfdan the Black marks a most important epoch in the
Heimskringla or History of the Kings of Norway.   Previous to his reign all the
history recorded therein is mythical, consisting chiefly of the history of the
Ynglings, a race of legendary sovereigns which include the Deities Odin, Niord,
Frey, and Freya.   After Halldan's reign, in the succession of his son Harald
Fairhair (about 860) the Heimskringla becomes historical, and Harald's reign
is most closely connected throughout with the "Book of the Settlement."

and

[PART V, CHAPTER IX.]

and was carried to Atli's-isle where he died of his wounds. After this Hastein kept to himself the rule of Sogn, until King Harald and Earl Sigurd drew together an army against him, whereupon Hastein fled away and betook himself to journeying to Iceland. He had for wife Thora, the daughter of Olvir, and their sons were Olvir and Atli. According to ancient fashion, Hastein shot overboard his seat-stocks out at sea and they drifted aland on Stalf-jara facing Stockseyri (Stocks Island), but Hastein came into Hastein-sound east of Stockseyri, and was wrecked there.

Hastein took to himself land between Rothay, and Olvis-river up to Full-brook, and the whole of Broadmere up to the Holts, and abode at Starstones, as did likewise his son Olver after him ; that place is now called Olver's-stead. Olver had all the land-take to the west of Grim's-river, Stockseyri to wit, and Asgaut's-stead, but Atli owned all between Grim's-river and Rothay, and abode in Trod-holt. Olver died leaving no children. Atli took after him lands and loose chattels ; a freedman of his was Bratt, in Brattholt, and another Leidolf of Leidolfstead. Atli was the father of Thord the Deaf, the father of Thorgils, the step-son of Errubein, the father of Grim Babbler, the father of Ingjald, the father of Grim, the father of Bork and of Einar, the father of Hallkatla, whom Rafn, the son of Sveinbjorn, had for wife ; their daughter was Steinun, the mother of Lord Rafn, and Herdis, the mother of Atli, the father of Steinun, whom Hauk, the son of Erlend, had for wife. Bork, the son of Grim, was the father of Ragnhild, whom Flosi, son of Bjarni, had for wife ; their children were Einar and Bjarni and Valgerd, the mother of Lord Erlend, the father of Hauk. Another daughter of Flosi was Thordis, the mother of lady Ingigerd, the mother of lady Gudrun and Hallbera the Abbess. Another daughter of Flosi was Halla, the mother of Lord Christophorus.

There

[PART V, CHAPTER IX.]

There was a man called Hallstein, who went from Sogn to Iceland, he was a brother-in-Law of Hastein, who gave to Hallstein the western part of Eyrarbank; he abode at Framness; his son was Thorstein, the father of Arngrim, who was slain as he was busy digging for withered wood-stumps; his son was Thorbjorn, who abode at Framness.

Thorir, son of hersir Asi, the son of Ingjald, the son of Hrvald, went to Iceland and settled the Rape of Kaldnessings all up from Full-brook and abode at Sealforce; his son was Tyrfing, the father of Thurid, the mother of Tyrfing, the father of Thorbjorn the Priest and the Priest Hamund of Goddales.

Hrodgeir the Sage, and his brother Oddgeir, whom Finn the Wealthy and Haven Orm bought out of his landtake, took to themselves the Rape of the Hraungerdings, and Oddgeir abode at Oddgeir's-holar; his son was Thorstein Ox-goader, the father of Hrodgeir, the father of Ogur in Kambakista, but the daughter of Hrodgeir the Sage was Gunnvor, whom Kolgrim the Old wedded, thence are sprung the Kvistlings.

Onund Bill, who was mentioned before, took land to the south of Hroar's-brook and abode at Onund's-holt; from him are sprung many men of greatness as is writ before.

Settlements of Ozur the White and his freedman Bodvar.
Bodvar summoned for sheep-lifting. After his death his
house at Willowwood became the source of a fatal feud to
rival claimants. Thord slays Rafn from an ambush.

CHAPTER X.   Ozur the White was the name of a man who was the son of Thorleif of Sogn. Ozur committed a manslaughter in holy places in the Uplands when he was tending the bridals of Sigurd Risi; on that account he
                                                              had

[PART V, CHAPTER X.]

had to flee away to Iceland, and there he settled first
all the land of the Holts between Steer's-river and
Hraun's-brook. When he committed the manslaughter
he was seventeen years old. He got for wife Hallveig,
the daughter of Thorvid ; their son was Thorgrim Cheekbeard, the father of Ozur, the father of Thorbjorn, the
father of Thorarin, the father of Grim, the son of Tova.
Ozur abode in Kamp-holt. A freedman of his was named
Bodvar, who abode at Bodvar's-tofts by Vidiskog (Willowwood), and Ozur gave him a share in the wood, which he
reserved for himself in case Bodvar should die leaving no
children. Orn of Vælagarth, already mentioned, summoned Bodvar for sheep-lifting, and for that reason,
Bodvar conveyed to Atli, the son of Hastein, all his
belongings, and Atli brought to nought the suit of Orn.
Ozur died whilst Thorgrim as yet was young, and then
Hrafn, the son of Thorvid, took over the guardianship of
Thorgrim's goods. After the death of Bodvar, Hrafn
laid claim to Willowwood and forbade it Atli, but Atli
deemed he was owner thereof. Atli went with three men
to fetch wood (faggots) and there was Leidolf with him ;
of this Hrafn's shepherd warned him (Hrafn) and he rode
after them with seven men. They met in Fight-dale and
fought there ; two of Hrafn's house-carles fell and he
himself was wounded ; but of Atli's side there fell one
house-carle, while he got wounds unto death and rode
home. Onund Bill parted them and bade Atli come into
his house. Thord the Deaf, the son of Atli, was then
nine winters old ; but when he was fifteen winters old,
Hrafn rode to meet a ship in Einar's-haven ; he had on a
blue cloak and rode home by night. Thord lay in
ambush for him alone by Howe-ford, a short way from
Trodholt, and slew him there with a spear ; there is the
howe of Hrafn to the east of the path, while to the west
of it is the howe of Hastein and the howe of Atli and
Olver

Olver. These manslaughters were allowed to stand each against the other. From this deed Thord rose in renown; he then married Thorun, the daughter of Asgeir East-men's-Terror, who slew a ship's crew in the mouth of Grim's-river, in revenge for a robbery he had to put up with in Norway. At the age of two-and-twenty, Thord bought him a ship in Knor-Sound, being minded to go claim his heritage; at the same time he hid (buried) a great deal of wealth and therefore Thorun would not go away with him, but took over his landed possessions. Thorgils, the son of Thord, was a little over two winters old. The ship of Thord was lost; and a winter thereafter came Thorgrim Errubein, the son of Thormod and Thurid, the daughter of Ketilbjorn to Thorun, to look after things with her. He wedded Thorun, and their son was Hæring.

Olaf Twinbrow was the name of a man who went from Lofot to Iceland; he took to him all the Skeid between Steer's-river and White-river unto Sand-brook; he was a man of exceeding great strength. Olaf abode at Olaf's-walls and he lies buried in Brow-howe beneath the Varda-fell. Olaf had for wife Ashild, and their sons were Helgi the Trusty and Thorir Snowdrift, the father of Thorkel "Gullkar," the father of Orm, the father of Helga, who was the mother of Odd, the son of Hallward. A third son of Olaf was Vadi, the father of Gerd. Thorgrim set his heart on Ashild when Olaf was dead, but Helgi would chide him therefore, and he lay in ambush for Thorgrim at the cross-roads below Ashild's-moor; Helgi bade him leave off coming to the house, but Thorgrim answered he was no longer a child in mind, and so they fought and Thorgrim fell there. Ashild asked where Helgi had been, he sang this verse:

On

[PART V, CHAPTER X.]

> On that spot was I present,
> Where Errubein fell earthward,
> The friend of hosts pushed forward,
> Where bright tongues sang loudly.
> I made a gift to Odin
> Of the stalwart son of Asmod,
> Gaut's [1] feast to Gallows wielder,[2]
> To raven corpse we yielded.

Ashild said he had cut for himself the undoing of his own head. Helgi went and got for himself a berth in Einar's-haven. Hæring, the son of Thorgrim, was then sixteen winters old, and he rode with two women to Head to see Teit, the son of Gizur. Teit and his rode fifteen in company to forbid Helgi taking passage abroad; they met in Mark-Hraun up away from Mark against Helgi's-hill and Helgi had three men. There Helgi fell, together with one of his fellows, and on Teit's side one man fell; these manslaughters were allowed to stand against each other. A son of Helgi was Sigurd of the Land, and Skefil out of Hawkdale, the father of Helgi Deer, who fought with Sigurd, the son of Ljot Lingback, in the holme of Axe-river at the Althing; on which fight Helgi wrote this:

> My right hand it is bound up,
> The Tyr of wave's bright fire
> Fetched me a wound, I lie not,
> Oh, Bil, o' the lea of serpents.

Another son of Skefil was Hrafn, the father of Grim, the father of Asgeir, the father of Helgi.

---

(1) Gaut=Odin, his feast=sacrifice made to him in the shape of a slain warrior.
(2) Gallows wielder=Odin.

[PART V, CHAPTER XI.]

Settlements of Thrand Much-sailing, Olvir Bairncarle, Thorbjorn Laxcarle, Thorbrand, and others who came out late in the Landnamtide.

CHAPTER XI. Thrand, the Much-Sailing, the son of Bjorn and brother to Eyvind the Eastman, who has been written of before, fought in Hafur's-firth against King Harald, and had to flee the land afterwards; he came to Iceland late in the tide of the landtakes, and he took land between Steer's-river and Lax-river up into Kalf-river and to Land-brook; he abode in Thrand-holt and his daughter was Helga, whom Thormod Shaft had for wife.

Olver Bairncarle was the name of a highly renowned man in Norway, he was a great Viking; he would not allow children to be tossed on spear points as was then the custom of Vikings; hence he was called Bairncarle. His sons were these: Steinolf, the father of Una, whom Thorbjorn Laxcarle had for wife, and Einar, the father of Ofeig Grettir and of Oleif Broad, the father of Thormod Shaft. A third son of Olvir Bairncarle was Steinmod, the father of Konal, the father of Alfdis of Barra, whom Olaf Feilan wedded. The son of Konal was Steinmod, the father of Haldora, whom Eilif, the son of Ketil One-handed, had for wife. Those kinsmen, Ofeig Grettir and Thormod Shaft, went to Iceland, and were the first winter with Thorbjorn Laxcarle, their kinsman-in-law, but in the spring he gave them the Rape of the men of Gnup. Unto Ofeig he gave the western part, between Thvera or Thwart-river and Calf-river, and abode at Ofeig's-stead by Stein's-holt, but to Thormod he gave the eastern part and he abode at Skapt-holt. The daughters of Thormod were these: Thorvor, the mother of Thorodd the godi, the father of Bjarni the Sage, who was the father of Skeggi, the father of Markus the Speaker-at-law, the father of Valgerd, the mother of

Bodvar

[PART V, CHAPTER XI.]

Bodvar, the father of priest Thord, the father of Thorleif of the Garths, and of Markus of Melar, and of Bodvar of By. Law Skapti was the father of Thorstein Hollowmouth, the father of Gunnhild, the mother of Jodis, the mother of Viborg, the mother of Magnus, the father of Snorri of Melar. Ofeig fell by the hand of Thorbjorn Earl's-Champion in Grettir's-lane by Heel. The daughter of Ofeig was Aldis, the mother of Wall-Brand.

Thorbjorn Laxcarle settled the whole of Steer's-river-dale and all of the Rape of the men of Gnup down to Calf-river, and abode the first winter at Midhouse; he had three different winter abodes before ever he came to Hagi, where he abode to his dying day. His sons were these: Ottkel in Steer's-river-dale, and Thorkel Trandil, and Thorgils, the father of Otkatla, the mother of Thorkatla, the mother of Thorvald, the father of Dalla, the mother of Bishop Gizur.

There was a man of Norwegian kindred called Thorbjorn Earl's-Champion; he left the Orkneys for Iceland and bought land in the Rape of the men of Hrani, from Mar, the son of Naddod, all down below Seals-brook, between it and Lax-river, and abode at Holar. His sons were these: Solmund, the father of Singed-Kari, and Thormod, the father of Finna, whom Thororm in Carle-firth had for wife; their daughter was Alfgerd, the mother of Guest, the father of Valgerd, the mother of Thorleif Beiskald, who was the father of Alfeid, the mother of Thorlak, the father of Priest Ketil, the father of Herdis, the mother of the children of Bishop Paul.

Brondolf and Mar, the sons of Naddod and Jorun, the daughter of Olvir Bairncarle, came to settle in Iceland at an early time; they took to them the Rape of the men of Hrani as far as the watershed. Brondolf abode at Berghyl, and his sons were these: Thorleif, the father of Brondolf, the father of Thorkel Skotakoll (Shooting-pate), the

[PART V, CHAPTER XI.]

the father of Thorarin, the father of Hall in Hawkdale, and Thorlak, the father of Runolf, the father of Thorlak the Bishop. Mar abode at Mar-stead; his son was Beinir, the father of Kolgrima, the mother of Skeggi, the father of Hjalti.

Thorbrand, the son of Thorbjorn the Dauntless, and Asbrand, his son, came to Iceland late in the tide of the landtakes, and Ketilbjorn showed them to a landtake above the Mull that juts into the river called Stack-river, and thence to Kaldakvisl, and they abode in Hawkdale. They found these lands too narrow, because the eastern-most Tongue was already taken possession of. So they eked out their landtake and took to them the upper part of the Rape of the men of Hrani by a straight sight line from the Mull to Ingjald's-gnup above Gyldarhagi. The children of Asbrand were Vebrand and Arngerd; Vebrand was the father of Oddlaug, whom Sverting, the son of Runolf, had for wife. Eyfreyd the Old settled the easternmost Tongue between Kaldakvisl and White-river, and abode at Tongue; with him came out Drumbodd, who abode at Drumbodd-stead.

Ketilbjorn from Naumdale in Norway with a ship (tne Ellidi) gives that name to the Ellidi's-river. His settlements at Grimness, Laugar-dale, Bishop's-tongue, and Mossfell. Settlement of Asgeir at Lithe, Eilif at Head. Grim, son of Vethorm, settles Bowerfell. Hallkel fights with and slays Grim for his land upon Hallkel's-hillocks.

CHAPTER XII. There was a man named Ketilbjorn, one of high renown, in Naumdale; he was the son of Ketil, and of Asa, the daughter of Earl Hakon, the son of Grjotgarth; he had for wife Helga, the daughter of Thord Skeggi. Ketilbjorn went to Iceland when already the land was settled wide about along the sea. He

steered

[PART V, CHAPTER XII.]
steered a ship called Ellidi ; he hove in at the mouth of
Ellidi's-river down below the Heath, and was the first
winter with Thord Skeggi, his father-in-law. In the
the spring he went up across the Heath in order to look
for some choice of land ; they made for themselves a lair
over night and put up a Skali, where now the spot is
called Scale Brink, and when they went thence they came
to the river, which they called Axe-river, because they
lost their axe ; they tarried a while under the Mull of a
fell, which they named Trout Mull ; for there they left
behind the river trout which they had caught in the
river. Ketilbjorn took to him the whole of Grimness all
up away from Hoskuld's-brook, the whole of Laugar-dale
and the whole of Bishop's-tongue up to Stack-river, and
abode at Mossfell. Their children were Teit and Thormod, Thorleif, Ketil, Thorkatla, Oddleif, Thorgerd,
Thurid ; a natural son of Ketilbjorn's was called Skæring.

Ketilbjorn was so wealthy in loose goods that he bade
his sons forge a cross beam of silver for the temple they
were building, and when they would not do that, he took
the silver by a yoke of oxen up to the top of the mountain,
he and his thrall Haki and his bondwoman Bot, and
there they hid the treasure so that it cannot be found.
Thereupon he killed Haki in Hakiskard and Bot in
Botskard. Teit had for wife Alof, the daughter of Bodvar of Vors, who was the son of Viking-Kari ; their son
was Gizur the White, the father of Bishop Isleif, the
father of Bishop Gizur. Another son of Teit was Ketilbjorn, the father of Kol, the father of Thorkel, the father
of Kol, the Bishop of the men in Wick (Norway.) From
Ketilbjorn and his wife many distinguished men have
sprung.

There was a man named Asgeir, the son of Ulf, to
whom Ketil gave his daughter Thorgerd, and bestowed
upon her as a dowry from home all the Lithe-lands above
Hagagarth ;

Hagagarth ; he dwelt at Lithe the westernmost ; their son was Geir the godi, and Thorgeir, the father of Bard of Mossfell. Eilif the Wealthy, the son of Onund Bill, got for wife Thorkatla, the daughter of Ketilbjorn, and as a dowry from home the lands of the Head were bestowed upon her ; they abode at Head ; their son was Thorir, the father of Thorarin " Sæling " (the Luxurious).

Vethorm, the son of Vemund the Old, was a mighty hersir ; he fled away from King Harald east into Jamta land and there cleared the woods for an abode. His son was called Holmfast, but Grim was the name of a sister's son of his ; they were out in the western Viking raid and in the Hebrides they slew Earl Asbjorn Skerryblaze, and took there for war booty Alof, his wife, and Arneid, his daughter, who fell to Holmfast's lot, and by him was handed over to his father to be a bondmaiden of his. Grim got for wife Alof, the daughter of Thord the Wagging whom the Earl had had for wife before. Grim went to Iceland and took to him all Grimness up to Swine-water and abode at Onwardness (Ondurtunes) for four winters, and afterwards at Bowerfell ; his son was Thorgils, who married Æsa, the sister of Gest, and their sons were Thorarin of Bowerfell and Jorund of Middlemead.

Hallkel, the brother of Ketilbjorn by the same mother, came to Iceland and stayed with Ketilbjorn through the first winter ; Ketilbjorn offered to give him land, but Hallkel deemed it the way of a mannikin to take gift land, so he challenged Grim either to give up his lands or to accept a Holmgang-fight. Grim fought on the Holm with Hallkel beneath Hallkell's-hillocks and fell there, and there Hallkel abode ever after. His sons were these : Otkel, whom Gunnar, the son of Hamundi slew, and Odd of Kidberg, the father of Hallbjorn, who was slain at at Hallbjorn's-beacons, and also Hallkel, the father of Hallvard, the father of Thorstein, whom Einar the Shet-
lander

lander slew. A son of Hallkel Oddson was Bjarni, the father of Hall, the father of Orm, the father of Bard, the father of Valgerd, the mother of Haldora, whom Bishop Magnus, the son of Gizur, had for wife. Now we come to the landtake of Ingolf, and the men who hereafter are told have taken up lands within his landtake.

Thorgrim Bill settles Bills-fell, and Steinraud, his freedman, gets the Waterlands. Hrolleif settles lands on the western side of the Axe-river, which flows across the Thingwall. Orm settles land east of the Warm-river (Hita). Alf of Agdir, from Norway, brings his ship into Alf's-os Inlet. Settles lands to west of Warm-river ; resides at Gnupar.

CHAPTER XIII. Thorgrim Bill, the brother of Onund Bill, settled all lands above Thvera and abode at Bills-fell. A freedman of his was was Steinraud, the son of Melpatrick in Ireland ; he got for his own all the Waterlands and abode at Steinraud's-stead. Steinraud was the goodliest of men ; his son was Thormod, the father of Kar, the father of Thormod, the father of Brand, the father of Thorir, who had for wife Helga, the daughter of Jon.

Hrolleif, the son of Einar, the son of Olvir Bairncarle, came into Miry Creek at a time when all was settled along the sea. He took all lands up towards those of Steinmod on the western side of the Axe-river which flows across the Thingwall (Thing Vellir) and abode at Heathby for sundry winters. Then he challenged Eyvind in Kviguvagar (Heifer-creek) to choose between Holmgang or exchange of land with him, and Eyvind chose rather that they should exchange the lands. For some winters afterwards Eyvind abode at Heathly and went afterwards out to Walrusness to By-Skerries, but Hrolleif abode afterwards at Kvigu-vagar and there he is laid in how. His son

[PART V, CHAPTER XIII.]

son was Sverting, the father of Grim, the Speaker-at-law at Moss-fell.

Orm the Old was the son of Earl Eyvind, the son of Earl Armod, the son of Earl Nereid the Old. Orm took land to the east of Warm-river unto Thvera and round about all Ingolf's-fell, and abode at Hvamm; his son was Darri, the father of Orn. Earl Eyvind was with Kjotvi the Wealthy against King Harald in Hafur's-firth.

Alf of Agdir ran away before King Harald out of Agdir in Norway, and went to Iceland, and brought his ship into an inlet which is named after him, being called Alf's-os. He took to himself all lands to the west of Warm-river, and abode at Gnupar. Thorgrim, the son of Grimolf, was a brother's son of Alf, and went west to Iceland with him and took heritage after him, Alf having no children. A son of Thorgrim was Eyvind, the father of Thorodd the godi, and of Ozur, who had to wife Bera, the daughter of Egil Skallagrimsson. The mother of Thorgrim was Kormlöd, the daughter of Kearbhal, the King of the Irish. The daughter of Thorodd the godi was Helga, the mother of Grim the Babbler, the father of Ingjald, the father of Grim, the father of Bork, the father of Ragnhild, the father of Valgerd, the mother of Lord Erlend, the father of Hauk.

Note to Chapter XIII. The Plain of Thing Vellir. The Axe-river (Oxard) and the Althing.

In connection with the Plain of Thing Vellir and the Axe-river, the following extract will be of interest :—

" Independently of its natural curiosities, Thing Vellir was most interesting on account of the historical associations connected with it. Here long ago, at a time when feudal despotism was the only government known throughout Europe, free Parliaments used to sit in peace and

and regulate the affairs of the young Icelandic Republic ; and to this hour the precincts of its Commons House of Parliament are as distinct and unchanged as on the day when the high hearted fathers of the Settlement first consecratep them to the service of a free nation. By a freak of nature, as the subsiding plain of lava (with a centre area of 50 square miles) cracked and shivered into twenty thousand fissures, an irregular oval mass of about two hundred feet by fifty was left almost entirely surrounded by a crevice so deep and broad as to be utterly impassable ; at one extremity alone a scanty causeway connected it with the adjoining level and allowed of access to its interior. It is true just at one point the encircling chasm grow so narrow as to be within the possibility of a jump ; and an ancient worthy named Flosi, pursued by his enemies, did actually take it at a fly, but as leaping an inch short would have entailed certain drowning in the bright green waters that sleep forty feet below, you can conceive there never was much danger of this entrance becoming a thoroughfare. This spot then, erected by nature almost into a fortress, the founders of the Icelandic Constitution chose for the meetings of their Althing or Parliament, armed guards defended tho entrance, while the grown bonders (bondi) deliberated in security within, to this day at the upper end of the place of meeting, may be seen three hummocks, where sat in state the Chiefs and Judges of the land.

From the Althing we strolled over to the Almanna Gja (chasm) visiting the Pool of Execution on our way. The river from the plateau leaps over the precipice into the bottom of the Gja, and flows for a certain distance between its walls. At the foot of the fall the waters linger for a moment in dark, deep, brimming pool, hemmed in by a circle of ruined rocks, and to this pool in ancient days all women convicted of capital crimes were

[PART V, CHAPTER XIII.]

were immediately taken and drowned. Witchcraft * seems to have been the principal weakness of ladies in those days throughout the Scandinavian countries.

A walk of about twenty minutes brought us to the borders of the lake—a glorious expanse of water fifteen miles long by eight miles broad, occupying a basin formed by the same hills, which must have arrested the further progress of the lava torrent. A lovelier scene I have seldom witnessed. In the foreground lay huge masses of rock and lava, tossed about like the ruins of a world, and washed by waters as bright and green as polished maluchite. Beyond a bevy of distant mountains, robed by transparent atmosphere in tints unknown to Europe, peeped over each other's shoulders into the silver mirror at their feet, while here and there from among their purple ridges, columns of white vapour rose like altar smoke toward the tranquil heaven."—*Lord Dufferin's Letters from High Latitudes.*

Thorir Harvestmirk settles Sealcreek (Selvag) and Creasywick. Steinun the Old buys from Ingolf, her kinsman, Walrusnes for a spotted cloak ; gives land to her kinsman Eyvind. Herjolf,† mentioned before, gets land from Ingolf between Reekness and Veg. Herjolf, his grandson, fares to Greenland and is drawn into the ocean-whirl. In his ship a man from the Hebrides writes the Poem of " The Ocean Whirl."

CHAPTER XIV. Thorir Harvestmirk took to him Sealcreek (Selvag) and Krysuvik (Creasywick) but his son Hegg abode at Vag. Another son of his, Bodmod, was father of Thorarin, the father of Sugandi, the father of

---

* It would seem from II, 9, page 44, that witches were at times tried by durádom or Court held at the door of the defendant, a sort of Court of the " first instance."

† The adventures and Settlement of Ingolf and his companions are related in Part I, Chapter V, page 7.

Thorvard

[PART V, CHAPTER XIV.]

Thorvard, the father of Thorhild, the mother of Sigurd, the son of Thorgrim. The sons of Moldagnup settled Grindavik (Porpoise Bay) as is written before.

Steinun the Old, a kinswoman of Ingolf, went out to Iceland, and was with Ingolf the first ˉwinter; he offered to give her the whole of Walrusnes west of Sharp-lava (Hvassahraun), but she gave for it a spotted cloak * and desired that that should pass for a bargain, as thus she would be more secure against disputes as to her title to the land. Herlaug, the brother of Skallagrim, had had Steinun for wife formerly, and their sons were Nial and Arnor.

There was a man named Eyvind, a kinsman and foster son of Steinun, to him she gave land between Heifsr-creek-fell and Sharp-lava ; his son was Egil, the the father of Thorarin, the father of Sigmund, the father of Thorarna, the mother of Thorbjorn in Krysuvik, and of Alof, the mother of Finn the Speaker-at-Law, and of Freygerd, the mother of Lopt, the father of Gudlaug the smith. Herjolf, he of whom the story is before recorded, was a kinsman and a foster brother of Ingolf, hence Ingolf gave him land between Reekness (Reykjanes) and Vag ; his son was Bard, the father of that Herjolf who went to Iceland and got into the ocean-whirl; on his ship was a man hailing from the Hebrides, who wrote the Ocean-whirl-drapa, a poem, whereof this is the beginning :

Let all listen to our skaldship
(The drink of the dwarf's hall).

Asbjorn, the son of Ozur, a brother's son of Ingolf, took land between Lavaholt-brook (Hraunsholts-lækr) and Sharplava, the whole of Swansness, and abode at

* Hecla=cloak or hood, hence Mount Hecla=the cloaked or hooded mountain ; its hood is mist or vapour.

Skuli's-stead ;

[PART V, CHAPTER XIV.]
Skuli's-stead: his son was Egil, the father of Ozur, the
father of Thorarin, the father of Olaf, the father of Sveinbjorn, the father of Styrkar, the father of Goatbjorn, the
father of Thorstein and Gizur of Sealtarnness (Seltjar-
narness).

*Names of the noblest landtakemen. The land completely
    settled in sixty years. Names of the greatest Chieftains
    in the four Quarters at the end of 120 years. Most
    settlers from the west (British Islands) were baptised
    Christians. Relapse of their descendants into heathenism
    for about 120 years.*

CHAPTER XV. Now have been gone over the landtakes which we have heard of as having taken place in
Iceland.

Of landtake men these have been the noblest in the
Quarter of the Southlanders: Hrafn the Foolish, Ketil
Salmon, Sighvat the Red, Hastein Atli's son, Ketilbjorn
the Old, Ingolf, Orlyg the Old, Helgi Bjola, Kolgrim the
Old, Bjorn Goldbearer, Onund Broadbeard.

So many men of lore aver, that the whole land was
settled in the course of sixty winters, so that since it has
not been further peopled.* Then there were still alive
many of the landtake men and their wives. But when
the land had been peopled for sixty years (more) these
were the greatest Chiefs of the land :--

In the Southlanders Quarter: Mord Gig, Jorund the
godi, Geir the godi, Thorstein Ingolf's son, Tongue-Odd.

---

* For census estimating bondi or landowners see III, 20; Page 162 note.
        Population in Iceland in A.D. 1801 was 46,240.
            „   „   „   1880 was 72,442.
            „   „   „   1888 was 69.224.
Since 1870 there has been very great emigration to America, especially to the
far north-west of Canada where an Icelandic community is formed and a news-
paper issued in Icelandic.

                                                              In

[PART V, CHAPTER XV.]

In the Westfirthers Quarter: Egil Skallagrimsson, Thorgrim Kjallak's son, Thord the Yeller.

In the North : Midfirth-Skeggi, Thorstein Ingimund's son, the Goddale men, the sons of Hjalti, Eyjolf, the son of Valgerd, Askel the godi.

In the Eastfirthers Quarter : Thorstein the White, Hrafnkel the godi, Thorstein, the father of Hall-o'-Side, Thord Freysgodi ; Hrafn, the son of Salmon, had at that time the Chief Speakership-at-law.*   '

Wise men say that sundry of the landtake men who took up their abode in Iceland were baptised, most indeed, of those who came from west beyond the sea ; among these are mentioned Helgi the Lean, Orlyg the Old, Helgi Bjola, Jorund the Christian, Aud the Deep-minded, Ketil the Foolish, and yet some more of those who came from west beyond the sea. Some of these held faithfully to their belief unto the day of their death, but in few cases did this pass on from parents to progeny, for the sons of some of these men reared Temples and did sacrifices, and wholly heathen the land remained for well-nigh a hundred winters.†

---

* Some of the names given in this list mark the time of the Sagas in whose events they took a very prominent part, *e.g.* Mord Gig in " Burnt Nial," and Egil the hero of the Egil Saga.

† The Icelandic has a duodecimal system of notation, so one hundred as here mentioned is equivalent to one hundred and twenty.—TRANSLATOR.

PLACE NAMES,

Being the Register of all the Place Names, Farm Names, and Tribe Names contained in the Book of the Settlement.

———

It was as a means of comparing the Icelandic Language and Place Names with the Place Names and Dialect of Cumberland, Westmorland, and Furness, that originally about eleven years ago I commenced this work. I intended when I started to translate a chapter, or perhaps two chapters, of the Book of the Icelandic Settlement for the purpose of such comment and comparison.

In the years that have elapsed since, the work has widened out to its present proportions; it is still, however, as a record of Icelandic Place Names in comparison with North English Place Names upon which it grounds its chief claim to consideration. Hence the following Index and Reference of Place Names has occupied weeks and months of careful thought and work, and has been most carefully gone over and revised again and again by me, and I have given a reference to Part and Chapter where each Place Name is found, so that the student interested in tracing out and following the connexion and history of such Place Names may at once turn to whereever it occurs in the body of the work. This has been a work implying much comparison and research. I have also from my own examination, or from the best authority available, given in *italics* the meaning of each Place Name, as such meaning is often of important service in following out the connexion of the history, and will be available also for use in comparing those Icelandic Place Names with our own Place Names in the north.

The

The Norsemen, as will be seen from the note at page 160, considered the giving of Place Names as a solemn ceremony in the act of Settlement, by which they dedicated the land to the God, and thereafter held it from him for their own use. Hence all Place Names were very carefully and very methodically given, and each marks some characteristic description, some distinguished chieftain, or some notable event in the early History of the Settlement.

The following Register * should be carefully compared with the names upon the map, commencing with the settlement of Kalman in þverar þing in the Quarter of the Western Firths, Part II, page 27. Some slight differences exist between the names in the index and those on the map—fjörd or fjardar on the map is generally *firth* in the index; and þ and ð on the map are represented by Th and d in the index ; map heiði=register *heath*, and á or ár in map is often *river*, as also is fljot, vatn, lækr, and straum.

Rivers, as will be seen, form an essential factor in the great work of the division of landtakes. The Place Names of Norway to be found in the Book of the Settlement, have been so annotated, either in the body of this work or in the following register, that their modern locality will be easily found upon a good modern map of Norway. The meaning of each Place Name is put in Italics immediately after the Place Name.

---

* Ferguson in his Northmen in Cumberland and Westmorland, expresses some doubt about how and when Norwegian Place Names as distinguished from Danish Place Names found their way to the north-west of our island. Anyone carefully reading the story of the Settlement and comparing the words in the following Register with North English Place Names, will find such doubt cleared up.

LIST OF PLACE NAMES.

A

Á, *River,* iv, 11 ; v, 7.

Adalvik, *Main Wick,* ii, 20-31.

Asvaldsnes, *Asvald's-ness,* ii, 31.

Agdanes, v, 7.

Agdir, ii, 19 *bis,* 21, 26 ; iii, 19.

Akrafell, *Cornfield mountain,* i, 15.

Akranes, *Cornfield-ness,* i, 15 *bis,* 17, 20, 21 *bis*; ii, 1.

Akrar, *Cornfields,* ii, 4.

Alfgeirsvellir, *Alfgeir's-field,* iii, 6.

Alfsnes, *Alf's-ness,* i, 11.

Alfsos, *Alf's-inlet,* v, 13.

All, iii, 6.

Almannafljot, *All men's river,* iv, 11.

Almannagja, *All men's gorge or rift*

Almdalir in Norway, *Elm-dale,* iv, 1.

Almenningar, *All men's land,* commons, ii, 20.

Alptafjordr, The Lower, *Swan-firth,* iv, 7.

,, The Southern, i. 4 ; iv, 4-7.

,, Off Broadfirth, ii, 59, 13 *bis,* 14.

,, In Greenland, ii, 14.

,, Off Icefirth, ii, 29.

Alptanes, *Swan's-ness,* i, 14, 19, 24; ii, 4 *bis,* 24 ; iv, 12.

Alptaver, *Swan's-haunts,* iv, 12.

Alvidra in Dyrafirth, *All weather,* ii, 27, 29.

Alvidra in Norway, v. 8.

Althing, iii, 1 ; 5, 10. For Althing, see note under iv, 7.

Alost in Sandnes, i, 18; v, 3.

Ambattara, *Bondmaid's-river,* iii, 1.

Anabrekka, *An's-brink,* ii, 4.

Anavik in Greenland, *Ani's-wick.*

Andakilsa, *Duck-pool-river,* i, 17, 19.

Andarkelda, *Duck Bog.*

Armenia, *Armenia.*

Arnallstadir, *Arnall(ld)'s-stead,* iv, 3.

Arnarbæli, *Eagles's-seat,* ii, 3.

Arnafell, *Arni's mountain,* iii, 8.

Arnarfjordr, *Eagle-firth,* ii, 26 *bis.* 27 ; iii, 13.

Arnarholt, *Orn's-wood,* i, 19 ; ii, 3, 13.

Arnarhvall, *Orn's-knoll,* i, 7.

Arnarhvoll, *Eagle's-hill,* iii, 16.

Arnarnes, *Eagle's-ness,* iii, 13.

Arnarthufa, *Eagle's-hummock,* iii, 20.

Arnbjargarlækr, *Arnborg's-brook,* ii, 3.

Arneidarstadir, *Arneid's-stead,* iv, 2.

Arnlaugsfjordr in Greenland, *Arnlaug's-firth,* ii, 14.

As, *The Ridge,* i, 21 ; v, 8 ; iii, 20.

Asar, *The Ridges,* iv, 11.

Asbjarnarnes, *Osbern's-ness,* iii, 4.

Asbjarnarstadir, *Osbern's-stead,* ii, 2.

Asbjarnavick, *Osbern's-wick,* iii, 19.

Asgautsstadir, *Osgaut's-stead,* v, 9.

Asgeirsa, *Osgar's-river,* iii, 1.

Ashildarmyri, *Ashild's-moor,* v, 10.

Asia, *Asia.*

Askelshöfdi, *Oskettle's-head,* v, 8.

Asmundarleidi, *Osmund's grave,* ii, 6.

Asolfskali, *Oswulf's house,* i, 15, 16.

Atlahaugr, *Atli's how,* v, 10.

Atley, *Atli's Isle,* ii, 5 ; v, 9.

Audarstein, *Name of stone marking Queen Aud's grave,* see ii, 19.

Audartoptir, *Aud's-tofts,* ii, 16.

Audbrekka, *Aud's-brink.*

Audbrekku-menn, *Aud's-brink-men,* iii, 13.

Audkulustadir, *Aud-knoll-stead,* iii, 5.

Audnar, *The Wastes,* v, 2.

Audolfsstadir, *Eadwulf's-stead,* iii, 5, 19.

Audsstadir, *Aud's-stead,* i, 21.

Audunarstadir, *Eadwin's-stead,* iii, 1.

Augastadir, *Eye-stead,* i, 21.

Aungley, *Angle (hook) island,* iii, 17.

Austfirdingafjordungr or *Eastfirth Settlements,* iv, 1, 13 ; v, 1, 15.

Austfirdingar. see above.

Austfirdir, *East-firths,* i, 1, 4; v, 1.

Austfjordr, *East-firth.*
Austmadr, *Eastman, Norwegian,* ii, 28.
Austmenn, *plural Eastmen,* ii, 31, 33 *bis,*
  v, 5, 10.
Austrbygd in Greenland, *East Settlement.*
Austrvegr, *Eastern Baltic,* iii, 1.
Axlarhagi, *Axle (shoulder) Haws,* iii, 8.
Axlhegingar, *Axlhegings,* iii, 8.

B.

Bakkaholt, *Bank wood.*
Balkastadir *Bulk (balk)-stead,* ii, 32.
Ballará, *Ball-river,* i, 21 ; ii, 24.
Bard, *Hill-edge,* i, 12 ; ii, 26 ; iii, 10, 11.
Bárdardalr, *Bard's-dale,* iii, 18 ; iv, 10.
Bardagata, *Battle toe,* iii, 18; iv, 10.
Bardastrond, *Fish (or Skield) Strand,* i, 2,
  14; ii, 25.
Bardsnes, *Edge-ness,* iv, 6 *bis.*
Bardsvik, *Edge-wick,* ii, 20.
Bardverjar, *Men of Bard,* iii, 11.
Bareyskr, *From Barra Island, Hebrides.*
Baugsstadir, *Ring-stead,* iv, 1 ; v, 4.
Beigadarhvoll, *Beigad's-knoll,* iii, 3.
Beigaldi, ii, 4.
Bekanstadir, *Bekan's-stead,* i, 17.
Belgsdalr, *Bag-dale,* ii, 21.
Belgsstadir, *Bag-stead,* ii, 21.
Berg, *Mountain,* iv, 7.
Berghylr, *Mountain Pool,* v, 11.
Bergthorshvall, *Bergthor's-hill.*
Berjadalsá, *Berriekle-river,* i, 17.
Bersastadir, *Bersir's-stead,* ii, 32.
Berserkseyri, *Bearsark's-isle,* ii, 10.
Berufell, see Burfell.
Berufirdingar, *Men of Berufirth,* iv, 7.
Berufjördr, ii, 22 *bis,* 26; iv, 7.
Beruvik, *Bear's (female bear's) wick.*
Beruvikrhraun, *Beruvik-lava,* ii, 7, 8.
Bjargaos, *Rocksmouth,* iii, 1.
Bjarkey, *Birch Island,* iii, 11.
Bjarmaland, *Perm in Russia,* ii, 19.
Bjarmar, *Perm,* ii, 19.
Bjarnardalr, *Bear-dale,* ii, 3.
Bjarnarfjördr, *Firth,* ii, 31, 32.

Bjarnarhöfn, *Bjorn's-haven,* ii, 11 *bis.*
Bjarnastadir, *Bjarni's-stead,* ii, 1.
Bjarneyjafloi, *Bear-isle Bay,* ii, 19.
Bildsa, *Axe-river, or from bild, a sheep
  with spotted cheeks,* iii, 12.
Bildsfell, v, 13.
Bishupstunga, *Bishop's Tongue,* v, 12.
Bitra, *Bitterness,* ii, 20, 32.
Björgin, *Bergen or the Precipices,* i, 1 *bis.*
Blanda, *Whey-river,* iii, 5,
Blasekr in Greenland, *Blue Shirt,* ii, 14.
Blaskogar, *Blue Woods,* i, 19.
Blaskogsa, *Blue Woods-river.*
Blesastadir, *Horse-stead,** ii, 3.
Blundsvatn, *Blund (slumber) Water,* i, 20.
Blöndudalr, *Whey-dale,* iii, 3, 5.
Blönduhlid, *The slope up from the river
  Blanda,* iii, 8.
Blöndukvislir, *Branches of Blanda,* iii, 7.
Blönduos, *Mouth of Blanda,* iii, 5.
Bolstadará, *Lairstead-river,* iii, 8.
Bolstad, *Lairstead,* v, 3.
Bolungarvik, *Wood-pile-wick,* ii, 29.
Bordeyri, *Boardors,* ii, 33 *bis.*
Borg or Burg, *A fortress,* i, 19 ; iii, 4.
Borgardalr, *Borgdale,* ii, 13.
Borgarfjardarfloi, *Inlet of Burgfirth,* i,
  12, in note.
Borgarfjördr, ditto, i, 2, 19, 20; ii, 5, 14,
  24; iii, 4 in Eastfirth ; iv, 4.
Borgarholt, *Burgh-wood,* ii, 6, 11.
Borgarhraun, *Burgh-lava,* i, 19; ii, 5.
Borgarhofn, *Burgh-water,* iv, 7, 9.
Borgarlækr, *Burgh-brook,* ii, 11.
Borgarsandr, *Burgh-sand,* iii, 7.
Botarskard, *Pass of Bót,* v, 12.
Botn, *Bottom,* i, 14.
Botnsa, *Bottom's-river,* i, 14.
Brjanslækr, *Brien's-brook,* i, 2.
Brattahlid in Greenland, *Steep Slope,* ii,
  14.
Brattsholt, *Copsewood of Bratt.*
Brautarholt, *Road wood,* i, 14.
Bravollr, *Brow field.*
Breidá, *Broad-river,* iv, 10.

---

* Blesi, a horse with a white star on his forehead.

Breidabolstadr in Fellhversi, *Broad-lair-stead*, iv, 9.
　　in Fljotshlid, v, 3, 4.
　　in Pappyli, iv, 10.
　　in Reykjardal, i, 20 *bis*.
　　in Sidu.
　　in Skogarstrond.
　　in Sokkolfsdal, ii, 17.
　　in Vestrhop, iii, 5.
Breidamyri, *Broad-moor*, v, 8 *bis*, 9.
Breidasandr, *Broad-sand*, iv, 10.
Breidavad, *Broad-ford*.
Breidavik, *Broad-wick*, ii, 13; iv, 4.
Breiddale, *Broad-dale*, iv, 3, 7 *bis*.
Breiddælr, *Men of Broad-dale*, iv, 7.
Breidfirdingr, *Men of Broad-firth*, iii, 10.
Breidifjördr, *Broad-firth*, i, 2; ii, 5, 12 *bis*, 14 *bis*, 16, 19, 24, 26; iii, 20.
Breidvikingar, *Men of Broad-wick*.
Brekka, *Brinks or Fairbrink*, ii, 28, 33 *bis*.
Brekkur, *Brink*, v, 3.
Brenna, *The burning ; marks a burning in*, ii, 2.
Brenningr, *The burning*, ii, 7.
Bretland, *Britain*, Prologue.
Brimar, *Bremen*.
Brimilsvellir, *Seal Field*, ii, 9.
Brimnesskogar, *Surfness Shaws*, iii, 8.
Brokey, *Black grass Island*, ii, 14.
Brunahaugr, *How of Bruni*, v, 10.
Brunastadir, *Brun-stead*.
Bryndælir, *Men of Brynjadal*, i, 14.
Brynjudalr, *Bryndale*, i, 14 *bis*.
Brynjudalsá, *Bryndale-river*, ii, 25.
Budardal, *Boothdale*, ii, 19.
Buland, *Home-land*, iv, 11, 12.
Bulandshofdi, *Home-head*, ii, 9.
Bulandsnes, *Home-ness*, iv, 7.
Burfell, *Bower-fell*, ii, 25.
Byrgisvik, ii, 32.
Bægisa, *Bægis-river*, iii, 14.
Barjarsker, *Farm Skerry*, v, 13.
Bær, *Dwelling*, ii, 32; iv, 7; v, 11.
Bödmodshorn, *Bodmod's-horn*, iv, ii.
Bodmodstunga, *Bodmod's-tongue*, iv, ii.
Bödmod, *Battle Mood*.
Bödvarsdalr, *Bodvar's-dales*, iii, 20; iv, 2.

Bödvarsholar, *Bodvar's-knolls*, iii, 1.
Bödvasholt, *Bodvar's-wood*, iv, 8.
Bodvarstopter, *Bodvar's-tofts*, v, 10.

D.

Dala lönd, ii, 16.
Dalir, *Dales*, ii, 5, 17, 18, 22; ii, 26; iii, 1.
Dalsfjördr, *Dale's-firth*, i, 3.
Danir, *Danes*, v, 1.
Danmörk, *Denmark*, i, 1; iii, 1; v, 1.
Deildara, *Dealing or Divide-river*, two streams so called, v, 2, 3.
Deildarey, *Divide-river Island*, ii, 19.
Deildargil, *Divide-river Gill*, i, 21.
Deildarhjalli, *from deild=dale or division of land ; and hjalli=hill;* iii, 4, 5.
Digranes, *Digra-ness*, iv, 1.
Dimunarvâgr, ii, 14.
Djupa, *Deep-river*, iii, 8.
Djupidalir, *Deep-dale*, iii, 16.
Djupifjördr, *Deep-firth*, ii, 23.
Drangaland, *Rock-land*, ii, 31.
Drangar, *used of lonely upstanding rocks, and in popular lore believed to be giants turned into stone*, i, 11, 14; ii, 31; iii, 14.
Drangarik, ii, 31.
Drapuhlid, ii, 11.
Drifandi, iv, 11.
Dritsker, *Dirt-skerry*, ii, 12.
Drumboddstadir, v, 11.
Dufansdalir, ii, 26.
Dufunefsskeid, *Doveneb's-course*, iii, 8.
Dufthaksholt, *Dufthak's-wood*, v, 3, 5.
Dufthaksskor, *Dufthak's-scar*, i, 7.
Dumbshaf, *Foggy Sea, i.e. the Polar Sea*, iii, 12.
Dyflinn in Ireland, *Dublin*, i, 1, 19; ii, 15.
Dyflinarskiri, *Dublin's shire or district*, ii, 15.
Dynskogar, *Din Shaws*, iv, 12.
Dyrafjördr, *Dyra-firth*, ii, 27.
Dögurdara, *Day-meal-river*, ii, 16, 19.
Dogurdarness, *Day-meal-ness*, ii, 9; ii, 16.

E.

Egdskr, v, 13.

Egilsstadir, *Egil-stead*, iv, 1.

Eid, *Isthmus*, i, 7.

Eilifsdalsa, *Elif's-dale-river*, i, 13.

Einarsfjördr in Greenland, ii, 14.

Einarshöfn, *Einar's-haven*, v, 10.

Einarssker, *Einar's-scar*, ii, 11.

Einarstadir, *Einar's-stead*, iii, 19.

Eingihlid, *Eingis lithe*, iii, 5.

Eingines, ii, 31.

Einhyrningsmörk, v, 3.

Eireksey, *Eirek's-isle*, ii, 14.

Fireksfjördr, *Eirek's-firth*, ii, 14.

Eireksholmar in Greenland, *Eirek's-holm*, ii, 14.

Eireksstadir, *Eirek's-stead*, ii, 14.

Eireksvagr, *Eirek's-bight*, ii, 14.

Eldgrimstadir, *Elgrim-stead*, ii, 3.

Eldueid, *Eldu's-isthmus*, v, 3.

Ellidaaros, *Ellidis-river-mouth*, v, 12.

Ellidæy, *Ellidis-isle*, ii, 19.

England, ii, 18; iii, 1.

Enni, *Steep crag or precipice, a mountain bluff near Frodis-water*, ii, 8.

Enskr, *English*, Prologue.

Esjuberg, i, 12, 13, 20; ii, 2.

Esjubergingar, *From Esjuberg*, i, 12.

Eskifjördr, iv, 6.

Eskiholt, ii, 4.

Espiholl, *Aspknott*, iii, 16, 20.

Exara, v, 13.

Ey or Eyja, *an island*.

Eyjorfjardará, *Island-firth-river*, iii, 12, 16.

Eyjafjoll, *Isle-fells*, i, 15.

Eyjafjördr, *Island-firth*, ii, 25, 29; iii, 12.

Eyjará, *Island-river*, iv, 12.

Eyjardalsá, *Island-dale-river*, iii, 18.

Eyjasandr, *Sand-island*.

Eyjasunda Breidafirdi, *Island-sound*, ii, 16.

Eyjasvelt, *Island's-ditch*, v, 4.

Eyrar, *Islands*, v, 4.

Eyrarbakki, *Island-bank*, v, 9.

Eyrarfell, *Island-fell*, ii, 13.

Eyrbyggjar, ii, 13. For explanation, see Note, page 57.

Eyri, i, 13, 20; ii, 13, 20, 25, 26, 29.

Eystri bygd á Greelandi, ii, 14.

Eyvindará, *Eyvind's-river*, iv, 3.

Eyvindardalr, *Eyvind's-dale*.

Eyvindarfjördr, *Eyvind's-firth*, ii, 31.

Eyvindarholar, *Eyvind's-hollow*, v, 4.

Eyvindarmuli, *Eyvind's-mull or crag*, v, 4.

F.

Fabeinsa, *Fabein's-river*, ii, 19, 20.

Fagrabrekka, *Fair-brink*, ii, 33.

Fagradalsa, *Fairdale-river*, iv, 7.

Fagradalsaros, *Fairdale-river's-mouth*, ii, 22.

Fagravik, *Fairwick*, iv, i.

Fagrdælar, *Fairdale*, ii, 21.

Fagridalr in Broadfirth, ii, 21.

by Hofdarsand, iv, 13.

In Weaponfirth, iv, 2.

Fagriskogr, *Fair-wood*, ii, 5.

Faskrudsfjördr, iv, 6.

Faxaos, *Faxis Inlet*, i, 2.

Feldarholmr, *Cloak-holm*, ii, 11.

Fell, ii, 19, 32.

Fellshverfi, *The Fell district*, iv, 9.

Fellsmuli, *Fell-mull or point*, iii, 18.

Fellskogar, *Fell-woods*, ii, 19.

Ferstikla, i, 14.

F'alir, *Planks*, i, 3; ii, 5; v, 8, 9.

Fjardará, iv, 11.

Fjardarhorn, ii, 10.

Fiflavellir, *Dandelion-fields*, v, 6.

Finnafjördr, *Finn's-firth*, iv, 1.

Finnar, *Finn*, iii, 2.

Finnmork, *Finmark*, ii, 19.

Finnskor, *Finn's scar*, v, 7.

Firdafylki, i, 4.

Firdir in Norway, ii, 1.

Fiská, *Fish-river*, v, 5.

Fiskilækr, *Fish-brook*, iii, 16, 19.

Fitjar in Norway, i, 17.

Fjöll, v, 4.

Flangastadir, iv, 4.

Flatatunga, *Flat-tongue*, iii, 8.

Flatey in Broadfirth, *Flat-island*, ii, 19.

Flateyjardalr, iii, 17.

Fljot, *The Fleet or river-mouth*, ii, 1, 29;
iii, 4; iv, 2; v, 2, 3, 4.

Fljotsdalr, *Fleet-dale*, ii, 1; iv, 2, 3.

Fljotshlid, *Fleet-lithe*, v, 3.

Fljotshverfii, *Fljots-hamlet*, iii, 18; iv, 10.

Floi, *The flowe*, i, 17, v, 3, 4.

Flokadalr, *Floki's-dale*, i, 13, 18, 20; ii,
24; iii, 11.

Flokadalsa, *Floki-dales-river*, i, 19, 20.

Flokavagr, *Floki's-bight*, in the Shetlands, i, 2.

Flokavardi, *Floki's-beacon*, i, 2.

Flugumyri, *Flymoor*, iii, 8.

Folafortr, ii, 29.

Forsvöllr, *Force-field*, iv, 2.

Forsæludalr, iii, 3.

Foss, *Force*, ii, 4, 8; iv, 11.

Fossá, *Force-river*, i, 14, 19; iii, 5.

Fossjördr, *Force-firth*, ii, 26.

Framnes, *Fore-ness*, v, 9.

Fridleifsdalr, *Fridleifsdale*, iii, 11.

Fridleifsdalsa, *Fridleif's-dales-river*, iii,
11.

Froda, ii, 8.

Frodaros, *Froda's-mouth*, ii, 9.

Fullækr, *Foul-brook*, iv, 5, 13.

Fura, ii, 6.

Fyllarlækr, v, 9.

Færeyjar, *Sheep Islands*, i, 1, 2; ii, 6, 7,
16.

G

Galmströnd, *Galm-strands*, iii, 13.

Galtarhamar, *Boar's-crag*, iii, 12

Gardar, *The Intakes*, i, 15; iii, 9; v, 11.

Gardarsholmr, *Isle of Gardar*, i, 1, 2.

Garpsdalr, ii, 21.

Gata in the Faroe Islands, i, 2.

Gaular in Norway, i, 3; v, 7, 8.

Gaulverjabær, v, 8.

Gaunguskard, *The Search Pass*, iii, 6;
in searching for sheep in autumn.

Gaunguskardsá, *Gaunga Skard's-river*,
iii, 6.

Gaunguskardsaros, *Gaunga Skard's-
river-mouth*, iii, 5, 6, 8.

Gautar, *Swedes*, iii, 12.

Gautsdalr, *Gaut's-dale*, iii, 5.

Gautland, *Sweden*, iii, 2, 12.

Geiradalr, iii, 20.

Geirastadir, *Geir-stead*, iii, 20.

Geirhildarvatn, *Geirhild's-water*, i, 2.

Geirland, iv, 11.

Geirlandsá, *Geirland's-river* in the Shetlands, iv, ii.

Geirmundarstadir, *Geirmund-stead*, ii,
19, 24; iii, 6.

Geirmundarvagr, *Geirmund's creek* or
bay, ii, 19.

Geirolfsgnupr, *Geirolf's-peak*, ii, 31.

Geirsa, *Geir's-river*, i, 20.

Geirshlid, *Geir's-slope*, i, 20.

Geirthjofsfjördr, ii, 26.

Geitland, i, 19, 21.

Geitlendingar, i, 19.

Gerpi, iv, 6.

Gil, *Gills*, i, 21.

Gilhagi, *Gil-how*, iii. 6.

Gilja, *Gill's-river*, iii, 3, 4, 6.

Gilsá, *Gil's-river*, iv, 3.

Gilsbakki, *Gil-bank*, i, 12.

Gilsfjordr, *Gil-firth*, ii, 21.

Gislavötn, *Gil's-water*, ii, 3.

Glera, iii, 15, 16.

Gljufrá, *Gorge-river*, ii, 4; iii, 8, 9.

Glodafeykisá, iii, 8, 9.

Gnupa, *The Peak*, frequent as farm name,
ii, 5, 6.

Gnupar, *The Peaks*, iii, 18; iv, 10, 11.

Gnupudalr, *Peak-dale*, ii, 5.

Gnupufell, *Peak-fell*, ii, 29; iii, 13, 16, 20.

Gnupverjahreppr, v, 11.

Goddalir, *Goddales*, ii, 5, 7, 11, 20; iv, 1;
v, 9, 15.

Gotalækr, ii, 8.

Greipar in Greenland, i, 1.

Grenitresnes, *Spruceness*, ii, 23.

Grettisgeil, v, 11.

Grimolfsvotn, *Grimolf's-water*, ii, 29.

Grimsá, *Grim's-river*, i, 19, 20; iv, 13;
v, 9.

Grimsaros, *Grim's-river-mouth*, ii, 30;
v, 10.

Grimsdalr, *Grim's-dale*, ii, 3, 5.

Grimsey, *Grim's-isle*, ii, 5.

Grimsgil, *Grim's-gill*, i, 21.

Grimsnes, *Grim-ness,* ii, 25; iv, 12.
Grindalækr, *Grind-brook,* iii, 5.
Grindavik, *Porpoise Bay,* v, 14.
Grindill, iii, 11.
Grindr, ii, 1.
Grjotá, *Grit-river,* ii, 4; iii. 9.
Grjotvallarmuli, *Grit-mead mull or point,*
    ii, 21.
Grisartunga, *Pig Tongue,* ii, 3.
Grones, *Groa's-ness,* ii, 23.
Groustadir, *Groa's-stead,* iii, 4.
Grund, *The Grounds,* iii, 3, 16.
Grunnifjördr, *Shallow-firth,* ii, 1.
Grænavatn, *Green-water,* iii, 20.
Grænland or Greenland, i, 1; ii, 14, 22,
    31; v, 14.
Grof, *The Grove,* ii, 3.
Gudbrandsstadir, *Gudbrand's-stead,* iii, 4.
Guddælir, *Goddale men,* v, 15.
Gudlaugshöfdi, *Gudlaug's-hof,* ii, 32.
Gudlaugsvik, *Gudlaug's-wick,* ii, 32.
Gufua (Gufa) *Vapour-river,* i, 18; ii, 4,
    24.
Gufudair, *Vapour-dale,* i, 18; ii, 24.
Gufutjördr, *Vapour-firth,* i, 18; ii, 20.
Gufunes, *Vapour-ness,* ii, 24.
Gufuskalar, *Vapour-scales,* ii, 24.
Gullberustadir, *Goldbearer's-stead,* i, 19.
Gunnarsholt, *Gunnar's-wood,* v, 4.
Gunnbjarnarsker, *Gunnbjorn-skerries,* ii,
    8, 14, 29, 30.
Gunnlaugsstadir, *Gunnlaug's-stead,* ii, 2.
Gunnolfsá, *Battle-wolf's-river,* iii, 11.
Gunnolfsfell, *Battle-wolf's-fell,* v, i.
Gunnolfsvik, *Battle-wolf's-wick,* v, i.
Gunnsteinar, *Battle-stones,* iii, 17.
Gunnsteinstadir, *Gunnstein-stead,* iii, 5.
Gyjarsporsá, *Trollspoor,* ii, 31.
Gyldarhagi, *Gyldar's-pasture,* v, 11.
Gotuskeggjar in the Faroe Islands, ii, 16.

H.

Haddingadalr, ii, 5.
Hafgrimsfjordr in Greenland, ii, 14.
Hafnarfjöll, i, 19.
Hafr in Holtum, v, 8.
Hafrafell off Gilsfjörd, *Goat-fell,* ii, 22.
Hafranes, *Goat-ness,* iv, 6.

Hafrsá, *Goat-river,* iv, 5, 13.
Hafrasfjördr, *Goat-firth,* ii, 19, 29, 32;
    iii, 2; v, 11, 13.
Hafsbotn, i, 1.
Hafslækr, *Hof's-river,* ii, 4.
Hagagardr, *Pasture-garth,* v, 12.
Haganes, *Pasture-ness,* iii, 11.
Hagi, *The Pasture,* ii, 30; iii, 13; v, 11.
Hakskard, *Skard=Mountain Pass,* v, 12.
Hakonarstadir, *Hacon's-stead,* iv, 2.
Hallarmuli, *Hall's-crag,* ii, 2.
Hallbjarnarvordur, *Hallbjorn's-beacons,*
    ii, 30; v, 12.
Hallgeirsey, *Hallgeir's-isle,* v, 4.
Hallkelsholar, *Hallkel's-hollow,* v, 12.
Hallkelsstadir, *Hallkel's-stead,* i, 17; ii, 1.
Hallsteinsnes, *Hallstein's-ness,* i, 23.
Halogaland, ii, 13, 29, 30; iii, 11, 14, 17,
    20; iv, 13.
Hals, literally *neck,* used of a Mountain
    Pass, iii, 16.
Halsar, *Hal's-river,* iii, 4.
Halsgrof, *Hal's-grove or pit,* iii, 9.
Hamarbyggjar, ii, 3.
Hamarr, *Cargo,* ii, 2.
Hamarsá, *Cargo-river,* iv, 7.
Hamrar, iv, 10, 13.
Hamundarstadir, *Hamund-stead,* iii, 12.
Hanatun, *Cockton or Cocktown,* iii, 14.
Hareksstadir, *Harek's-stead,* ii, 3.
Hasteinshaugr, *Hastein's-how,* v, 10.
Hasteinssund, *Hastein's-sound,* v, 9.
Haugar, *The Hows,* ii, 4.
Haugavad, *Hows-ford,* v, 10.
Haugr, *The How,* iii, 11.
Haukadalr, *Hawk-dale,* ii, 14, 17, 27;
    v, 11.
Haukadalsá, *Hawkdale-river,* ii, 18.
Haukagil, *Hauk-gill,* iii, 4.
Hauksgrafir, *Hauk's-pits,* iii, 5.
Havararlon, *Havor's-lagoon,* iii, 20.
Hedinshöfdi, iii, 6, 18.
Hefni in Norway, v, 7.
Hegranes, iii, 7.
Hegrastadir, iii, 7.
Heidabær, v, 13.
Heidi, *Moss-fell, heath,* i, 1.
Heinabergsá, iv, 10.

Helgafell, *Holy-fell*, ii, 12.
Helgahvoll, *Holy-knoll*, v, 10.
Helgasker, *Helgi-skerry*, ii, 33.
Helgastadir, *Helga's-stead*, iii, 18, 19.
Helgavatn, *Helga's-water*, iii, 2, 3, 4.
Helkunduheida, iv, 1.
Hella, iii, 13.
Hellir, *Caves*, ii, 7.
Hellisdalr, *Cavern-dale*, ii, 3.
Hellisfirdingar, *Cave-firthers*, iv, 6.
Hellisfitjar, *Cave-foot*, i, 20
Hellisfjördar, *Cave-firth*, iv, 6.
Hellishraun, *Lava-cave*, ii, 7.
Hellismenn, *Cave-men*, i, 20; ii, 1.
Hengifossá, *Hengi-foss-river*, iv, 2, 3.
Hergilsey, *Hergil's-isle*, ii, 19.
Herjolfsfjördr, *Herjolf's-firth*, ii, 14.
Herjolfshöfn, *Herjolf's-haven*, i, 2.
Herjolfsnes, *Herjolf's-ness*, ii, 14.
Hestfjördr, *Horse-firth*, ii, 29.
Hjallaland, *Hill-land*, iii, 4.
Hjallanes, *Hill-ness*, ii, 27.
Hjalli, *Hill*, v, 8.
Hjaltadalr, *Hjalt's-dale*, iii, 10, 20.
Hjaltæyri, *Hjalt's-island*, iii, 14.
Hjaltdælalaut, iii, 10.
Hjaltdælær, iii, 10.
Hjaltland, *Shetland*, i, 1, 2.
Hjardarholt, *Herd-holt or Herd-copse*, ii, 27.
Hjardarnes, *Herd-ness*, ii, 20, 25.
Hjardarvatn, *Herd-water*, ii, 10.
Hildisey, *Hildi's-isle*, v, 4.
Hildishaugr, *Hildi's-how*, iv, 11.
Hisgargafl, *Hisgar's-gable*, i, 4.
Hitá, *Warm-river*, ii, 4, 5.
Hitadalr, *Warm-river-dale*, ii, 4, 13, 14.
Hjörleifshöfdi, *Hjorleif's-head*, i, 6, 7; iv, 5.
Hladhamarr, *Ledge-crag*, i, 14.
Hleidrargardr, *Illeidar's-garth*, iii, 17.
Hlid, *The Slope*, ii, 19; iii, 6; iv, 2; v, 3, 4.
Hlidar in Norway, *Slope*, see Lidar.
Hlidarendi, iv, 4, 11; v, 3, 4, 5.
Hlidmenn, *Men from the fell*, iii, 14.
Hlymrek, *Limerick*, ii, 22.
Hlödvik, ii, 29.

Hnappfellingar, *From Hnappfell*, iv, 10.
Hnjóska, *Hnjosk-river*, iii, 17.
Hnjoskadalr, *Hnjosk-dale*, iii, 16.
Hnjoskadalsa, *Hnjosk-dales-river*, iii, 16.
Hof, *Temple*, i, 11; iii, 2, 4, 6, 10; iv, 1, 10; v, 3, 15, 17.
Hofgardar, *Temple-garth*, ii, 6.
Hofsfell, *Temple-fell*, iv, 10.
Hof-fellingar, *From Temple-fell*, iv, 10.
Hofsmenn, *Temple-men*, iii' 4.
Hofstadir, *Temple-stead*, i, 21; ii, 12, 19; iii, 8.
Hofsteigr, *Temple-feig*, iv,-2;
Hofsvogr, *Temp'e-creek*, ii, 12;
Holar, *The Knolls*, ii, 22; iii, 1, 4; v, 10, 11, 12.
Holmgardr, *Novogorod in Russia*, iii, 1.
Holmkelsá, *Holmkel-river*, ii, 8.
Holmr, *Holm or Isle*, i, 15, 21; ii, 32; v, 5.
Holmsá, *Holm-river*, iv, 11, 12.
Holmslatr, *latr*, place where animals as seals, whales, lay their young, ii, 13, 14.
Holmsmenn, *Holms-men*, i, 19, 20.
Holt, *Wood or copse*, in common Icelandic usage, any *rough stony hill or ridge*, iii, 5, 11; iv, 11; v, 4, 9.
Holtastadir, *Holt-stead*, iii, 5.
Horn, *Cape or headland*, i, 1, 2; ii, 20, 29, 31; iv, 5, 8, 9, 10.
Hornafjardarströnd, iv, 9.
Hornafjördr, *Horn-firth*, iv, 9; v, 1.
Hornfirdingar, *From Horn-firth*, v, 9.
Hornstrandir, *Horn-strand*, ii, 14.
Hrafnista, found in Hauksbook in connexion with Arnahvol, i, 7.
Hrafnkelsdalr, *Hrafnkel's-dale*, iv, 3.
Hrafnsfjordar in Greenland, ii, 14.
Hrafnshaugr, *Ravens-how*, v, 10.
Hrafntoptir, *Raven-toft*, v, 3.
Hranafall, *Raven-fall*, ii, 3.
Hranastadir, *Raven-stead*, i, 21; iv, 12.
Hraun, *Lava*, ii, 1, 8, 10.
Hraunaheida, *Lava-heath*, iii, 1, 9.
Hraundalr, *Lava-dale*, ii, 4.
Hraundælar, *Lava-dales*, ii, 4.
Hraunfirdingar, *Lava-firth*, ii, 10,

Hraungerdi, *Lava-garth*, i, 17.

Hraungerdinga hreppr, *The Rape of the men of Lava-garth*, i, 17; v, 9.

Hraunhafnará, *Lava-havens-river*, ii, 6.

Hraunhofn, *Lava-haven*, ii, 6; iii, 20.

Hraunas, *Lava-ridge*, i, 21; ii, 1.

Hraunsfjördr, *Lava-firth*, ii, 10.

Hraunsholtslækr, *Lava-woods-brook*, v, 14.

Hreduvatn, *Bugbear-water*, ii, 3.

Hreggsgerdismuli, *Tempest-garth-mull*, iv, 9.

Hreidarsgerdi, *Garth of Hreidar*, ii, 7.

Hringariki, *Ring-realm*, i, 11; ii, 11.

Hringsstadir, *Ring-stead*, iii, 1.

Hrip, *Wooden basket of laths*, ii, 5.

Hris, *The copse-wood*. i, 20.

Hristeigr, *Copse-land*, iii, 17.

Hrisey, *Copse-isle*, iii, 12.

Hroarslækr, *Hróar's-brook*, v, 3, 6, 7, 9.

Hrolleifsdalr, *Hrolleif's-dale*, iii, 4, 10.

Hrolleifsdalsá, *Hrolleif-dales-river*, iii, 10.

Hromundarstadir, *Hromund-stead*, ii, 2.

Hrossagardr, *Horse-garth*, iv, 12.

Hrunamanna hreppr, *The Rape of the men of Hrani*, v, 11.

Hrutafjardarstrond, *Ramfirth-strand*, iii, 1.

Hrutafjördr, *Ram-firth*, i, 19; ii, 4, 32; iii, 1, 2, 4, 5, 20.

Hrutsstadir, *Ram-stead*, ii, 18.

Hunavatn, *The water of the young bears*, for full explanation see iii, 3, 20.

Hunavatnsthing, iii, 4, 5.

Hundadalr, *Hounds-dale*, ii, 17.

Hundsnes, *Hounds-ness*, iii, 20.

Husagardr, *House-garth*, v, 7.

Husavik, *House or wick*, i, 1; iii, 18; iv, 5.

Husvikingar, *House-creeker*, iv, 5.

Hvaleyri, *Whale-island;* in Hawksbook this is name of island in Borgarfirth where Heyjolf found a whale.

Hvalfjördr, *Whale-firth*, i, 8; ii, 1.

Hvallatr, *Whale-litter*, ii, 26; iii, 17.

Hvalsey, *Whale-island*, ii, 14.

Hvalseyjarfirdingar, *Whale-island-firther*, or *Hvalsey frithers*, ii, 14.

Hvalseyjarfjördr, *Whale-island-firth*, ii, 14.

Hvalsnesskridur, *Whaleness-screes*, iv, 7.

Hvalvatnsfjördr, *Whale-water-firth*, iii, 17.

Hvammr in Hvammsveit, ii, 6, 16, 18, 23, 27; iii, 10, 15, 16.

Hvammr in Kjos, i, 14.

— in Mydal, iv, 11.

— in Nordrardal. ii, 4.

— in Skagafirdi, iii, 9.

— in Ölfusi, v, 13.

Hvanná, *Angelica-river*, iv, 2.

Hvanndalir, *Angelica-dale*, iii, 11.

Hvanneyri, *Angelica-island*, i, 19; ii, 8; iii, 2.

Hvarf in Greenland, *Cape Past*, i, 1; ii, 14.

Hvarsgnypa in Greenland, ii, 14.

Hvassahraun, *Sharplava*, v, 14.

Hvatistadir, iii, 3.

Hvini, *Windy*, iii, 12, 15.

Hvinistjördr, *Windy-firth*, iii, 15.

Hvinnerjadalr, iii, 15.

Hvinverskr, iii, 15.

Hvitar *White river* at Hinessthing, v, 10, 11.

Hvitar in Borgarfirth, i, 20, 21; ii, 1, 2.

Hvitarbakki, *White-rivers-bank*, ii, 1.

Hvitarsida, *White-river-side*, i, 17; ii, 1.

Hvitbjörg, *The white precipices or rocks*, ii, 2.

Hvitramannaland, *Whitemen's-land*, ii, 22.

Hvoll, *The hill*, v, 5.

Hæll, *The heel*, v, 11.

Hofdabrekka, *Head-brink*, iv, 12.

Hofdarsandr, *Head-river-sand*, iv, 13.

Hofdaströnd, *Head-strand*, iii, 4, 10.

Höfdi-*head*, ii, 19, 18; iii, 6, 9, 9, 11, 17, 20; iv, 11, 13; v, 4, 10.

Höfn, *Haven*, i, 17; ii, 11.

Högnastadir, *Hogni=Tom-cat*, ii, 2.

Hökustadir, *Chin-stead*, iii, 8.

Hördadalr, *Hord's-dale*, ii, 17.

Hördadalsá, *Hord's-dale-river*, ii, 17.

Hördaland in Norway, i, 2; iii, 19; v, 1.

Hördá, *Hord's-river*, ii, 19.

Hördholar, *Hord's-hills*, ii, 2.

Hörgá, *Temple-river*, iii, 13.

Hörgardalr, *Horg-river-dale*, iii, 13, 14; see Note, iii, 14.

Hörgardalsá, *Horg-dales-river*, iii, 13.

Höskuldsarorm, *Hoskuld's-river*, ii, 8,

Höskuldslækr, *Hoskuld's-brook*, v, 12.
Höskuldsvatn, *Hoskuld's-water*, iii, 18.

I.

Ingjaldsnupr, *Ingeld's-peak*, v, 11.
Ingjaldshvall, *Ingeld's-hill*, ii, 8.
Ingjaldssandr, ii, 28.
Ingimundarholt, *Ingimund's-wood*, iii, 2.
Ingolfsfell, i, 7; iv, 9.
Ingolfsjördr, ii, 31.
Ingolfshofdahverfi, iv, 10.
Ingolfshöfdi, *Ingolf's-head*, i, 6.
Irar, i, 11.
Irafell, iii, 6.
Irland, i, 1, 5, 6; ii, 15, 22; iii, 12; iv, 11; v, 13.
Ireland the Great, *America*, ii, 22.
Irskr, *Irish*, Prologue, i, 6, 14, 15; ii, 24.
Isafjardardjup, ii, 29.
Isafjördr, *Ice-firth*, ii, 29.
Isfirdingar, *From Ice-firth*, ii, 29.
Islandsbygd, *Iceland-settlement*, v, 11.
Islandsför, *Expedition to Iceland*, iii, 17; v, 2, 3, 9.
Islandshof, *Icelandic-sea*, iv, 10.
Isleifsstadir, ii, 2.
Israudarstadir, ii, 2.

J.

Jadar in Norway, *The Borderland*, iii, 11.
Jafnaskard, *The Even Pass*, ii, 3.
Jamtaland, v, 12.
Jardfallsgil, *Landslip-gill*, ii, 27.
Jardlangsstadir, *Earth-long-stead*, ii, 4.
Jolduhlaup in Ireland, *Mare's-leap*, i, 1.
Joldusteinn, *Mare's-stone*, v, 2, 3.
Jolgeirsstadir, *Jolgeir's-stead*, v, 8.
Jorunnarstadir, *Jorunn's-stead*, iii, 16.
Jökulsá, *Glacier-river*, iii, 8; iv, 2, 5, 10, 13.
Jökulsdalr, *Glacier-dale*, iv, 2.
Jökulsfirdir, *Glacier-firth*, ii, 31.
Jörundarfell, *Jorund's-fell*, iii, 3.
Jörundarholt, *Jorund's-wood*, i, 15.
Jörvi, *Gravel-land*, ii, 11.

K.

Kaldá, *Cold-river*, ii, 4, 5.
Kaldakinu, *Cold-cheek*, ii, 19.
Kaldaklofsá, *Cold-fording-river*, v, 1.
Kaldakvisl, *Cold-river*, v, 11.
Kaldaros, *Cold-river's-mouth*, ii, 5.
Kaldbakr, *Coldback*, ii, 32.
Kaldbaksvik, *Coldback's-wick*, ii, 32.
Kaldnesingahreppr, *The Rape of the Kaldnessings*, v, 9.
Kalfá, *Calf-river*, v, 11.
Kalfagrafir, *Calf-pits*, iv, 4.
Kalfborgará, *Calfburg-river*, iii, 18, 20.
Kalfskinn, *Calf-skin*, iii, 13.
Kalmansá, *Kalman's-river*, i, 14, 15, 17; ii, 1.
Kalmanstunga, *Kalman's-tongue*, ii, 1.
Kambakista, *Combs'-kist*, v, 9.
Kambr, *Comb*, ii, 8, 9.
Kambsdalr, *Comb-dale*, iv, 7.
Kambsnes, *Comb or Combness*, ii, 4, 16, 18.
Kampahol:, v, 10.
Karlafjördr, *Carle (men's) fjord*, v, 11.
Karlastadir, *Karlis-stead*, ii, 1; iii, 5.
Karlsá, *Karl's-river*, iii, 13.
Karlsbrekká, *Karl's-brink*, ii, 2.
Karlsdalr, *Karl's-dale*, ii, 3.
Karlsfell, *Karl's-fell*, ii, 3.
Karstadir, *Karl's-stead*, ii, 13.
Katanes, *Caithness* in Scotland, ii, 15; v, 2.
Katneskr, *From Caithness*, i, 13.
Keflavik, *Cliff vik, or creek*, ii, 26.
Keldudalr, *Bog-dale*, ii, 27.
Keldugnupr, *Bog-peak*, iv, 11.
Kelduhverfi, *The Bogs*, iii, 19, 20.
Keldunes, *Bogness*, iii, 19, 20.
Kerlingará, *Old woman's-river*, iv, 13.
Kerlingarfjördr, *Old woman's-firth*, iv, 13.
Kerseyri, i, 33.
Ketilseyri, *Ketil's-isle*, ii, 27.
Ketilsfjördr in Greenland, ii, 14.
Ketilsstadir, *Kettle-stead*, ii, 17; iv, 3.
Kjalarnes, i, 9, 11, 12; ii, 16.
Kjalkafjördr, *Sledge-fjord*, ii, 25.
Kjallaksholl, *Kjallak's-hill*, ii, 19.
Kjallaksstadir, *Kjallak's-stead*, ii, 19.
Kjaransvik, ii, 20.

Kjarrá, *Copse-river*, ii, 1.
Kjarradalr, *Copse-wood-dale*, ii, 2.
Kidjaberg, *Kid-mountain*, i, 20; ii, 30; v, 12.
Kidjafell, *Kid-fell*, i, 13.
Kjos, *The Hollow*, i, 13.
Kirkjubær, *K rkby*, ii, 9.
Kirkjufell, *Kirk-fell*, ii, 10.
Kirkjufjördr, *Kirk-firth*, ii, 9.
Kjóir, *The Keel Mountain*, iii, 5, 8, 15.
Kjölvararstadir, *Keelvar's-stead*, i, 20.
Kleifar, *The Cliff-pass*, ii, 21, 32.
Kleifarlönd, *Cliff-lands*, iv, 7.
Klif, same as Kleifar, ii, 2.
Klofa-teinar, *Cloven-stones*, ii, 19, 21.
Klofnigar, *The Clefts*, ii, 19, 20.
Knafaholar, *Neif-hills*, v, 5.
Knappadalr, *Button-dale*, ii, 4, 5.
Knappsstadir, *Button-stead*, iii, 11.
Knararnes, *Shipness*, i, 19.
Knararsund, *Ship-sound*, v, 10.
Knefilsdalsá, *Knefil's-dale-river*, iv, 2.
Kolbeinsaros, *Kolbein's-inlet*, iii, 8, 9.
Kolbeinsdalr, *Kolbein's-dale*, iii, 9.
Kolbeinsey, *Kolbein's-island*, i, 1.
Kolbeinstadir, *Kolbein's-stead*, ii, 5.
Kolbeinsvik, *Kolbein's-creek*, i, 32.
Kolgrafir, *Coal-pits*, ii, 10.
Kolgreflingar, *Men of Kolgrafir*, ii, 10.
Kolknmyrar, *Kolka-moors*, iii, 5.
Kollafjardarheidi, *Kollis-firth-heath*, ii, 21.
Kollafjördr, *Kollis-firth*, ii, 24, 30.
Kollavik, *Kollis-wick*, iii, 20.
Kolshamarr, *Koll's hammer (rock)* ii, 1.
Kollslækr, *Koll's-water*, i, 24.
Kollsveinsstadir, *Collswain's-stead*, iii, 8.
Kollsvik, *Koll's-wick*, i, 12.
Kolsonafell, *Kollson's-fell*, ii, 10.
Kopanes, *Sealcubness*, ii, 25.
Koranes in Myra, ii, 24.
Kornhaugr, *Corn-how*, ii, 8.
Kornsa, *Corn-river* iii, 3, 4.
Kristnes, *Christness*, iii, 11, 14.
Krokr in Nordradal, *Crook*, ii, 3.
Kroksfjardanes, ii, 23.
Kroksfjördr, *Crook-fjord*, ii, 21, 22; iii, 20.
Kroppr *Bunch* in Egjafirth, iii, 14, 19.
Kroppsmen, i, 20.

Krossa *Cross-river* in Markfleet, v, 2, 3.
Krossa in Axfirth, iii, 20.
Krossavik *Cross-wick* in Ragdarfirth, iv, 6.
the inner in Vopnafirth, iv, 1.
Krossavik the outer in Vopnfirth, iv, 2.
Krossholar, *Cross-hills*, ii, 16.
Krossvikingar, *Cross-wick-men*, iv, 6.
Krysuvik, *Greasy-wick*, v, 14.
Kræklingahlid, *Shell-slope*, iii, 14, 15.
Krofluhellir, *Krafla-cave*, iii, 4.
Kudafljot, *Trout-fry-fleet*, iv, 12.
Kudafljotsos, *Trout-fry-mouth*, iv, 11.
Kernvogastrond, ii, 9.
Kvia ia Hornafirth, *Sheep fold-river*, iv, 9, 10.
Kviabekkr in Olafsfirth, *Sheep-fold-brook*, iii, 11.
Kviamid in Isafjardarfirth, ii, 29.
Kvigandafirth, ii, 25.
Kvigandanes, ii, 25.
Kviguvogabjorg, *Heifer-creek-mountain*, v, 14.
Kvigubogar, *Heifer-bends*, v, 13.
Kylansholar, *Kylans-hollow*, ii, 1.

L.

Lagarfljot, *Mere-fleet*, iv, 2, 4.
Lagarfljotsstrandir, *Mere-fleet Strands*, iv, 2.
Lagey, *Low-isle*, iv, 12.
Lageyingar, *Low islander*, iv, 12.
Lambafellsa, *Lambfell-river*, v, 1.
Lambastadir, *Lambistead*, ii, 4, 24; v, 3.
Landamot or Londsmot, *Land-meet (boundary)* iii, 18.
Landbrot, *Land-broken*, iii, 8.
Landverskr, *From Landeyjar*, v, 10.
Langá, *Long-river*, ii, 4.
Langadalsá, *Longdale-river*, ii, 13, 30, 31.
Langaholt, *Long-wood*, ii, 6; iii, 6.
Langanes, *Long-ness*, i, 1; ii, 26; iv, 1.
Langavatnsdalr, *Langwater-dale*, ii, 4; iii, 3, 2.
Langdælir, *Langdale*, ii, 13.
Langidalr, *Langdale*, iii, 5.
Laugarbrekka, *Bath-brink*, ii, 7, 17.
Laugardalr, *Bathdale*, i, 20.

Laxá, *Salmon-river*, i, 14, 17; ii, 5, 13, 15; iii, 18; v, 11.
Laxardalr, *Salmon-river-dale*, ii, 17; iii, 6, 19.
Leidarskeid, *Leet-race*, v, 5.
Leidolfsfell, *Thingwolf's-fell*, iv, 11.
Leidolfsstadir, *Thingwolf's-stead*, iv, 11; v, 9.
Leikskalar, *Game-scales*, ii, 14.
Leirá, *Miry-river*, i, 17.
Leirhofn, *Miry-haven*, iii, 20.
Leirulækr, *Miry-brook*, ii, 4.
Leiruvagr, *Miry-creek*, i, 10, 11; iv, 7.
Leiruvagsa, *Miry-river*, i, 10.
Linakradalr, *Flaxfield-dale*, iii, 1.
Ljosavatn, *Lightwater*, iii, 17, 18; v, 5.
Ljosavatnsskard, *Lightwater-pass*, iii, 17, 18.
Ljotarstadir, *Ljot's stead*, v, 4.
Ljotolfsstadir, *Ugly wolf's-stead*, ii, 19.
Lodmundarfjördr, *Shaggyhair-hands-fjord*, iv, 5.
Lofot in Norway, v, 10.
Lomagnupströnd, iv, 11.
Lon, *Inlet, sea-loch, or lagoon*, ii, 7; iii, 14; iv, 7, 8.
Lonsheida, *Lagoon-heath*, iv, 7.
Lunansholt, *Lunan's-woöd*, v, 7.
Lundar, *The Groves*, iv, 10.
Lundarbrekka, *Grove-brink*, iii, 18.
Lundr, *The grove*, i, 21; ii, 3; iii, 17, 19.
Lysa, *Bright-river*, ii, 6.
Lækjarbotnar, *Brook-bottoms*, v, 7.
Logberg, *Law-hill*, where the Laws were annually rehearsed; not found in Book of Settlement but occurs frequently in Islandinga Bok and Appendix to Book of Settlement.

M.

Mafahlid, *Sea-gull (mew's) slope*, ii, 9, 13.
Mafhlidingr, *man of sea-gull (mews's) slope*, ii, 9.
Mána, *Mani's-river*, iii, 20.
Manafell, *Mani's-fell*, iii, 20.
Manavik, *Mani's-wick*, iii, 5.
Manathufa, *Mani's-hummock*, iii, 5.
Mannafallsbrekka, *Manfalls-brink*, ii, 7.

Marbæli, *Sea-lair*, iii, 14.
Markarfljot, *Mark-fleet*, v, 2, 3.
Marsstadir, *Mew's-stead*, iii, 3; v, 11.
Medalfarssund, *Middle-Jaring-sound*, ii, 19.
Medalfell, *Middle-fell*, i, 13; iv, 10.
Medalfellströnd, *Middlefell-strands*, ii, 19.
Medallönd, *Mid-lands*, iv, 11.
Melahverfi, * i, 17.
Melar in Borgarfirth, *Passim*.
  in Hellisdale, ii, 3.
  in Krulufirth, ii, 32, 33.
Melrakkadalr, *Foxdale*, ii, 1.
Melrakkanes, *Foxness*, iv, 7.
Merkigil, *Landmark-gill*, iii, 13, 16.
Merkrhraun, *Wood-lava*, v, 10.
Merrhæfi (Murray) in Scotland, ii, 15.
Mideingi, *Middle-meadow*, ii, 25; v, 12.
Midfell, *Mid-fell*, i, 17.
Midfjördr, *Mid-firth*, iii, 1.
Midhus, *Middle-house*, v, 11.
Midjokull in Greenland, ii, 14.
Midskali, *Mid-scale*, i, 16.
Migandi, *The dripping*, iii, 13.
Mikilsstadir, *Mickle's-stead*, iii, 5.
Miklagil, *Mickle-gill*, iii, 4.
Mikligardr, *Mickle-garth* (Constantinople) i, 1; iii, 19.
Minnhakseyri, *Minnthak's-beach*, i, 6; iii, 4.
Mjodælingr, *Narrow-dale-man*, iii, 11.
Mjofadalsa, *Narrow-dale-river*, iii, 11.
Mjofidalr, *Narrow-dale*, ii, 3.
Mjofifjordr, *Narrow-fjord*, iv, 6.
Mjola, iii, 14.
Mjosyndi, *Narrow-sound* (Pass), v, 5.
Mjors in Norway, iii, 8.
Moberg, *Peat-rock*, iii, 5, 11.
Mobergsbrekkur, *Peat-brink*, iii, 5.
Modolfsgnupr, *Moodwolf's-peak*, iv, 11.
Mogilsá, *Peatgill-river*, i, 11, 12.
Mogilslækr, *Peatgill-brook*, iii, 3.
Moldatum, *Mouldy-field*, iv, 12.
Mor, *Peat*, iii, 11.
Mosfell et efru in Grimsness, iii, 7; iv, 7; v, 12.

* *Melr is bent grass, arundo arenaria,*

Mosfell et nedra in Mosfellssveit, ii. 8; v, 12; v, 13.
Mosfellingar, v, 12.
Mostr, an island off South Hordaland, in Norway, with a great temple of Thor in it, ii, 12.
Muli, *A jutting crag*; for explanation see ii, 32, page 103; vid Alptafjorl Sydra in Austfjördum, iv, 7.
Muli in Bryjudal, i, 14 in Hauk.
in Mosfellsveit, i, 11.
in Saurbæ, ii, 32.
hja Stakksa, v, 11.
Munadarnes, *Joyness*, ii, 4.
Mydalr, *Midge-dale*, iv, 11.
Mydalsá, *Midge-dale-river*, i, 11.
Myramenn or Meremen, *Fen-men*, iv, 10.
Myrar, *The Fens*, vid Borgarfjord, i, 19; ii, 24.
in Dyrafjord, ii, 27.
in Hornafjord, iv, 10.
Myri, *The Fens*, ii. 20
Mvrin, v, 3.
Myrka, *Mirk or Dark-river*, iii, 13.
Myvatn, *Midgewater*, iii, 18, 20.
Mælifell, *Measure-fell*, iii, 7.
Mælifell-á, iii, 7.
Mælifellsdalr, iii, 7.
Mælifellsgill, ii, 3.
Mæri, iv, 6, 8.
Modrufell, *Madder-fell*, iii, 16.
Modruvellir, *Madder meads*, iii, 16.
Mörk, iv, 13; v, 10.

N.

Narfasker, *Narfi's-skerry*, iii, 13.
Nattfaravik, *Nightfarer's-wick*, i, 1; iii, 19.
Naumdælafylki, *Narrowdale-district*, v, 3.
Naumdælar, *Narrowdale-men*, v, 3.
Naumudalr, *Narrowdale*, iii, 9, 13; v, 3, 12.
Nautabu, *Cattle-booths*, iii, 9.
Nes, *Ness*, i, 8; ii, 24; iv, 6, 9.
Neshraun, *Ness-lava*, ii, 8.
Nesmenn, *Nesmen.*, iv, 6.
Njardey, *Niord's-isle*, ii, 19.

Njardvik, *Niord's-wick*, iv, 2, 4.
Nordlendingafjördungr, *Northlunders' Quarter*, iii, 1, 5, 7, 20.
Nordmanndi, *Normandy*, iv, 8.
Nordmenn, *Northmen*, Prologue.
Nordmæri, *North Mæri*, iv, 12.
Nordrá, *North-river*, ii, 3; iii, 7, 8.
Nordrardalr, *North-river-dale*, ii, 3.
Nordfjördr, *North-firth*, iv, 6.
Norrænn, *Norse*, v, 7, 11.
Norvegskonungr, *King of Norway*, i, 11.
Nykomi, *Newcome*, iv, 11.

O.

Oddaverjar, *Family of Oddi*, iii, 5; v, 3.
See note at page 3.
Oddbjarnarleidi, *Oddbjorn's-hows*, v, 3.
Oddgeirsholar, *Oddgeir's-hollows*, i, 17; v, 9.
Oddi, *The Point*, v, 5, 6, 7.
Oddsas, *Odd's-ridge*, called also "*The Ridge*," iii, 4.
Odeila, *Undivided*, iii, 17.
Ofeigsfjördr, *Firth of Ufsig*, i.e un-death fated, ii, 31; compare Scottish "*fey*"
Ofeigsstadir, v, 11.
Ofrustadir, *Stead of Ofra*, iii, 1.
Ofæra, *Impassable*, ii, 32.
Olafsdalr, *Olaf's-dale*, ii, 21.
Olafsjordr, *Olaf's-firth*, iii, 11.
Olafsvellir, *Olaf's-field*, v, 10.
Olafsvik, *Olaf's-wick*, ii, 8, 21.
Oleifsburg, iv, 11.
Orkneyjar, *Orkney Islands*, i, 1; ii, 22; iv, 8.
Ormsá, *Orm's or serpent's-river*, iv, 2, 7.
Ormsdalr, *Orm's-dale*, iii, 1.
Orrastadir, *Battle-stead*, ii, 19.
Os, *River's-mouth or Inlet*.
vid Bruddal, iv, 7.
in Hunavatn's thing, iii, 1.
vid Tjörnes, iii, 19.
Osar, *The River's-mouth*, i, 15.
Ostjöll, iv, 2.
Osomi, *Mischief*, ii, 28.
Osta, ii, 18; iii, 1.
Osvifslækr, *Osvif's-brook*, i, 12.

P.

Papey, *Father's-isle*, abode of Anchorite fathers from Great Britain and Ireland, Prologue.

Papyli, *Seat of a Papa or Anchorite*, Prologue iv, 10.

Patreksfjördr, *Patrick's-firth*, i, 12.

R.

Rangá, *Wrong (awry) river*, iv, 2; v, 3; v, 5.

Rangadarvarda, *Raungad's-beacon*, iii, 7; see note there.

Rangaros, *Rang-river-mouth*, v, 3, 6.

Rangarvellir, *Wrong-river-plain*, v, 6, 7.

Raptalækr, *Rafter's-brook*, iv, 11.

Rauda, *Red-river*, compare Rothay, v, 8, 9.

Raudabjarnarstadir, *Red bear's-stead*, ii, 4.

Raudafell, *Red-fell*, v, 1.

Raudagnupr, *Redgnuf, Red-peak*, iii, 20.

Raudalækr, *Red-brook*, ii, 2; iv, 10; v, 8.

Raudamelr, *The Red Sandhill*, ii, 5, 19.

Raudamels lönd, ii, 6.

Raudaskrida, *Red Screes*, iii, 20.

Raudaskridu lönd, *Red Screes lands*, iii, 20.

Raudaskridur, *Red Screes*, iv, 7.

Raudisandr, ii, 26.

Raudkollsstadir, *Red-pate-stead*, ii, 6.

Raudlækingar, *Red-brook-men*, iv, 10.

Raudsgil, *Red-gill*, i, 20, 21.

Raufarfell, *Rift-fell*, see Raudafell.

Raumsdalr, *Raum's (giant) dale*, iii, 2.

Raumsdælafylki, *District of Raumsdale*, v, 2.

Refrstadir, *Fox-dale*, iv, 1.

Reistará, *Twisted-river*, iii, 13.

Reistargnupr, *Twisted-peak*, iii, 20.

Reydarfell *Whale-fell*, i, 19.

Reydarfjall, do. i, 1.

Reydarfjordr, *Trout-firth*, i, 1; iv, 3, 6.

Reydarmuli, *Trout mull or head or point*, for derivation of name see this passage, v, 12.

Reydarvatn, *Trout-water*, v, 3, 5.

Reykjaá, *Reek-river*, iii, 11.

Reykjadalr, iii, 19.

Reykjadalsá, i, 20.

Reykjahlid, iii, 20.

Reykjaholar, *Reek hills*, ii, 19; v, 3.

Reykjaholt or Reekholt, *Smoke or vapourwood*, i, 21; ii, 30.

Reykjanes off Broadfirth (*Reek-ness*) ii, 26. In the South, ii, 14; v, 1, 14.

Reykjardalr, *Reek-dale*, i, 20, 21.

Reykjarfjordr, *Reek-firth*, ii, 26.

Reykjarholl, iii, 11.

Reykjarvik, i, 8.

Reykjavellir, iii, 7.

Reykir, *Reekie*, i, 20.

Reyknesingar, *The men of Reekness*, ii, 22.

Reynir, *The Rowan trees*. i, 15.

Reynisnes, *Rowan-ness*, iii, 12.

Reyrvöllr in Norway, *Reed-field*, ii, 11.

Rodreksgil, *Roderek's-gill*, iii, 6.

Rogaland, *A district of Norway, corresponding to the present governorship of Stavanger*, i, 2; ii, 19, 26; iii, 18.

Rom, *Rome*, i, 1.

Ros, *Ross in Scotland*, ii, 15.

Rosmhvalnes, *Walrus-ness*, ii, 2, 4; v, 13, 14.

Rudajarls, *Descendants of Rolf the Ganger, Earls of Rouen*, iv, 8.

Ryta-gnupr, *Squealing-peak*, ii, 20.

S.

Salteyraros, *Salt-reef-mouth*, ii, 9.

Sandá, *Sand-river*, ii, 3, 6.

Sandbrekka, *Sand-brink*, ii, 5.

Sanddalr, *Sand-dale*, ii, 3.

Sandeyrara, *Sand-eyrr-river*, ii, 31.

Sandfell, *Sand-fell*, iv, 10.

Sandfellingar, *Dweller on Sand-fell*, iv, 10.

Sandgil, *Sand-gil*, v, 5.

Sandlækr, *Sandy-stream*, v, 10, 11.

Sandnes, *Sand-ness*, i, 18; v, 3.

Sandvik, *Sand-creek*, iv, 1.

Sandvikingar, iv, 6.

Saudá, *Sheep-river*, iii, 6.

Saudafell, *Sheep-fell*, ii, 17.

Saudanes, *Sheep-ness*, iii, 20.

Saubær in Eyjafjord, iii, 16.

in Gilsfjord, ii, 21, 32.

Saxahvoll, ii, 8.

Sel, *Shieling*, ii, 11.

Selæyri, *Seal-ise*, i, 19.

Selalon, *Seal-lagoon*, i, 19.

Selasund, *Seal-sound*, ii, 11.

Selardalr, *Seal-river-dale*, ii, 20; iv, 1.

Selfors, *Seal-force*, v, 9.

Seljalandsá, *Seljaland-river*, v, 2.

Seljalandsmuli, *Selja'and's-head*, v, 2.

Selslækur, *Seal's-river*, v, 11

Seltjarnarnes, *Seal-tarn-ness*, v, 14.

Selvagr, *Seal-creek*, v, 14.

Seydarfjordr, *Seydis*=a fire pit or fire, iv, 3; see i, 2, where firestead=Seydis.

Seydfirdingar, *Seydis-firther*, iv, 6.

Sida, *The Side, Slope*, ii, 1; iii, 20; iv, 9.

Siglufjördr in Greenland, *Sail-firth*, ii, 14; iii, 11.

Siglunes, *Sail-ness*, iii, 11, 12.

Sigluvik, *Mast-wick*, iii, 16.

Sigmundarhaugr, *Sigmund's-how*, ii, 7.

Sigmundarnes, *Sigmund's-ness*, ii, 4.

Sigmundarstadir, *Sigmund's-stead*, i, 21.

Signyjarstadir, *Signey-stead*, i, 20.

Silfrastadahlid, *Silver-stead-slope*, iii, 8.

Silfrastædingar, *Silver-steadings*, iii, 8.

Sjoland, *Sealand*, iii, 1.

Sireksstadir, *Sirek-stead*, iv, 1.

Skagafjördr, *Scaw (ness) firth*, iii, 4, 7.

Skagastrond, *Scaw-strand*, iii, 6.

Skagi, iii, 3.

Skal, iv, 11.

Skalabrekka, *Scale-brink*, v, 12.

Skalafell, *Scale-fell*, i, 8; iv, 10.

Skalmyri, *Scale-moor*, iii, 7.

Skalanes, *Scale-ness*, ii, 24.

Skalavik, *Scale-wick*, ii, 29.

Skaldskelmisdalr, ii, 1.

Skali, *Scales*, iv, 7.

Skallanes, *Baldpate-ness*, ii, 9.

Skalmarkelda, *Skalm's-bog*, ii, 5.

Skalmarnes, *Skalm's-ness*, ii, 5.

Skaney, *Scania*, i, 20.

Skaptá, *Shaft-river*, iv, 11, 12.

Skaptafells Thing, *compare Shap Fell*, iv, 11; iv, 13.

Skard, *Mountain-pass*, see note iii, 6; ii, 4, 19, 20; iv, 11; v, 6.

Skardsbrekka, *Mountain-pass-brink*, iv, 9

Skeggjastadir, *Skeggi's (Bearded) stead*, i, 10; iv, 1, 2, 7.

Skeid, *The run, the race*, i, 9; v, 10.

Skeidsbrekka, *Shell-brinks*, ii, 14.

Skjaldabjarnarvik, *Shield-bear-wick*, ii, 31.

Skjaldey, *Shield-island*, ii, 11.

Skjalfandafljotsos, *Mouth of the shivering-river*, iii, 17, 18.

Skjalfandi, *That which shivers*, i, 1.

Skjalgdalsá, *Skjaldales-river*, iii, 16.

Skidadalr, *Skid (snow-shoe) dale*, iii, 4.

Skidastadir, *Skid-stead*, iii, 4.

Skjöldolfsnes, *Shield-ness*, iv, 7.

Skjöldolfsstadir, *Shield-stead*, iv, 2.

Skogahverfi, *Hverfi = hamlet*, iv, 4.

Skogar, *The Shaws*, i, 17; ii, 19; iv, 5; v, 1.

Skogarströnd, *Shaws-strand*, ii, 13.

Skorradalr, i, 19.

Skorraholt, ii, 24.

Skorrey, *Scaur-isle*, ii, 24.

Skotar, *Scots*, i, 11; ii. 15.

Skotland or Scotland, ii, 11, 16, 23.

Skrattafell, *Scratch-fell*, iii, 19; see note at page 156.

Skraumuhlaupsá, *Hlaup = flood of river*, now Skrauma, ii, 15, 17.

Skridnisenni, ii, 32, 33.

Skridudalr, *Screes-dale*, iv, 3.

Skrudey, iv, 6.

Skufslækr, *Skaf's-brook*, v, 8.

Skuggabjörg, *Shadow rocks*, iii, 17.

Skutastadir, *Skuta-stead*, v, 14.

Skutilsfjördr, *Harpoon-firth*, ii, 29.

Skutr, *Harpoon*, ii, 23.

Skötufjördr, *Scate-firth*, ii, 29.

Sleg-julækr, *Sledge brook*, ii, 2.

Sleggustadir, *Sledge-stead*, iii, 4.

Sletta, *The Flat*, ii, 31; iii, 20.

Slettahlid, *Smooth-slope*, iii, 11.

Slettubjarnarstadir, *Smooth-bear's-stead*, ii, 21; iii, 9.

Smidsstadir, *Smith's-stead*, iii, 4.

Snjallsteinshofdi, *Snellstein's-head*, v, 4.

Snæfell in Greenland, *Snow-fell*, ii, 14.

Snæfellsjokull, *Snæfell-glacier*, i, 12; ii, 14.

Snæfellness, *Snowfell-ness*, i, 1, 2; ii, 24.
Snæfjöll, *Snow-fell*, ii, 31; iii, 1.
Snæland, *Snow-land*, name given to Iceland by Naddod the Viking, i, 1.
Sogn, *A bay and the surrounding country in Norway, now Sognefjord*, i, 10; ii. 29, 31; iii, 5, 11, 19; iv, 10; v, 5, 9.
Soknadalr, *Sokn-dale*, iii, 15.
Solarfjall in Eyjafirth, *Sun-fell*, iii, 12.
Solheimar, *Sunhome*, iv, 5, 13.
Solheimsandr, *Sunhome's-sands*, i, 5, 13.
Solundir, iv, 1, 5, 13.
Sotafell, *Sooty-fell*, i, 18.
Sotanes, *Sooty-ness*, ii, 32.
Stad in Norway, *Stead*, i, 1.
Stardarholl, *Stead-hill*, ii, 21.
Stafá, *Staff-river*, ii, 11, 12.
Stafaholt, *Staff-wood*, ii, 3.
Stafaholtstunga, *Staff-wood's-tongue*, ii, 3
Stafanesvogr, *Staff-ness-creek*, v, 9.
Stafangr, *Staff-ness*, i, 17.
Stafhyltingr, *A Staf-holt man*, ii, 30.
Stafngrimsstadir, i, 24.
Stafsholl, iii, 11.
Stakksá, *Hack-river*, v, 11, 12.
Stalfjara, *Steel foreshore*, v, 9.
Stangarholt, *Stang-wood*, ii, 4.
Stapi, *Steeple-rock*, in Arnarfirdi = *Eaglefirth*, ii, 26, 27.
Steinar, *Stones*, ii, 3.
Steinfinnsstadir, *Steinfinn-stead*, v, 2.
Steingrimsfjordr, *Steingrim's-firth*, ii, 5, 20, 32; iii, 10.
Steinolfsdalr, *Stonewolf's-dale*, ii, 21, 22.
Steinolfshjalli, *Stonewolf's-slope*, ii, 21.
Steinraudarstadir, *Steinred-stead*, iv, 3; v, 13.
Steinsholt, *Stone-wood*, v, 11.
Steinslækr, *Stoney-brook*, v, 8.
Steinsstadir, *Stone-stead*, iii, 7.
Stifla, *The dam (of a river)*, iii, 11.
Stigandahrof, *Stead of Stigandi*, iii, 0.
Stigi, *The Steep*, i, 29.
Stjornusteinar, *Star-stones*, v, 9.
Stokkahladir, *Stocks-lathe*, iii, 17.

Stokkseyri, *Stock's-isle*, v, 9.
Storolfshvoll, *Great Wolf's-hill*, see hvoll.
Storolfsvöllr, *Great Wolf-field*, v, 5.
Stotalækr, *Stutterer's-brook*, v, 5.
Strandarheidi, *Strand-heath*, ii, 30.
Strandir, *Strands*, ii, 20, 31; v, 6.
Straumfirdingar, *Men from Straum-firth*, ii, 6.
Straumfjordr, *Stream-firth*, ii, 4.
Straumnes, *Stream-ness*, ii, 20, 31.
Straumsfjardara, *Streamfirth-river*, ii, 6.
Strind, iv, 1.
Strugsstadir, *Stew-stead*. ii, 5.
Strönd, *Strand*, iii, 13.
Sturlustadir, *Sturls-stead*, ii, 1.
Stödfirdingar, iv, 6.
Stodvarfjördr, iv, 6.
Stödverjar, iv, 6.
Sudrey in Faroe Islands, ii, 14.
Sudreyjar,* *The Hebrides*, i, 11, 12; ii, 6, 11, 15; iii, 4, 12, 15, 18; iv, 8, 11; v, 12.
Sudreyskr, *From the Hebrides*, ii, 1, 14; iii, 2.
Sudrjöklar, i, 21.
Sudrland, *Sutherland in Scotland*, ii. 15.
Sugandafjördr, *Soughing's-firth*, ii, 29..
Suluholt, *Solan goose wood*, v, 8.
Sumarlidabær = *Samarlidis-by or Sailorshome*, v, 3,
Sunnlendinga-fjordungr, iii, 11; v, 1, 15.
Sunnmæri, ii, 27; iv, 11.
Sunnudalr, *Sundale*, iv, 1.
Surnadalr, *Sorreldale*, iii, 15.
Surtr, *The cave of Surt* = *the dark cave*, iii, 10.
Svalbard, i, 1.
Svarfadardalr, *Desolation-dale*, iii, 12; iv, 1.
Svartardalr, *Dark-dale*, iii, 6.
Svartfellsmyrar, *Dark-fell-moors*, iii, 4.
Svartsmyri, *Swart's-moor*, iii, 4.
Svartssker, *Dark-scar*, ii, 24.
Svefneyjar, *Slumber-isle*, ii, 23.
Sveinungseyri, *Sveinung's-island*, ii, 30.
Sveinungsvik, *Sveinung's-wick*, iii, 20.

---

*Called also Sudor, which is Latin translation of Sudreyjar. For full explanation see ii, 19, page 72.

Svertinsgstadir, *Sverting's-stead*, v, 3.
Svidinhornadalr, iv, 7.
Svinadalr, *Swinedale*, ii, 19, 21; iii, 3, 5.
Svinanes, *Swineness*, ii, 20.
Svinavatn, *Swine-water*, *vid* Giimness, v, 12.
  vid Hrunsfjord, ii, 10.
  vid Svinadal, iii, 3, 4, 5,
Swiney, *Swine-island*, ii, 18, 19.
Svinhagi, *Swine-pasture*, v, 5, 6.
Svithjod, *The people or land of the Swedes*, i, 1; iii, 9.
Sydridalr, *Southern-dale*, i, 21.
Sognafylki, *People of Sogn*, v, 9.
Sygnakleif, *Sygn-cliff*, ii, 29.
Sæmundarhlid, *Sæmund's-slope*, iii, 6.
Sæmundarlækr, *Sæmund's-river*, iii, 6.
Sokkolfsdalr, *Sokkolf's-dale*, ii, 17.
Solmundarhofdi, *Solmund's-head*, ii, 1.
Sölvadalr, *Solvisdale*, in Greenland, ii, 14.
  in Eyjafjord, iii, 12.
Sö"vafjordr, *Solvis-firth*, ii, 14.

T.

Talknafjordr, ii, 26.
Teigará, *Teig-river*, iv, 2.
Thordisholt, *Thordis-wood*, iii, 2.
Tjaldanes, *Tentness*, in Arnarfjord, ii, 26.
  in Breidafjord, ii, 21.
Tjaldastadir, *Tent-stead*, v, 6.
Tjaldavöllr, *Tent-field*, iv, 12.
Tili or Thule, Prologue. Strabo speaks of a voyage made by a citizen of Marseilles, time of Alexander the Great, up the English Channel, and so up the North Sea past an Island he calls "Thule."
Tinnudalsá, *Flint-dale-river*, iv, 7.
Tjornes, *Tar-ness*, iii, 19, 20.
Toptavöllr, *Toft-field*, iv, 1.
Torfastadir, *Torfi's-stead*, iv, 1.
Torfnes, *Turf-ness*, ii, 21.
Torgar, v, 3.
Trajarholt, *Trod-holt*, v, 9, 10,
Tradir, *Trodden-lane*, ii, 11.
Trekyllisvik, *Woodbag-wick*, ii, 31.
Trostansfjordr, ii, 26.
Tröllahals, *Troll's-neck or Hause*, ii, 10.

Tröllatunga, *Troll-tongue*, ii, 32.
Tunga, *Point of land between two rivers*,
 In Arness Thing, v, 11.
 In Nordrardal, ii, 3.
 In Vatnsdal, iii, 4.
Tunga, ii, 1.
Tungardr, *Home-field-garth*, ii, 19.
Tunguá, *Tongue-river*; Tungu=a tongue of land formed by the meeting of two rivers, iii, 11, 19.
Tungufell, *Tongue-fell*, i, 20; ii, 4.
Tunguheida, *Tongue-heath*, iii, 18.
Tungu-land, iv, 11.
Tungu-lönd, iv, 2.

U.

Ulfarsfell, *Ulf's-fell*, ii, 13.
Ulfsdalir, *Ulf's-dale*, iii, 11.
Ulfsstadir, *Ulf's-stead*, i, 21.
Unadalr, iii, 4.
Unadalsá, iii, 10.
Unadsdalr, *Delight-dale*, ii, 29, 31.
Unalækr, *Uni's-brook*, iv, 4.
Unaos, *Uni's-inlet*, iv, 4.
Undirfell, *Underfell*, iii, 4.
Undir-Brekkum, *Under-brinks*, v, 3.
Upplendingar, ii, 15; iii, 11; iv, 8; v, 9.
Upplendingr, iv, 11.
Upplenzkr, ii, 29.
Upplond, iii, 2; v, 10.
Uppsalir, *Upper-halls*, iii, 9.
Upsar, *Fish-place*, iii, 13.
Urdavatn, *Stony-water*, iii, 2, 3.
Urdir, *Stone-heaps*, iii, 11.

V.

Vadill, *Shallow-water*, ii, 28, 30.
Vag, *Creek*, v, 14.
Vallanes, *Field-ness*, iv, 3.
Valldres in Norway, iv, 13.
Vallverjar, *Men of Vellir*, v, 7.
Valthjofsstadir, *Valthjof-stead*, ii, 14.
Vardgja, *Ward-gorge*, iii, 16.
Varmá, *Warm-river*, v, 13.
Varmadalr, *Warm-dale*, v, 6.
Varmalækr, *Warm-brook*, i, 20.
Vatn, *Water*, ii, 17, 18.
Vatnahverfi, *The Waters*, in Greenland, ii, 14.

Vatnlausa, *Waterless*, i, 13, 20.
Vatnsá, iii, 14.
Vatnsdalı in Hunavatnsthing, iii, 2, 4, 11.
Vatnsdalsá, iii, 4.
Vatnsdælär, *Water-dale-men*, iii, 4.
Vatnsfell, *Water-fell*, v, 3.
Vatnsfjördr, vid Bardarstrond, i, 2; ii, 25.
    Isafirdi, iii, 5.
Vatnshorn, ii, 14.
Vatnsnes, *Water-ness*, ii, 29; iii, 1.
Vatnsskard, *Water-pass*, iii, 4, 5, 6.
Veggir, *The Walls*, ii, 2.
Veidilausa, *Fish-less*, ii, 31.
Vekelshaugar, *Vekell's-howes*, iii, 7.
Vellir, v, 7.
Veradalr, iv, 2.
Vermaland, *A county in Sweden*, iii, 1.
Vestarsness, *Vestar's-ness*, ii, 20.
Vestdalsá, *West-dale-river*, iv, 6.
Vestfirdinga-fjordungr, ii, 33.
Vestfirdir, *Western-firths*, ii, 1.
Vestfold in Norway, iii, 9.
Vestmannaeyjar, *Westmen's-islands*, i, 7; v, 5.
Vestmannsvatn, *Westmen's-water*, iii, 19.
Vestmenn, Prologue; i, 7.
Vestradalsá, *West-dale-river*, iv, 1.
Vestrhop, *Westhope*, iii, 1, 4, 6.
Vestri-bygd in Greenland, ii, 14.
Vestri-obygd in Greenland, ii, 14.
Vestrlönd, v, 4.
Vidbord, iv, 10.
Vidfirdingar, *Wood-firthers*, iv, 6.
Vidfjördr, *Wood-firth*, iv, 1, 6.
Vididalr, *Wide-dale*, iii, 1, 2.
Vididalsey, *Wide-dale-island*, iii, 4.
Vidilækr, *Willow-brook*, ii, 3.
Vidimyri, *Willow-mire*, ii, 4, 25.
Vidiskogr, *Willow-wood*, v, 10.
Vidvik, *Wood-wick*, iii, 9.
Vifilsdalr, *Vifil's-dale*, ii, 17.
Vifilsfell, i, 8.
Vifilstoptir, *Vifil's-toft*, i, 8.
Viggjar in Norway, *The Steeds*, v, 2.
Vigrafjördr, *Vigra-firth*, ii, 9, 13.
Vik, *A small bay, creek, or inlet*, ii, 31; also Vikr, found in Husa vik, Reykja-vik.

Vikarsskeid, ii, 16.
Vikingslækr, *Viking-brook*, v, 5, 6.
Vikr, *The Wicks*, ii, 26.
Vikverjar, *Men of Vikin*, v, 12.
Villingadalr, iii, 16.
Vinland the good, *Wineland*, ii, 22; iii, 10.
Vinverjadalr, iii, 18.
Vogar, *The Voss*, ii, 9.
Vogr, *Vos or creek*, v, 14.
Vonarskard, *Hope-pass*, iii, 18; iv, 10.
Vopnafjardará, *Weaponfirth's-river*, iv, 1.
Vopnafjardarstrond, *Weaponfirth's-river-strand*, iv, 2.
Vopnafjordr, *Weaponfirth*, ii, 3; iv, 1.
Vopnaferdingar, *Weaponfirther*, iv, 2.
Vors in Norway, iv, 5, 6, 7; v, 8, 12.
Vorsbær, v, 8.
Vorskr, iv, 10.
Vælagerdi, *Væla-garth*, v, 4, 10.
Vætleifsholt, v, 8.
Vardafell, *Ward-fell*, v, 10.

Y.

Yrarfell, *Wet-fell*, iii, 6.
Yrjar, *Wetting*, iv, 1.
Ytrafjall, formerly called Skrattafell, iii, 19. Ytrafjall is "outer" fell— Skratti the name of a demon supposed to haunt this mountain; compare Crossfell in Cumberland, formerly Fiends Fell.

Th.

Theigjandadalr, *Hushed-dale*, iii, 19.
Thelamörk ın Norway, v, 6.
Thernanes, *Bondmaid's-ness*, iv, 6.
Thingeyrar, *Thing-island*, iii, 3.
Thingeyra, iii, 3.
Thingnes, *Thing-ness*, ii, 18; ii, 30.
Thingvollr, *Thing-field*, see note, v, 13.
Thjorsá, *Steer's-river*, iii, 20; v, 7, 11.
Thjorsardalr, *Steer's-river-dale*, iii, 20; v, 7, 11.
Thjorsarholt, *Steer's-river-wood*, v, 7.
Thjorsaros, *Steer's-river-mouth*, v, 8.
For origin of name *Steer's-river*, see v, 8, where Thorarin brings his ship with

a Steer's-head carved upon its stem into the river's mouth, which thence takes its name.

Thjorsdælir, *Steer's-dale*, iii, 20.

Thistilsfjördr, *Thistle-firth*, ii, 7 ; iii, 20.

Thorbrandsstadir,*Thorbrand's-stead*, iii, 8

Thordisarholt, *Thordis-river-wood*, iii, 2.

Thoreyjargnupr, *Thorey's-peak*, iii, 4.

Thorfinnsstadir, *Thorfinn's-stead*, ii, 3.

Thorgautsstadir, *Thorgaut's-stead*, ii, 1.

Thorgeirsfjordr, *Thorgeir's-firth*, iii, 17.

Thorgerdarfell, *Thorgerd's-fell*, iii, 19.

Thorgilsstadir, *Thorgil's-stead*, ii, 23.

Thorisbjörg, ii, 5.

Thorisholar, *Thoris-holes*, i, 14.

Thorisstadir, *Thoris-stead*, ii, 19.

Thormodseyri, *Thormod's-island*, iii, 11.

Thormodssker, *Thormod's-skerry*, ii, 24.

Thorodsstadir, *Thorodd's-stead*, iii, 1.

Thorolfsfell, *Thorolf's-fell*, v, 2.

Thorormstunga,*Thororm's-tongue*, iii, 3, 4

Thorsá, *Thor's-river*, ii, 12, 13.

Thorskafjordr, *Cod-firth*, ii, 19, 22.

Thorskfirdingar saga, ii, 19.

Thorsmörk, *Thor's-mark*, v, 2.

Thorsnes, *Thor's-ness*, ii, 12.

Thorsnesingar, *from Thor's-ness*, ii, 12,, 29.

Thorsness-lönd, ii, 9, 13, 14.

Thorunnarey, *Thorunn's islet*, iii, 12.

Thorunnarhalsar, *Thorunn's-hause-river*, v, 6.

Thorunnarholt,*Thorunn's-holt or wood* ii, 3

Thorunnarhylr,*Thorunn's-hole or pool*, ii, 3

Thorunnartoptir, *Thorunn's-tofts*, ii, 19.

Thorvaldsdalr, *Thorvald's-dale*, iii, 13.

Thorvaldsdalsá, *Thorvald's-dale-river*, iii, 13.

Thorvardsstadir, *Thorvard's-stead*, i, 20; ii, 1.

Thrandarholt, *Thrand's-wood*, v, 11.

Thrandheimr, *Thrand's-home*, iv, 1, 6; v, 1, 2.

Thrihyrning, *Three corner*, v, 3, 5.

Thruma in Norway, v, 6.

Thrælavik, *Thrallwick*, ii, 7.

Thufa, *Hummoek*, ii, 27.

Thufubjörg, ii, 7.

Thulunes, iv, 5.

Thurssta lir, *Giant-stead*, ii, 4.

Thverá, *Cross or Thwart-river*, from flowing athwart or across into the main river.

In Arness Thing, v, 11, 13.

In Borgarfirth, ii, 2, 3.

In Eyjafirth, iii, 14, 16.

In Rangar Thing, v, 3, 4.

In Skagafirth, iii, 8.

From Vatnsness, iii, 1.

Thverardalr, ii, 2.

Thverarhlid, *Cross-river-slope*, i, 12 ; ii, 1, 2.

Thverfell, *Crossfell*, ii, 21.

Thykkvibær, *Thick-by*, iv, 10.

Thykkviskogr, *Thick-wood*, ii, 18.

Æ.

Ægissida, *Ægir's side*, iii, 1.

Ævarsskard, *Ævar's-pass*, iii, 5.

Ö.

Ögrvik, ii, 29.

Öldugrof, *Alda's-grove or pit*, v, 5.

Ölfusá, *Olfu's-river*, i, 7, 8.

Ölfusvatn, *Olfu's-water*, i, 8.

Ölvisstadir, *Olver's-stead*, v, 9.

Ömd, in Halogaland, iii, 14.

Öndurtnes, *Onward-ness*, v, 12.

Öndverd-eyri, *Onverd's-eyr or beach*, ii, 9.

Önundarfjördr, *Onund's-firth*, ii, 29.

Önundarholt, *Onund's-wood*, v, 9.

Örlygshöfn, *Orlyg's-haven*, i, 12.

Örlygsstadir. *Orlyg's-stead*, ii, 13.

Örnolfsdalr, *Ornolf's-dale*, ii, 2.

Örnolfsdalsá, *Ornolf's-dale-river*, ii, 2.

Örnolfsstadir, *Ornolf's-stead*, ii, 2.

Örridaros, *Char-river* in Hvammsfirth, II, 16.

in Leirarsveit, i, 15, 17.

Öxará, *Axe-river* in Bardardal, iii, 18.

in Thingvöll, i, 8 ; v, 12.

Öxararholmi, *Axe-river-island*, v, 10.

Öxarfjördar, *Axfirth*, ii, 31 ; iii, 20.

Öxl in Snæfellsness, ii, 6.

Öxney or Oxey, *Ox-island*, ii, 11.

Öxnadalr, *Oxen-dale*, iii, 14.

Öxnalækr, *Ox-brook*, iv, 3.

In drawing up and interpreting the foregoing Register of Place Names, two objects have throughout been especially kept in view; *first*, to make the meaning of the Place Name as clear as possible, more especially as illustrating the conditions under which it was first given, and *secondly*, in order to make a reference to the map easy and obvious, it was necessary, as near as possible, to give the exact form of the word in the original Norse. To secure this, the list given in the Landnama (original Icelandic volume) Copenhagen 1843, has been adhered to. In the renderings and elsewhere, possibly in some instances, fjördr for *firth* or *vice versa*, or shaw, holt, or wood, or other partly synonymous words are made interchangeable, or the concluding letters r or ar may be found in some forms and left out in others.

I would, however, remind critics about spelling, that the variations introduced into Norse words by the old forms of declension, often unsettles in the original the spelling of the same word. Moreover in the Book of the Settlement, the Norse language is used in prose composition for the first time and almost before it can be said to have acquired the consistency of a language at all. The two original Icelandic copies that I have used to supplement each other are often themselves at variance about the spelling of the same word or Place Name, and I can point out instances in which the same Place Name is differently spelled in different passages of the same copy. Moreover the most eminent Icelandic philologists differ about the exact rendering of the spelling of the same term in Place Names, nor would it be difficult to show, if required, that in the spelling of Place Names from Ari himself downwards, the same writer is not at all times consistent with himself.

In order to be quite sure about the originals of the work, I have kept almost all the MSS. of the translations, almost every scrap of the copying, alterations, and Place-Names, together with the corrections of proofs and correspondence about them, and a voluminous mass they are.

T. ELLWOOD.

SOME ADDITIONS AND CORRECTIONS.

The Map represents Iceland from the beginning of the Settlement A.D. 874 to the close of the 10th century, and during the opening years of the 11th century.

In Table of Contents, page v, and also at page 75—for " A.D. 885 " *read* " A.D. 872," as date of Battle of Hafursfirth.

Also Table of Contents, page v—for " South America " *read* " Southern America," generally understood to refer to a more southern portion of the North American continent than that originally discovered by the Norsemen.

Page x—for " Sunholme " *read* " Sunhome."

Page xvii—for " Ornæfa " *read* " Oræfa."

Page xxi—for " Alfdis of Barna " *read* " Alfdis of Barra."

At page 4, Chapter II, line 12—for " Aft over the stem " *read* " Aft over the stern."

LIST OF SUBSCRIBERS.

ADAMS, J. R., Esq., 66, Cannon Street, London.
ADAIR, JOSEPH, Esq., Egremont.
ALCOCK-BECK, MAJOR, Esthwaite Lodge, Hawkshead.
AINSWORTH, LIEUT.-COLONEL, Broughton Hall, Grange-over-
Sands, Cartmel.
ATKINSON, JAMES, Esq., King Street, Ulverston (2 copies).
AYRE, REV. CANON, Holy Trinity Vicarage, Ulverston.

BALFOUR, R., Esq., Bridge House, Torver.
BARNES, H., Esq., M.D., LL.D., 6, Portland Square, Carlisle.
BARRATT, W. I., Esq., Broom Hill, Broughton-in-Furness.
BARRATT, J. W. H., Esq., Holy Wath, Coniston, R.S.O.
BARON, Miss, Bank House, Bury-St.-Edmunds.
BARROW-IN-FURNESS, THE LORD BISHOP OF, How Foot,
Grasmere, R.S.O.
BARROW-IN-FURNESS FREE PUBLIC LIBRARY (per Ernest
Beck, Esq., Librarian.)
BELL, JOHN, Esq., Haws Bank, Coniston.
BENSON, T., Esq., Stable Harvey, Torver.
BLANC, HIPPOLYTE J., Esq., F.S.A., Scot., 73, George Street,
Edinburgh.
BROWNE, Miss, the Square, Broughton-in-Furness.
BROWN, S. D., Esq., Souterstead, Torver.
BROCKBANK, Mrs., The Croft, Kirksanton.
BUTLER, THOMAS, Esq., Solicitor, Broughton-in-Furness.

CAVENDISH, VICTOR, Esq., M.P., Holker Hall, Cartmel.
CARLISLE, THE LORD BISHOP OF, Rose Castle, Carlisle.
CARLISLE PUBLIC LIBRARY, Tullie House, Carlisle.
COLLINGWOOD, W. G., Esq., M.A., Coniston.
COWARD, JOHN, Esq., Fountain Street, Ulverston.
COWPER, H. S., Esq., F.S.A., Outgate, Ambleside.
CLOUSTON, T. G., Esq., M.D., Morningside Place, Edinburgh.
CLARK, JOHN, Esq., Solicitor, Broughton-in-Furness.
CRANKE, M. I., Esq., Midtown, Urswick, Ulverston.
CROWDER, W. J. R., jun., Esq., 3, Marine Terrace, Silloth.

DICKSON, A. B., Esq., Abbots Reading, Haverthwaite, Ulverston.

DOUGLAS & FOULIS, Messrs., 9, Castle Street, Edinburgh.

DUNN, J. M., Esq., 61, Harcourt Terrace, South Kensington, London, S.W.

DUNN, Miss, 61, Harcourt Terrace, South Kensington, London, S.W.

EASTHOPE, JAMES, Esq., Barrow-in-Furness (2 copies).

ELLWOOD, G. B., Esq., York Street, Chorlton-on-Medlock, Manchester. (2 copies)

ELLWOOD, Rev. T. E., Hawes Vicarage, Yorkshire.

ELLWOOD, Rev. R. D., St. George's, Barrow-in-Furness.

ELLWOOD, J. F. A., Esq. Arrow Field, Coniston.

FAWCETT, Dr., Broughton House, Broughton-in-Furness.

FELL, JOHN, Esq., Flan How, Ulverston.

FERGUSON, The Worshipful Chancellor, F.S.A., Carlisle.

FISKE, WILLARD, Esq., c/o E. G. Allen, 28, Henrietta Street, Covent Garden, London.

FOTHERGILL, JOHN, Esq., Brownber, Newbiggin, R.S.O.

FORD, JOHN R., Esq., Quarry Dene, Weetwood, Leeds.

GARNER, JOHN, Esq., The Garner, Broughton-in-Furness.

GAYTHORPE, HARPER, Esq., 12, Harrison Street, Barrow-in-Furness.

GLAISTER, T., Esq., Saltcoats, Abbey Town, Carlisle.

GRANT, MRS., Kenilworth, Camberlay, Surrey.

GRAINGER, F., Esq., Southerfield, Abbey Town, Carlisle.

GREENWOOD, R. H., Esq., Bank House, Kendal.

HARGREAVES, J. E., Esq., Beezon Lodge, Kendal.

HARRISON, JAMES, Esq., Sand Area House, Kendal.

HARRISON, JAMES, Esq., Newby Bridge, Ulverston.

HARRISON, G., Esq., Beck Stones, Torver, Coniston, R.S.O.

HASLAM, REV. J., Thwaites, Millom.

HOUSMAN, R. F. Esq., Liverpool.

HIBBERT, PERCY, Esq., Plumtree Hall, Milnthorpe.

HILLS, H. W., Esq., Storrs, Windermere.

HOARE, REV. J. N., St. John's Parsonage, Keswick.

HODGSON, JAMES, Esq., Britain Place, Ulverston.

HOLT, Miss EMMA G., Sudley, Mossley Hill, Liverpool.

HOLMES, W., Esq., Lightburn Road, Ulverston.

HUDLESTON, F., Esq., 57, Inverness Terrace, Hyde Park, London.

IDDON, THOMAS, Esq., Market Street, Ulverston.
IRVING, REV. JOHN, Holy Trinity Vicarage, Millom.

JACKSON, THOS., Esq., M.D., Hazel Bank, Yanwith, Penrith.
JACKSON, S. HART, Esq., 49, Market Street, Ulverston.
JOWETT-BURTON, REV. J., Stanton-by-Dale, Nottingham.

KEGAN PAUL, TRENCH, TRUBNER & Co., Ltd., Charing Cross
    Road, London (2 copies).
KEWLEY, REV. W., Natland Vicarage, Kendal.
KEY, THOMAS, Esq., High Wray, Ambleside.
KITCHIN, REV. G. W., D.D., DEAN OF DURHAM, The Deanery,
    Durham.

LAMONBY, W. F., Ballaarat, Kitto Road, New Cross,
    London, S.E.
LEHMAUN U STAGE, Herr, Buchhandlung, Copenhagen.
LEWIS, REV. L. OWEN, Lindal-in-Furness, Ulverston.
LITTLE, WILLIAM, Esq., Chapel Ridding, Windermere.
LONGTON, E. J., Esq., M.D., Brown How, Torver.
LUMB, JAMES, Esq., Homewood, Whitehaven.

MADDEN, The Venerable Archdeacon, Archdeacon of War-
    rington, St. Luke's, Liverpool.
MACKERETH, H. W., Esq. Market Place, Ulverston.
MACHELL, Lieut.-Col., Whitehaven.
MAGNUSSON, E., Esq., University Library, Cambridge (3
    copies).
MANDALL, T., Esq., Coniston (2 copies).
MARSHALL, STEPHEN A., Esq., Skelwith Fold, Ambleside.
MARSHALL, Mrs., Patterdale Hall, Penrith.
METCALFE, Rev. C. F., Claremont, Ambleside.
MIDGELEY, J., Esq., Grange-over-Sands.
MILLARD, REV. F. L. N., Aspatria Vicarage, Carlisle.
MILLOM PUBLIC LIBRARY, per W. T. Lawrence, Esq.
MOORE, REV. C. A., All Saints Parsonage, Gustav Adolphe
    Strasse, 6, Dresden Shehlen, Saxony, Germany.
MORRIS, JOHN, Esq. (for Coniston Institute), School House,
    Coniston.

NASH, J. R., Esq., The Mount, Cark-in-Cartmel.
NORRIS, F. T., Esq., 31, Adolphus Road, South Hornsey.

PEACHE, THE REV. ALFRED, Wimbledon, London.
PHILLIPSON, J., Esq., Emlin Hall, Torver.

PHILLIPS, The Venerable Archdeacon, St. George's Vicarage, Barrow.

PORTEOUS, Messrs. R. J. & Co., Grainger Street West, Newcastle-on-Tyne.

PREVOST, E. W., Esq., PhD., Newnham, Gloucester.

RAWNSLEY, REV. CANON, Crosthwaite Vicarage, Keswick.
REMINGTON, REV. T. M., Aynsome, Cartmel.
RENTON, W., Esq., Wray, Ambleside.
REE, J. ROGERS, Esq., Winterbourne, Penarth.
RHODES, MR. JOSEPH, 54, Drewery Terrace, Keighley.
RIDLEY, REV. G., Crosby Garrat Rectory, Westmorland.
ROBINSON, JOHN, Esq., M.Inst. C.E., Dock Works, Middlesbrough.
ROBINSON, J., Esq., Westwood Hall, Leek, Staffordshire (4 copies).
RUSKIN, PROFESSOR, Brantwood, Coniston.

SEVERN, ARTHUR, Esq., Brantwood, Coniston.
SEWELL, COL. FREDERICK R., Brandling Ghyll, Cockermouth.
SMALLPIECE, REV. J., Meppershall Rectory, Shefford.
SMITH, J. J., Esq., Abbey Town, Carlisle.
SPEDDING, M., Esq., Coniston, Lancashire.
STEAD, Miss A., 3, Belgrave Place, Southport.
STEFANSSON, DR. JON, National Liberal Club, Westminster.
STOCK, ELLIOT, Esq., 62, Paternoster Row, London (2 copies).
STUART, REV. J. C., Liverpool.
STUART, WILSON, Esq., M.A., Liverpool.
SUART, W., Esq., St. John's College, Cambridge.
SYKES, Rev. W. SLATER, Millom, Cumberland.

TAYLOR, REV. RICHARD, Bromfield Vicarage, Wigton.
THRELFALL, W., Esq., Blawith, Ulverston.
THOMAS, K. G., Esq., High Wray, Ambleside.
THORNLEY, Rev. CANON, The Vicarage, Kirkoswald, R.S.O.
THE CHURCH AGENCY, 6, Southampton Street, Strand, London.
THE CLERGY LIBRARY for the Archdeaconry of Furness.

WALKER, Miss A., Oak Lea, Whitehaven.
WILSON, Miss, Abbey Town, Carlisle.
WILSON, Mrs., Aynam Lodge, Kendal.
WOODHOUSE, REV. CANON, Canon of Manchester Cathedral, 65, Ardwick Green, Manchester.
WORKINGTON FREE LIBRARY.
WRIGHT, MRS. DR. HODGSON, Park Lane, Halifax.